D1601708

DESIRE AND CRAVING

SUNY Series in New Social Studies on Alcohol and Drugs
Harry G. Levine and Craig Reinarman, Editors

DESIRE AND CRAVING

A Cultural Theory of Alcoholism

PERTTI ALASUUTARI

STATE UNIVERSITY OF NEW YORK PRESS

Published by
State University of New York Press, Albany

For information, address State University of New York
Press, State University Plaza, Albany, N.Y., 12246

Production by E. Moore
Marketing by Theresa A. Swierzowski

Library of Congress Cataloging-in-Publication Data

Alasuutari, Pertti.
    Desire and craving : a cultural theory of alcoholism / Pertti
Alasuutari.
        p.   cm. — (SUNY series in new social studies on alcohol and
drugs)
    Includes bibliographical references and index.
    ISBN 0-7914-1097-8. — ISBN 0-7914-1098-6 (pbk.)
    1. Alcoholism—Finland—History. 2. Alcoholism—Social aspects.
I. Title. II. Series.
HV5515.5.A75   1992
362.29'2'094897—dc20   91-22457
                                                                  CIP

10 9 8 7 6 5 4 3 2 1

CONTENTS

ACKNOLWEDGMENTS

Over the years when I worked on this book, several people have helped me by reading all or parts of the text in draft, and supplied me with advice, comments and ideas. Jon Cruz, Mike Hilton, Terry Macdonald, Robin Room, Ron Roizen, and Constance Weisner provided helpful comments during my Fulbright year at Berkeley. Parts of the work have been read also by Jari Aro, Risto Heiskala, Brian Lutz, Merja Kinnunen, Matti Peltonen, David Silverman, and Peter Stromberg. The whole manuscript was read by Risto Alapuro, Ilkka Arminen, Heikki Lehtonen, Markku Salo, and Pekka Sulkunen. I would particularly like to express my gratitude to Harry Levine for his support and innumerable helpful comments throughout the later history of this book. I also got invaluable comments from the people who reviewed the manuscript for the State University of New York Press: Professor Norman K. Denzin, Doctor Bryan M. Johnstone, and two others who wanted to remain anonymous. I also want to use the opportunity to thank Editor Rosalie M. Robertson and other people from the State University of New York Press for their help and support. Many others have also either commented on earlier versions of the texts published in this book helped me in gathering the data, or have used their time and energy as informants. I am grateful to them all for their contribution. I would also like to thank Karen Armstrong for patiently going through the manuscript several times, correcting my English, and giving me comments about my style and clarity of thought. Financially, this work has been made possible by the Finnish Foundation for Alcohol Research and by the University of Tampere, for which my family and I are grateful. Finally, I want to thank my wife Maarit for her help. It is with her that I have most often discussed my work, and also been able to take distance from it.

Chapter 1

INTRODUCTION

THE ALCOHOLISM FRAME AND THE EVERYDAY-LIFE FRAME

The studies of this book distinguish two frameworks used in interpreting and accounting for drinking, especially socially unacceptable drinking. I call these the *alcoholism frame* and the *everyday-life frame*.

The concept of frame was developed first by Erving Goffman (1974). My use of the concept is influenced by Anthony Giddens (1984, 87) who emphasizes its cognitive dimension. Frames can be understood as clusters of rules which help to define and constitute specific activities. In everyday life, when we enter a situation and get an answer to the question "what is going on here," we have found a frame from our stock of social knowledge that fits with at least certain characteristics of the situation. Such a loose definition of "frame" makes it possible to apply several noncontradictory frames to any situation by paying attention to different aspects of what is going on. When I speak about the everyday-life frame for drinking, I refer to an aggregate of more specific frames that people use to interpret drinking.

In the everyday-life frame, drinking is to a large extent taken for granted. The everyday-life frame focuses attention on the place and functions of drinking in social interaction. For example a drink may be used to convey meaning—a glass of champagne drunk to celebrate an anniversary. Banquets and other special occasions are naturally part of the everyday-life frame and an essential part of "ordinary" drinking situations. In Finland, in fact, it seems that alcoholic drinking makes almost any situation special. Drinking also may be an occasion for social interaction as, for instance, when two colleagues go "to have a drink" after a hard day's work. In this case, drinking symbolizes freedom and release from work (and perhaps home), and from the self-discipline needed in carrying out one's duties..The everyday-life frame focuses attention on social context and meaning.

The alcoholism frame, on the other hand, shifts attention from the situation to individuals and their drinking habits or style. Along with this focus on individual drinking patterns, three additional things stand out about the alcoholism frame. First, the alcoholism frame distinguishes between normal and abnormal (or pathological) drinking. This way of dividing drinking is characteristic of some modern Western societies.[1] The alcoholism frame does not interpret frequent, unacceptable drinking an extreme case of "normal" behavior, but as something altogether different. Second, alcoholism is seen as a weakness or disease of the will. According to the alcoholism frame, alcoholics are unable to prevent themselves from drinking, because they have an overwhelming craving for drink. If a person believed to be an "alcoholic" goes for a drink after work, the alcoholism frame interprets the behavior as proof of craving and of addiction. It does not use the notions of freedom and relaxation to interpret the drinking of an "alcoholic." Rather, it sees drinking as the result of craving and of the inability to refrain. Third, the alcoholism frame portrays heavy drinking as a long-standing problem which can be managed and handled, but not cured. As this book will show, in all three of these aspects, alcoholism is a Western culture-bound syndrome.

It should be noted that the alcoholism frame is similar to other frameworks that assess behavior and situations by focusing on individual style, manner, or behavior. It is a special case of the frames by which the modern individual and individuality is socially produced and reproduced. On a more general level we could talk about the *personality frame* as a cluster of frames that construct the modern individual as a personality. We could also talk about the craving for alcohol as part of the *addiction frame* which itself is a cluster of frames that construct the modern individual as a desiring subject.

I am not suggesting that frames are grids or lenses through which "reality" is more or less accurately perceived. And I am not saying that someone who perceives an alcohol problem has an unreal or false belief.

Rather, this book suggests that frames constitute and organize social thought and social situations. As with any frame, the alcoholism frame is, in part, a self-fulfilling prophecy. When it is applied to a person, it generally structures social relations and situations, and gives them new meanings.

The two interpretive frameworks, the everyday-life frame and the alcoholism frame, are not equal, alternative ways of viewing drinking. The everyday-life frame is the basis for taken for granted attitudes toward social situations. When something is perceived within the everyday-life frame, it is usually not done reflexively, self-consciously. People are not deliberately applying a particular frame; they simply understand what is going on as competent members of a culture. Within the everyday-life frame, "ordinary drinking" consists of everyday-life situations such as having a party, or going to the tavern. Ordinary drinking occasions are not understood as "normal" drinking. The alcoholism frame, on the other hand, is usually a more conscious, second-order interpretive framework applied to a situation or to behavior that can not easily be made intelligible within the everyday-life frame. It distinguishes between normal and abnormal drinking, and then develops further interpretations of abnormal drinking—of "alcoholism." The studies in this book analyze the history and logic of the alcoholism frame, its interpretations of alcoholism, and the ways that it structures our drinking habits and notions of drinking.

DESIRE AND THE MODERN PERSON

This is also a book about the modern individual as a subject of desire. Drawing upon the research tradition dealing with the concepts of desire and self-control, this book consists of theoretically informed empirical analyses of the way we are constructed and reconstructed as desiring subjects.

In the social science literature, the theme was first taken up by Sigmund Freud, particularly in his essay *Civilization and Its Discontents* (1978, first published in 1930). In that work, Freud suggests that civilization develops by imposing constraints on the natural instincts of men and women. The influence of Freud and psychoanalysis probably cannot be overestimated since Freud has provided the Western world with the vocabulary with which to talk about the psyche.

Norbert Elias's two-volume study entitled *The Civilizing Process*

(Elias 1978; 1982, first published in 1939) was an important work in the Freudian tradition. Elias showed that the psychic structure, so eloquently described by Freud, is a historical construction. According to Elias, modernization has meant an ever greater need for self-restraint. The civilizing process is best understood as a gradual internalization of outer constraints into self-restraint. This development is due to the growing importance and strength of the central power of a nation— that is, the state—as a power monopoly. Along with state formation, and the growing importance of an exchange economy, networks of mutual dependence have become denser, and that has been the reason for individuals' need for greater discretion.

Michel Foucault has also studied the formation of the modern person in a number of his studies (for instance Foucault 1973; 1979; 1980; 1986). Foucault insists that it is insufficient to treat the modern psyche as a historical construction, to trace the history by which humans have developed an ever stricter self-discipline over their instincts. We must also realize, said Foucault, that "desire" and "self-control" are *notions* Western culture uses, notions that produce us in their own image as desiring subject.[2]

The concepts of self-control, addiction, and dependence have also been discussed in sociological alcohol research (Room 1985b). Of particular interest are Harry Levine's studies dealing with the social history of temperance and alcoholism (Levine 1978a; 1978b; 1980; 1984; 1990). According to Levine, the eighteenth and nineteenth centuries saw the rise of an "obsession with self-control" (Levine 1978a), especially among the American middle class, an obsession that contributed to producing the modern concept and experience of addiction (Levine 1978b).

The case studies of this book analyze the ways in which we are constructed or constituted as modern, desiring subjects by the notions of desire and self-control. As modern individuals, we have available to us at least two different sets of understandings. We can talk about "desire" in the everyday-life sense, or we can treat wants and wishes as alien "cravings" in the alcoholism and addiction sense. In many situations and for many individuals, we take the everyday-life frame for granted and barely recognize the way "desire" shapes our understandings and interpretations. In other situations and with other individuals, a compelling desire—a "craving"—seems to break beyond the interpretations provided by the everyday-life frame and the notion of abnormality or pathology seems most appropriate.

ORGANIZATION OF THIS BOOK

This book is a collection of theoretically informed studies dealing with one theme, the social and cultural character of alcohol problems. The studies are experiments in empirically grounded theory-building and do not try to exclude other interpretations of the phenomena. The studies concentrate on specific cases in one country, Finland; but the theoretical material draws upon a broad range of sociological, anthropological, social psychological, philosophical, and historical literatures, and addresses broad questions about the character of life in modern society.

From the vantage point outlined in the previous sections, I have tried to provide answers to certain questions. In chapter two I analyze the role of the Finnish temperance movement and ideology in the rise of the distinction between normal and pathological drinking. The chapter shows that the stages through which heavy drinking began to be considered an illness coincided with changes in alcohol legislation. Along with a gradual shift, first from a collective control to state-control, and later to individual control of drinking, the responsibility for drinking habits has shifted from the collective or the state to the individual. At the same time, it became common to think that abnormal drinking must be due to a personal pathology.

In chapter three I report on two case studies of Finnish local taverns, analyze the way in which the desire to go to the tavern and to drink is rooted in Finnish working-class culture, and discuss the role of the alcoholism frame in these cases. Although the alcoholism frame is seldom explicitly used by the men studied, they are well aware that they may be deemed "drunks" or "alcoholics" by outsiders, and they themselves also have their moments of doubt about the "real" motive for their pub-going. In that sense, the alcoholism frame structures their behavior to some degree.

Chapter four further develops these themes. It analyzes the "cultural grammar" of Finnish male working-class drinking by using the life stories of alcoholic and nonalcoholic men. It shows that the men's drinking habits are guided by a distinct cultural notion of *freedom*. They believe that total personal freedom is achieved, paradoxically, only when every kind of self-control and self-discipline is delegated to other people or externalized to outer constraints. However, when they interpret their drinking as expressing the desire to be personally free, it contradicts their will to preserve good relations with their significant others.

To solve this contradiction, the men redefine their drinking within the alcoholism frame as proof of their uncontrolled craving for alcohol.

Chapter five is a study of a Finnish alcoholism treatment institution called the A-clinic. It examines the way that different explanatory models of alcoholism are used as a means of making sense of the lived experience of both clients and therapists, and how these explanations are rooted in the specific social conditions. A case analysis of a family treatment group, applying the ideas of family systems theory, shows how insistently a medical model of alcoholism suggests itself, even if not offered by the therapists.

Chapter six is a case study of a Finnish self-help group called the A-guild. It looks at the way these men try to unthink the alcoholism frame and resolve their drinking problems by relating them to the meaning of drinking in Finnish working-class culture.

Chapter seven discusses three ways in which the alcoholism frame is linked with the modern notion of person. First, alcoholism is seen as a personal problem, and this presupposes an individualist worldview. Second, in the alcoholism frame, alcoholism is seen as a disease of the will, and this presupposes the modern notion of a person as a desiring subject. Third, the alcoholism frame presents an individual's heavy drinking pattern as a long-standing personal problem. This is rooted in the way in which the modern individual is constructed as a personality with the help of "autobiographical reasoning."

Chapter eight outlines a cultural theory of alcoholism. It suggests that theories about drinking problems are efforts to deal with them, and that is why such theories restructure the problems themselves. Theories of alcohol related problems, therefore, have to be seen as part of the problems themselves.

The theoretical appendix discusses theories of the modern individual as a desiring subject. It develops an account of modernization and character modification, the role of the notions of "desire" and "self-control" in it, and discusses its methodological implications. By taking examples of the studies of this book, it also discusses the different functions and meanings of explicitly stated regulative rules may have.

The studies in this book deal with Finland. It seems that in Finland the alcoholism frame does not organize everyday life so much as, say, in the United States. Therefore it may appear easier for me to relate unacceptable drinking to the social and cultural meanings that structure everyday life, to the meaning structures in terms of which ordinary drinking situations are perceived. However, I think that the ease with which the excessive drinking habits of the men studied here are shown to be intelligible in terms of the meaning of ordinary drinking is largely an illusion, created by painstaking cultural analysis. The cultural structures of everyday-life are constitutive of men and women's interaction and mutual understanding, but they are rarely if ever discussed and reflected on. In this regard, Pierre Bourdieu (1977) talks about doxa, the universe of undiscussed and undisputed knowledge, on the basis of which people's discourse, arguments, and attitudes arise. The everyday-life frame resides below a horizon of taken for grantedness; its rules are obvious only after they have been expressly articulated. Further, from without, these men's "alcoholic" drinking and other behavior seems quite as irrational as that of, say, American alcoholics. So, I would like to say to a reader who thinks that these cases are "ethnic" exceptions: *De te fabula narratur*; it's you that the tale tells about.

METHODOLOGY

The construction of this work is due to the subject and to my conception of the role of theories, methods, and empirical material in cultural studies. To me, sociology is a genre of literature rather than a form of social engineering. This book does not seek to provide the state, or other groups, with useful, reliable background information for planning and policy-making. That does not imply that all references to concrete reality are in vain. Neither do I think that "methodic sincerity" (Malinowski 1961, 3) is unimportant. I have been careful in making observations.

Nonetheless, the point of cultural studies, in my view, is to find new ways of seeing, to create possibly confusing and hopefully fresh, but nevertheless grounded points of view for understanding and explaining social phenomena. By revealing the social and historical form and logic of limits and constraints that are often taken for granted and conceived as universal and natural, sociology can help the reader find new ways of thinking and acting. This kind of effort requires a lot of thinking, but it also takes devices and conceptual tools that help one to succeed.

I perceive a theoretical framework as a way of thematizing and understanding phenomena in a way that differs from that of lay thinking. A research method is a way of applying that framework to a particular subject and material. A developed and explicitly defined method is a way of protecting oneself from being carried away by one's own prejudices, by the constraints of lay thinking. A method is like a telescope or a microscope that presents the material in a way that differs from the one we are used to. It may raise into the fore things that cannot be seen with the "bare eye," details that may give us a hint of a totally new theoretical framework. And the same can be said of the so-called empirical data, since any material organized by the rules of research methodology may represent the "empirical material" of a study. Empirical data, therefore, have a double role. They provide us with direct or mediated information about a phenomenon. In addition, empirical material, whether it be based on interviews or observation, a sample of cultural artifacts, or a collection of essays written by other social scientists, is food for thought. By arranging and interpreting the material the researcher can clear his or her thoughts and sharpen the conceptual and methodological tools.

In my search for new ways of thinking, I have been influenced by several trends in cultural studies. My debt to Michel Foucault is great and will become clear in later chapters. I also want to pay tribute to the Birmingham school, especially the ethnographic studies of Paul Willis. The Birmingham school must be especially appreciated for its ability to cross, or at least narrow, the gap between structure and agency, between subjects and their external limits and conditions. On the one hand, human subjects search in an active and creative way for a view of the social world that makes sense. On the other hand, the tools available for our cultural construction of social reality and identity are themselves part of that world. The way social life appears to us is pre-structured by cultural distinctions, classifications, and discourses. I have sought to hold on to both ends of the chain at once; to treat way of life—or, to use Pierre Bourdieu's concept, habitus—as a structured and structuring structure.

Even though this book can be classified as alcohol sociology, I would like to place my work in a broader context, and treat it as a work in the cultural studies of complex society. To paraphrase Michel Foucault (1986, 9), the case studies that follow are studies of alcoholism by reason of the domain they deal with, and the references they appeal to. But my interest in drinking is of a philosophical nature. The primary object has been to learn to what extent the efforts to think about drinking can "free thought from what it silently thinks, and so enable it to think differently."

Chapter 2

THE UTILITARIAN ETHIC
AND THE CULT OF SELF-CONTROL:
FROM TEMPERANCE TO ALCOHOLISM

This chapter analyzes the function and importance of the idea of self-control in Finnish culture and the Finnish temperance movement. Temperance ideology's emphasis on self-control is seen here legitimizing an increasing use of a utilitarian framework or worldview. I will discuss the growing importance of self at the end of the nineteenth century and the beginning of the twentieth century, the era of the strength of the Finnish temperance movement. Then I will briefly analyze the way in which conceptions about drinking changed when the temperance movement lost its appeal to the masses.

FROM BOTTOMLESS THIRST TO SELF-CONTROL

The rise of the temperance cause as a mass movement in the late nineteenth century coincides with a change in drinking habits that Oiva Turpeinen (1975; 1977) has documented in his studies dealing with alcohol mortality in Finland, 1802-1917. In his first study (1975), he reveals a pattern that is elegant in its simplicity. The number of alcohol-related deaths was strongly associated with total alcohol consumption and with the overproduction of distilled spirits. The better a season, and the more successful a region was with respect to agricultural production, especially that of grain, the more such deaths there were. There was higher mortality in the autumn, after harvest. Those who died of alcohol poisoning were more likely prosperous farmers rather than farmworkers or tenant farmers. In other words, whenever there was any grain left over beyond the amount stored for food, it appears that it was fermented, distilled, and practically drunk on the spot. There seemed to be a bottomless yearning and thirst for distilled spirits (see Mäntylä 1985, 169-79).

The whole pattern changed after the late 1870s. In the second part of his study, dealing with alcohol-related mortality in Finland in 1878 to 1917, Turpeinen (1977) can no longer employ the simple materialist explanatory model. Differences in grain production no longer explained the regional differences in alcohol mortality and consumption. Now alcohol mortality was noticeably greater in towns than in rural areas. And in towns, it was not the affluent middle- or upper-class people but rather the factory workers who had the highest alcohol mortality rates. On the basis of these mortality figures and other sources, Turpeinen inferred that rural alcohol consumption—especially that of farmers—sharply decreased whereas alcohol consumed by the industrial population increased with industrialization and urbanization.

This shift was in part the result of changed alcohol legislation. The acquisition of spirits became more difficult in the countryside due to the legislation of 1865 and 1886. The 1865 law denied the farms the right to distill spirits. The 1886 law enforced further restrictions on the sales of beer and spirits, and denied country towns the right to produce and sell spirits. On top of this, the law raised the tax on alcohol production (Turpeinen 1977, 63-65). When the peasants' license to make distilled spirits was transferred to the bourgeoisie of the towns, alcohol mortality diminished. Although farm income and prosperity in rural areas grew in the latter period, farmers did not spend the extra money on alcohol but used it for other purposes, such as on various forms of investment. On the other hand, industrial workers in towns spent a large part of their increasing income on spirits.

But there was a more profound shift as well. Take for instance the 1865 change in alcohol legislation. Previously, every farm used to have a set quota, a set amount of grain it produced. That quota was shared among the people who lived off the farm—both the owners and the farmworkers—and was consumed in traditional ways according to rituals that emphasized a collective ownership of alcohol (I. Sulkunen 1986, 276-77). After the change of the legislation, individuals had to buy their spirits personally in the towns. In other words, alcohol became a commodity with a certain price. The new situation made it easier to think of drinking in terms of a utilitarian framework. However, the application of the utilitarian framework to drinking habits had to be ideologically legitimized.[1]

TEMPERANCE AS A MOVEMENT AND AS AN IDEOLOGY

The late nineteenth-century change in the patterns of alcohol consumption corresponds with the rise of the Finnish temperance movement. According to Turpeinen (1977), the decrease in total alcohol consumption in Finland for 1878 to 1900 occurred mainly among the rural population, industrial workers did not decrease their consumption until after the turn of the century.[2] The principal Finnish temperance organization, Raittiuden Ystävät (the friends of temperance), was founded in 1884. Temperance was the biggest mass movement in Finland at the time, reaching a peak in the number of its members between the years 1900 and 1905 (Sulkunen and Alapuro 1987, 142).

There are certainly several reasons for the unique Finnish phenomenon of massive working-class support for temperance and prohibition. First, it has been argued that the working class used the temperance movement as an umbrella under which it organized as a political movement (I. Sulkunen 1986, 260-72). Second, since the license for the sale of spirits was in the hands of the bourgeoisie of the towns, they were branded with the name "liquor mafia." The abuse was not an accusation of illegal activity. According to the labor movement's temperance ideology, the bourgeoisie profited from the sale of liquor in two ways. On the one hand, some capitalists produced and sold it as a profitable article, and on the other hand, it kept the working class content and passive. Alcohol was perceived as "the opium of the people." This articulation of the temperance ideology with class interests estranged some of its middle-class supporters. Third, temperance was also a gender issue. As early as in 1876, a group of women demanded restrictions to the alcohol legislation in an attempt to protect religion, family, and the fatherland (I. Sulkunen 1986, 33-35). A similar incident took place in 1916 at the Kymmene paper factories. The wives of factory workers organized a meeting, and decided to demand that the sale of beer be prohibited. When the lists were placed at the factory gates, they were signed by 1,337 people, most of whom were men (Talvi 1979, 298). Working-class solidarity crossed gender boundaries. According to the prevailing ethics, the interests of the working class overrode individuals' own preferences; they were prepared to make personal sacrifices.

According to Irma Sulkunen (1986), the temperance movement was a major force for the adoption of new habits and ways of life among the working class. She maintains that temperance was a civic religion:

> [It] acted as a tool by which the entire view of life of the working class, which was recruited from the countryside, sought its ideological character. Or to be more precise: it *was* the workers' central ideology during that stage of history in which there occurred the shift from the old class system, from the religion-oriented view, and from the collective concept of man to individualist secular citizenship.

While the temperance movement redefined the people as individuals and as citizens of the modern state, the ideology of temperance provided them with the legitimations of the individualist behavioral code. The temperance ideology made the modern worldview and the corresponding codes of conduct seem like every individual's and real Christian's moral duty. Let us study how the new ethics was achieved.

THE IDEOLOGIES OF SELF-CONTROL

Temperance was first raised as a central issue by the Fennoman movement. This originally upper-class movement began in the conviction of some Swedish-speaking upper class and intelligentsia that their group had become too detached from the ordinary, Finnish-speaking folk, whose needs it did not know, and whose best interests it did not promote. The Fennoman movement proposed that the upper class start speaking Finnish (a language the upper class had not mastered) and develop it into a civilized language. As a result of its efforts, public elementary schools were established, Finnish language newspapers were established in increasing numbers, Finnish books began to appear, and libraries were founded (Hästesko 1931; Numminen 1961; Suuniitty 1976; Raivio 1975). The Fennoman movement promoted literacy, knowledge as opposed to superstition, and humanist in addition to religious values.

The Fennoman movement made the fight against drunkenness a central part of their program. They contended that drunkenness was widespread among the population and especially the working class, causing poverty, misery, negligence at work, and an overall moral decline. The Fennoman intelligentsia launched a campaign against drunkenness and published many pamphlets or "temperance tales" (see Lender and Karnchanapee 1977). The first pamphlet told the story of a fictitious person called Turmiolan Tommi, or "Paul of Perdition Place," of the year 1858. This picture story shows that bad morals lead to bad ends. In the story Tommi leads a happy family life until he goes to a barroom, brawls at home, loses his fortune, and finally beats up and kills his wife. He ends up in prison, and the story closes with the moral, imitating the meter of Kalevala, the national epic of Finland: "The Booze did its deed/Menaced the mind/And fettered the feet."

The Fennoman intelligentsia promoted various kinds of cultural activities including the founding of temperance societies in order to raise the public morals among the working class. The Fennoman newspaper *Uusi Suometar* urged its readers:

> Establish a temperance society in your region; may the members of the estates and the employers be in the forefront. Make rules which the members are forced to obey. Have the courage to be the first to sign your name in the document; I'm sure the good example attracts others to follow. Here the ministers have the chance to be the first to set out to noble work, to remove brutality from our dear Finland; also the public school teachers have opportunity to show that they want to exterminate darkness, to bring light and civility to our folk. [Sulkunen 1986, 37]

The aim of the intelligentsia demands was the crusade to teach the folk more civilized habits.

Temperance ideology was also associated with the ideologies of other movements of the time, especially the revivalist religious movements of the nineteenth century. Two main points distinguished revivalists from ordinary Protestant religious life. First, like the temperance movement, the revivalist movements were proponents of a new form of societal organization (Sulkunen 1986, 18; 1983). The movements had a rebellious relation to the church as an institution. They more or less challenged the position and authority of Protestant ministers, and had their own preachers and leaders. It has been said that the

Lestadian sect was the most radical in this respect.[3] The revivalist movements have been often considered prepolitical social movements (Alapuro 1977; Suolinna 1975; 1969).

The revivalist movements also strongly promoted an individualist view of life by emphasizing the total and personal nature of being in the faith. Around 1800 Paavo Ruotsalainen, one of revivalism's most influential and legendary characters, started to preach that true faith is based on a daily fight for it; one must not fool oneself into thinking that one is sacred and that knows God; one has to do penance every day (Rosendal 1902, 26-27).[4] In short, this pietist movement supported the growing importance of self-reflection:

Another movement that contributed to building temperance ideology was the youth societies (*nuorisoseura*) movement founded in the countryside after 1881. In the 1890s the youth societies movement then started to spread all over the country. Compared to the Fennoman movement the youth movement was more in the hands of the peasantry itself, but it also sought to refine the "uncivilized" or "immoral" folkways. One of the youth movement's main enemies was traditional heavy-drinking habits and drunkenness. Other immoralities included dancing and the tradition of night courting (*yökosinta*)[5] (Turunen 1979, 24-25). To fight these immoralities, the youth associations organized choirs and amateur theater groups, so that the youth would become more cultivated, and develop a taste for more mental activities.

A cult of self-control was a shared theme in the ideology of all these social movements. This was the case clearly with the thinking of one of the leading ideologists of the time, Santeri Alkio, the leader of the youth societies movement. His central concept was self-education (*itsekasvatus*). By that concept he synthesized the various indicators—temperance, public education, sexual morality—of the ideological change into a whole.

According to Alkio's individualist worldview, both social and individual faults were caused by lack of knowledge and education. Therefore the "folk youth"—by which he referred mainly to the peasantry—needed education and guidance in civilized manners. The function of education was not, however, to change only external behavior, but rather to awaken the individual's personal activity and yearning for knowledge and mental cultivation. By self-education Alkio meant that individuals have to take care of their own growing (Turunen 1979). In other words, an individual should learn to conceive of his or her life as an endless striving for better, and as a "sublimation" of desires.

The same idea of "sublimation" was also present in the ideology of the Russian novelist, Leo Tolstoy. Among the intelligentsia, "Tolstoyism" was a well-known and rather popular ideology at that time and influenced Alkio. In the youth societies movement two presidents of the central organization were, in addition to Alkio, interested in and influenced by Tolstoyism. It also had an influence on the workers' movement, since many of the leading figures of the socialist movement admired Tolstoy and read his books. Matti Kurikka, one of the socialist leaders and an editor of the workers' newspaper *Työmies*, in 1897-99, spoke and wrote openly for Tolstoy's ideas.[6] In this creed, there were three main points. The first was pacifism. The second one has a ring from socialism: according to it, we must not live on others' work. And according to the third point, we must not let our sex drive control us (Nokkala 1958).

SELF-CONTROL AND THE NATURE/CULTURE OPPOSITION AS LEGITIMIZING TECHNIQUES

The previous section suggested that self-control was a key concept used by a number of social movements at the turn of the century for assessing individual behavior and promoting civilized habits. In what way did the cult of self-control affect people? Did they simply get the message and begin to control their urges and impulses more effectively? That is how Norbert Elias (1978; 1982) perceives the change. According to him, the civilizing process can be best understood as the emergence of self-control, whereby natural instincts and urges are kept in check. In this respect he shares the views of the Finnish late nineteenth-century popular movements, whose members also perceived themselves as proponents of "culture," of civilized conduct as opposed to "nature" or primitive behavior. That does not prove the theory either right or wrong. However, the popularity of the nature/culture opposition makes us ask how it is socially and historically constructed. What made it appealing to the public as an essential element of the temperance ideology?

I suggest that the cult of self-control had a legitimizing function. It contributed to rendering the individualist behavioral code morally acceptable. The cult of self-control was articulated through two pairs of value oppositions, in terms of which individual behavior was assessed. There was an opposition between utilitarian self-seeking and a code of

conduct serving the interests of a community, and there was an opposition between nature and culture.

During the rise of the temperance movement, people were apt to
consider their drinking habits from an individualist, utilitarian perspective. However, this was a new frame to be applied to drinking occasions which were traditionally structured by a collectivist frame. And
utilitarian self-seeking was morally disapproved by the working class
and the peasants. In this situation, the temperance ideology provided
the people with a way of accepting the individualist frame. In the temperance ideology, personal moderation or abstinence was associated
with class solidarity among free and equal individuals. In other words
in temperance ideology the individualist frame was not in contradiction
with communal values.

The emphasis on the value of self-control also justified the individualist behavioral code by stressing the strong willpower it takes to be
able to resist the temptations of individual drives and needs. This is
expressed in Tolstoyism's third point by saying that we must not let
our sex drive freely control us. Take, for instance, methods of birth control adopted by large numbers of people in late nineteenth-century Finland (Notkola 1989). Along with the extension of capitalist exchange
relations, the value of a child could—and often had to—be counted in
money, and that certainly influenced the spread of birth control methods. However, to account for birth control in terms of a utilitarian
framework would have made it morally and ethically questionable to
many people. The emphasis on the heroic willpower and self-denial it
required presented the situation in a new, more favorable light.

The other ideological technique pictured traditional habits associated with social solidarity as savage, animalistic, and uncivilized. Here
the nature/culture opposition came into play. People's desire to behave
in the old ways was interpreted as less "civilized," nearer to the state of
nature, than the new ones. Those who still clung to the old ways were
therefore perceived as savage, childlike people with a weak willpower.

The ideology of these social movements worked by creating these
new oppositions: the individualist and collectivist frameworks on the
one hand, and the nature/culture opposition on the other. By associating traditional habits with selfishness, savagery, and hedonism, and
individualism with civilization and solidarity, individualist behavior
was presented as a socially appropriate and beneficial code of conduct.

The late nineteenth-century Finnish temperance movement used
self-discipline and the nature/culture opposition as instruments in legit-

imizing the modern, individualist code of conduct. The cult of self-control constructed the competition and conflict between traditional habits and modern ways of life as a struggle between nature and culture, between natural instincts and civilized manners. In that way, the utilitarian frame was portrayed in a new light by interpreting it as individuals' heroic fight over their internal nature.

Because it became a mass movement, the temperance movement helped spread the cult of self-control: propagated and legitimized the individualist behavioral model. And the temperance cause, in turn, was adopted by practically all social and political movements at the turn of the century. As an ideology it housed many traditional, spiritually powerful, elements and borrowed many of its features from Protestant religion and from the revivalist movements of the mid-nineteenth century. Temperance branded traditional drinking habits as sinful and hedonistic, a violation of both religious and civic standards. The believers in this new civic religion were shaped as individual, self-controlled citizens embracing individualism.

FROM TEMPERANCE TO ALCOHOLISM

What has changed since the end of the nineteenth century? As trivial as it seems, the most important change is that there is no more such thing as the temperance movement, hardly even a temperance ideology. The organizations still exist, and they get funding from the state,[7] but they cannot really be called social movements. They are now institutions doing health education, and as important as health has become to the people recently, it does not give rise to social movements.[8]

However, the decline of the temperance movement is a sign of a qualitative shift in the civilizing process. The traditional temperance ideology, based on a cult of self-control, does not appeal to people any more. People are not fascinated by sacred self-denial; they want to feel free to behave according to their own desires. Nor do people feel defensive about seeking their own interests. The whole situation has been reversed in that individuals' own best, "self-realization," and the fulfillment of their own needs and desires is now used as a legitimizing device of a present behavioral model. Asceticism is no more approvable or valued, because it is associated with paternalism and militant narrow-mindedness. Instead, the present temperance ideology cherishes the values of Romanticism, the right and duty of every person to find one's own ways and true self.

The shift can be seen in the changes of the temperance movement's programs. From "civic religion" or convictional teetotalism to rationalist temperance (of the types of temperance ideology, see Kirsi 1988) and "healthyism" has been the general trend at least on the programatic level. Until the 1950s, the programs of the temperance movement were based on an ideal picture of a "healthy, natural, and positive way of life," and alcoholic beverages did not belong to it. But the ideal of a good life included also other things: cultural education, taking care of one's physical fitness, and being a good, law-abiding citizen. The programs warned of "diversions that idealize and maintain an unhealthy life," and advised to be cautious of "asocial individuals who spread drunkenness."

In the 1980s the programs shifted to emphasize individual values, needs, and decisions: they stressed that one can lead a natural and positive life in a number of ways. The goal of temperance work nowadays is understood as "to support people in their own aspirations to be healthy and to increase their control over their life." Temperance is understood as a means to control one's own life (Kirsi and Piispa 1985, 16). Therefore, since instructions about a proper way of life are excluded, almost the only message the temperance movement has got is information about health issues, especially about the dangers of intoxicants and about alcoholism.[9] In other words, the empty space left by the disappearance of an outspoken moral ideal has been filled in by an increased interest in the areas usually taken care of by state officials—that is, health care and social policy.

There are no paternalistic instructions in the present-day ideologies, only a vaguely expressed wish that every individual is provided the chance for self-realization. The notion of "self-control" even has a bad ring.

This shift is produced, I suggest, by a transformation of the civilized/primitive distinction into that of normal/pathological. It is taken for granted that every individual acts according to his/her own best interests, that everybody leads a normal, "healthy" life. Forms of behavior thought to be bad for the individual's health are taken as proof of an individual pathology, of a mental disorder. Aberrations from the normal are no longer interpreted as immoral, sinful, or hedonist, but rather as sick.

Consequently, a concern for moral, civilized conduct—expressed in the late-nineteenth century social movements, such as the temperance movement—has been replaced by a concern about behavioral pathologies such as alcoholism. Because of this shift, views of heavy drinking have changed. During the days of glory of the temperance movement, drinking was understood as a moral question concerning the whole community. Since then, it has been increasingly perceived—both by the individual and by others—as a personal question. As Kettil Bruun (1971) summarizes it in his analysis of the development of the Finnish alcoholism treatment system, at the turn of the century alcoholism was perceived as a crime or a sin, then as a bad habit, and finally as a disease.

This line of development is not a new observation in social theory and many modes of behavior are now viewed in medical terms.[10] In the social science literature, this shift goes by the name of medicalization of deviance and social control, wherein a form of nonnormative behavior is labeled first a "sin," then a "crime," and finally a "sickness" (Conrad and Schneider 1980; Schneider 1978).

In light of the history of the Finnish temperance movement discussed in this chapter, it seems fruitful to approach medicalization as the replacement of the earlier civilized/primitive opposition by that of normal/pathological. In the previous distinction, "primitive" behavior was condemned as "sinful," "immoral," or "hedonist," and "civilized" conduct was cherished as being controlled and socially constructive. In terms of the normal/pathological opposition, moral evaluation of human behavior is perceived as irrelevant, or even inhuman. It is now the right of individuals to set their own values and to rationally seek to fulfill their needs and desires. It is taken for granted that such "normal" behavior is for the good of the whole society. Should, then, an individual's behavior be harmful to the society, or especially to that individual, it is taken as proof of a disease or disorder. Such disorders are not condemned; rather they are treated by various forms of therapy.

It seems that the new "temperance," or rather "healthyism," ideology is based on a changed conception of "human nature." Unlike the Christian religious doctrines, where it was thought that people are bad, or "wild," by nature, and reflected in the nineteenth-century temperance movement, the new "healthyism" reflects the modern, secularized concept that all "evil" in a human being is caused by a "disorder," either induced by bad social conditions or by an individual's inheritance.[11] As Sulkunen (1986, 312) notes, the temperance movement was indeed, even in this sense, a civic religion, a transition stage "from the religion-oriented view, and from the collective concept of man to individualist secular citizenship."

The shift from asceticism to hedonism and from a religious or criminological to a medical view on heavy drinking seems to be linked to the repeal of prohibition in 1932. As drinking was no longer criminalized, more responsibility for the negative consequences of drinking was delegated to the individual. However, the shift from the cult of self-control to an ethic of hedonism has been a gradual one. That may be because, from the days of total prohibition onward, the liberalization of Finnish alcohol policy has been a slow process.

The prohibition act entered into force in 1918 after the Finnish Civil War, when the bourgeoisie had completely defeated the working class. The smuggling and sale of alcohol soon became an organized business and public opinion turned against prohibition. Drinking and smuggling took on the flavor of a revolt against authorities, and smugglers were hailed almost as national heroes. For working people, the prohibition act had now taken on a completely new meaning: drinking became associated with protest and defiance of the "White Finland" of the bourgeois classes. This meaning of drinking did not die out right after the repeal of prohibition, since the state alcohol monopoly, which was established as the only authority to take care of the sales of alcohol, adopted a strict alcohol control policy. According to the liquor act of 1932, trade in spirits had to be so regulated that all illegal trade was prevented, and the consumption of spirits reduced to as low a level as possible (Simpura 1982; Sulkunen, Alasuutari, Nätkin, and Kinnunen 1985, 32-33). Even though the control policy has been gradually liberalized, drinking today still carries a connotation of protest.

Social theorists from Daniel Bell to Christopher Lasch have suggested that modern society has witnessed a shift from asceticism to hedonism. It seems that the rise and fall of the Finnish temperance movement can be partially interpreted in terms of this transformation. Asceticism seemed to be a central element in the ideology of the temperance movement during its days of glory, whereas its decline seems to be associated with the rise of some sort of hedonism.[12] However, along with the shift from asceticism to hedonism on the ideological level, there is a shift from state control to individual control on the organizational level. The latter shift means that people attempt to develop themselves into subjects that behave within the limits of "normality." In the modem hedonist era, the crossing of the limits of normality is defined as pathological.[13]

Chapter 3

PUB-GOING AND DESIRE

Because of historical changes in the cultural and political meaning of drinking and temperance in Finnish society, public attitudes toward drinking are highly ambiguous. The old temperance ideology, which disapproves of the alcohol trade and treats spirits as the opium of the people, is still alive, but it is balanced against the individual hedonism, and symbolic defiance and freedom that may be represented by drinking. This ambiguity is reflected in the tradition of heavy weekend drinking, coupled with total abstinence during the rest of the week. Most of the drinking takes place in the privacy of homes.

Against this background, it is no wonder that the local taverns established in newly built suburbs in the end of the 1960s or early 70s acquired a bad reputation. The regulars of these taverns have broken many traditional norms; even though they may drink moderately, they go to the tavern several times a week.

That is why the local taverns were an extremely interesting object of study. The idea of the local tavern research project (see Alasuutari and Siltari 1983; Sulkunen, Alasuutari, Nätkin, and Kinnunen 1985), which was started in the early 1980s, was to study the place of alcohol in everyday life. Of course that was not the only objective; it was also to tackle the meaning for ordinary people of the great structural changes of the 1960s and 70s in Finnish society. The people studied—especially the regulars of the two local taverns selected as objects of case studies—do not represent "typical" individuals or "normal drinkers." Given the research setting, it would have been impossible, because local taverns of the newly built suburbs were and still are places with a fairly bad reputation, or at least open to moral debate. However, the point of departure was to relate drinking and pub-going—both as a habit and as a topic—and the problems and conflicts they generate, to a larger societal and cultural context. From the viewpoint—and often literally from the windows—of decent, middle-class suburbanites, the lifestyle of the local tavern's regular patrons certainly looked strange, but as a deviation of norms, their lifestyle probably revealed much more of the norms and cultural structures of everyday life than an analysis of "normality" would have done.

In other words, the local tavern is a middle ground between decency and normal drinking on one hand and shabbiness and alcoholism on the other. The tavern and the group of regulars that was the object of the first ethnographic case study was more "respectable" in this respect, whereas the other pub was deliberately chosen to represent a more severe case, more heavy-drinking regulars of a lower-grade tavern. The vague initial idea was—by comparing the two cases—to study what becoming an alcoholic means as a process of cultural change. Let me briefly report the two cases,[1] and let us then discuss the implications that eventually could be drawn of the two case studies.

THE DARTS CLUB

The first of the two case studies dealt with the regulars in the darts club at a tavern called Vapaavuoro. The game of darts was introduced to Vapaavuoro in the early 1970s; at that time Metsäkylä was still under construction and the tavern was quite new. Ten years later most of the club's original founders and other long-established members were still actively involved.

The total membership is about thirty persons, and club officials are duly elected each year as required by Finnish law. The members can be divided into two groups, the "pros," who were the founders and still are among the best players, and "juniors," who have joined the club later on. Additionally, there are occasional darts players, but they are of no real importance to the cultural forms of the club.

The formal organization of the club at Vapaavuoro is actually of little importance. The club members form a loose, informal group whose members come together to enjoy a few beers and play darts in a relaxed atmosphere. The group members have different backgrounds and different motives for using their leisure time in this way; in fact, an individual's motives may differ from one day to the next. Nevertheless, participation in a game of darts is a social activity characterized by conformity, regularity, and agreement. Its regularity has no superimposed set of rules, its unity derives from no external source, and the agreement that it represents has no specific external aim. For these reasons the darts club can be studied as what is called here a miniculture.

The implicit orderliness to be found in the club members' behavioral patterns is not due to regulative but rather to constitutive rules (Winch 1958): the rules stem from an implicit agreement on the symbolic meaning attached to certain cultural artifacts and to the group's activities. These cultural meanings are made more explicit by the way people talk about their group. They lay particular stress on certain things that are meaningful elements of their miniculture.

Elements of the Miniculture

One of the things that the men emphasize when discussing the meaning of pub-going and darts for them is action and sociability. The members of the darts club go to the tavern mainly for the game, but the acquaintances and friendships that build up around the game combine with the activity of beer drinking to produce an integral whole. Every element is important: if one is missing, the activity as a whole no longer meets the expectations of the participants:

> Darts is very important. That's why I come here. You can always play darts at home with the neighbors, but here you can meet new people as well. It's no life just sitting at home watching the telly. That's why I come out.

This is how Eino (40), an industrial worker with two children, explains what the game means for him. Darts is a chance to relax and forget the problems of everyday life. As a social activity darts always involves some degree of competition. "That's human nature," is the explanation often cited by the members, but the game is not to be taken too seriously. The significance of the darts game for social intercourse is taken for granted.

The regular customers and the darts club thus form a sort of local community, an arena for mutual interaction and communication. Its role can thus be compared with that of the mass media, which in modern society have largely replaced direct interpersonal relationships. The men seem to have considerable reservations about a family-centered way of life.

The men's activity is not restricted to the tavern. Some members have several hobbies and many of them were active sportsmen during their younger days. For them, darts represent something of a "cooling-off" activity, an enjoyable way of satisfying their desire for action. And in addition to action, the game also provides excitement.

One indication of the need for excitement is that all games, even on weekdays, are played for money. The amount involved is small, generally one mark, or two in the case of "harder" games; the regular members do not usually play for larger amounts. The men stress that the excitement is not created by the fear of losing money or the desire to win; they feel the amounts they put in are too small for that. It is more a question of honor.

Accuracy is only one of the skills needed by darts players. A certain amount of mental arithmetic is necessary for many games, and this proves difficult for some. "That's it, you've got it" was the comment when a younger player finally managed to work out the right result with a lot of help from the others. The ability to work out scores quickly and accurately is a highly regarded skill at least in the eyes of the regular players who can add and subtract fairly complicated numbers to work out their scores in an instant.

Another feature of the darts club that the men like to emphasize is their moderate drinking habits. To an external observer the members of the darts club indeed seem more sober than the other customers. The shouted, drunken conversations so typical of male groups in taverns are lacking, and the group of players has an air of silent concentration, even though they are all generally drinking beer.

There are no unusual features in the drinking habits of the darts players. On weekdays they usually drink four or five bottles of beer, but their consumption is much higher at the weekends and especially during long competitions. The men have a tendency to understate the amount they drink, but they also exaggerate the amount of money they spend.

Darts requires self-discipline, and players who are too drunk simply cannot play. Indeed, every now and then a player who has had a few too many decides to give up and either goes home or moves to a table to join other nonparticipants in the game. Most members, however, want to stay in the game; they are not interested merely in drinking. Therefore they ensure that they remain sober enough to take part. This is even more important when the game is played in teams of two, since a player who is too drunk spoils his partner's chances as well. If the game is one where players pay to participate, the drunken partner may be liable to pay for his teammate, too. Thus the game functions as an external form of self-discipline, a norm that limits participants' drinking. This norm is consistent with Finnish drinking culture; normally it is completely inappropriate to try to limit your friend's drinking. "When you play darts you have to pull yourself together . . . it keeps you sharp, even if you've drunk a fair lot," says Aki.

The men nevertheless say that playing darts does not actually limit their drinking; they are hardly sober even if they appear to be. However, drinking and getting drunk are not the main reasons why the members go to the tavern. They go to play darts and meet their mates. For the darts players, their state of intoxication and its public expression are not matters of great importance.

The men also stress that home and family come first, then darts. In their opinion, they fulfill their domestic duties first, and only then do they go to the tavern. They also stress that drinking has not severely affected their household. Many of the club members own their apartment, and some even have a summer place.

The men admit that beer does cause some friction at home with the wife. And although the darts players consider meeting their mates as more important than drinking beer, they are not quite sure about the priorities. Aki thinks that they are all quite close to being alcoholics but says that "it's been very close, but one way or another we've managed to steer clear of it." All the darts players have nevertheless managed to avoid any interference with their work. That work has priority and drinking must not be allowed to interfere with it is, in their opinion, of primary importance. All in all, it seems that the dangers connected with pub-going are part of the fun and excitement; they bring a sense of skillful mastery and self-control into one's life.

The club members also stress solidarity and strong ties of friendship between themselves. They may occasionally argue among themselves, but their disagreements are never stronger than a few harsh words, even though the game is by nature a kind of contest for superiority.

The solidarity is not limited to members. Anyone in the tavern can enter the game even if their previous experience of darts has been restricted to the simpler Finnish game. The regular players may joke about a newcomer's lack of experience in the proper game, but never in his presence; newcomers always receive a genuinely friendly welcome.

The open attitude toward newcomers does not imply that they are immediately fully accepted into the group. The solidarity and openness are actually part of the general attitude the long-standing members have adopted toward others. A real friendship will develop between a newcomer and the established members only if the newcomer is fully compatible with the group.

The maintenance of solidarity is also the main reason behind the unwritten rule that members avoid discussions on subjects that could easily lead to disputes. A good example is the subject of politics. There is no categorical rule, but politics is almost never discussed during the game. If someone raises a subject that leads to a lively discussion or an argument, those involved usually adjourn to another table. Some members also occasionally go and sit in the "top booth," which is occupied by a group of older men who continually talk politics or recount their exploits during the war:

> *Ossi:* Politics doesn't come into it. We're not playing with red or blue darts . . . there's no reason to bring politics into the game. It doesn't matter whether somebody's come over from the east or whether they're from the west. It makes no difference whether their politics is red, black, blue, or white. It just doesn't matter.

There is simply no room for politics in the game: skill is the only thing that matters. In the light of Ossi's reply it is also evident that the members are not very interested in politics, at least when they want to relax and play darts.

The fourth characteristic of the darts club's own miniculture is independence. Like the features discussed above, it is complex and not without its own inherent contradictions. In part this independence is manifested as the independence of the darts club from the other customers and from the tavern personnel.

The club's independence from the tavern is a subject that frequently comes up in conversation. One reason is that the members are not actually on very friendly terms with the management. They are tolerated but not particularly welcomed; according to the members, the management would like to turn Vapaavuoro into a "better class place where stylish people come to wine and dine." The members firmly believe that the money they spend finances the tavern, and that they are entitled to something in return.

With their officially registered association the darts players form a sort of interest group that defends the interests of certain of the customers. They have common interests to pursue and demands to make, and these demands carry extra weight because the players are regular customers. Although the players do not enjoy any special prestige at Vapaavuoro, they are nonetheless unwilling to give in to the management.

The club's independence from the tavern's other customers is less pronounced than its independence from the management. The club members make jokes about the political debates and stories of war exploits that the other customers favor; other customers for their part fail to understand what is so special about the game. Nevertheless, as tavern regulars the two groups do have something in common.

This independence on the part of the darts club members also involves a certain degree of individuality, since the men tend to stress how important it is to manage one's affairs properly. The members may occasionally borrow money from each other, but the one who does makes sure that he pays it back as soon as possible.

Most members consider that a private darts club—with booze and everything else—would not be a good idea. In a small group with the same faces the game would become more of a duty than a spontaneous pastime. For the same reason the men do not like to fix the time for their next session in advance, because this would commit them too much.

Miniculture as a Common Organization of a Way of Life

As strange or accidental as the cultural features outlined above may appear, they could nonetheless be made intelligible by relating them to the living conditions and cultural tradition of the group members. The elements of the miniculture have a relation to the men's world outside the pub; the values, behavioral patterns, and social meanings of artifacts or activities in the group of dart players are like another language in terms of which issues of everyday life are indirectly dealt with, discussed, and "magically" reorganized and resolved (Clarke and Jefferson 1973). That is why one could find homologous relations between the meanings attached to the activities of the darts club, on the one hand,

and those attached to other aspects of their everyday life, on the other. One could put it this way: the pub environment, in the way it is symbolically and collectively worked out and "marked" by the members of the cultural group, is a reality that, in terms of a symbolic language, contains the most valued sides of one's everyday life in a form that further clarifies their value. Negative sides of one's life are deemphasized or presented in a form where expressions of opposition are permitted and where opposition is successful. It is this symbolic system of meanings that is the reason for their drinking and related activities like playing darts. Therefore, by studying these socio-symbolic homologies (see Willis 1978) one can grasp the inherent logic in the men's way of life. Let us now look at the homological analysis.

Manual Labor and Professionalism

With very few exceptions the darts players are manual laborers, and in this sense they represent Finnish working-class culture. Within this culture the distinction between mental and manual labor is extremely important. This is then overlaid by a further distinction concerning the performance and control of work: workers who are autonomous in terms of instructions and controls tend to classify supervisors as mental workers. Workers who are told exactly what to do, and how to do it, maintain their self-esteem by putting value on the practical implementation of any given task, rather than on theoretical knowledge:

> PA: How do these blokes with all the training and education get on in more practical jobs?
> *Aki:* Most of them, they're all thumbs. At least those blokes.
> *Ale:* Take the boss of a workshop or a paintshop . . . they always try to get a technician or an engineer or something—but you try working under someone like that for a few weeks, you soon get fed up with the way they carry on.

However, the rejection of mental work as "theoretical garbage" is by no means simple and straightforward. There is a high regard for intelligence and education—but the principles of action that apply to darts are also relevant in this context. Professional skill is indeed greatly respected, on the condition that it produces practical results. If manual workers criticize those who are better trained, it is not because they consider learning and intelligence to be of no value; on the contrary, any mockery is directed at a lack of common sense. This forms the basis of an entire genre of antisupervisor jokes:

> *Aki:* There was this case at Tamrock. They were making some parts—the total run was something like two hundred thousand. So along comes this supervisor, and he thinks the lathe operator isn't going fast enough. So he says, can't you work any faster. And so the lad on the lathe screwed up the whole bloody lot—all two hundred thousand. It had to be done steadily—just as he was doing it. And he had the balls to screw it up on purpose . . . with a real technician telling him how to do his job. Or was he a fucking engineer.

Juniors are even more resolute in this respect. The younger players in the darts team associated manual labor with masculinity and mental work with femininity, and they showed the same kind of determination as the British working-class kids in Paul Willis's study, *Learning to Labour* (1977). Jouko is one of the junior players:

> Most students are somehow different, they're awkward. You know, they're not really any good at practical things, they couldn't cope with the kind of things I do. Say a plane crashed on a desert island, they just couldn't take care of themselves, they wouldn't survive. I would.

The juniors in this group are members of the unskilled working class and they tend to emphasize brute force in their model of masculinity. By contrast, the older workers, and especially the skilled workers, tend to focus their criticism of mental labor on the impracticality of the knowledge that is learned at school, not on the knowledge itself. They look askance at mental work because they are critical of the kind of theoretical thinking that is completely divorced from practical action. They insist that their own job also requires intelligence and creativity. They do not reject mental labor per se as feminine, because they value it as part of their own occupation. But intelligence must be practical; intelligence is useless unless it can be translated into practical action.

At the workplace, as in darts, skilled workers have a high regard for accuracy and common sense. In this sense the game is a homologous equivalent to work:

> *Aki:* It's the same with darts as it is at work, you can get better even if you don't have a talent for it. You need skilled hands. Somebody who does a skilled job that involves detailed work can be good at darts, too.

Aki's own job does not require a steady hand (he is a calibrator), but his mental arithmetic comes in handy for the game:

> *Aki:* After you've thrown you can quickly figure out how much more you've got to go (like in 501 when you count down to zero). It's the same sort of simple arithmetic that I need at work. That's what I really like about darts, the way you can play around with numbers.

Skilled workers do not regard their job merely as external coercion and necessity, even though they are in wage employment and thus very much dependent on their daily toil. For them, work is a source of pride, but at the same time they are well aware that they do it mainly for the money. This is why another aspect of the miniculture—independence—occupies a special position for them in the way they perceive their work. Most of them work independently, without any direct supervision, or in small groups where they are on an equal footing with highly trained colleagues.

The third main characteristic of the darts players' miniculture, self-discipline, is an integral element in their whole way of life. Although the ideal of heavy drinking has still not completely disappeared from the darts players' miniculture, it is moderated by another meaning attached by the skilled workers to drinking. In the same way as they carry responsibility for demanding tasks in the work place, they also regulate their drinking in the tavern so as to be able to play a good game.

Work, One-Upmanship, and Politics

The homology between the world of work and the miniculture of the tavern also extends to the human relations at the work place, to organizational activities and to politics. The Finnish working class has relatively strong traditions of political organization, even though its history is rather short. With the growing social influence of working-class parties and the centralization of the trade union organization, they have ceased to be popular movements and have become bureaucracies; indeed, they have to a certain extent been integrated into the state apparatus. The members are significant only as numbers in election results. Party and trade union officials have become part of the massive bureaucratic apparatus. They have made their careers in the organization.

The darts players' attitudes to these developments are also reflected in their miniculture, in its activity, independence, and mutual harmony. They equate organizational and political activity with study and social climbing, and at the same time compare it with their own work. In politics and large organizations, people seek success through deception; the same applies to those who aspire to high social status through studying.

Their relation to trade union officials is similar. No one denies the importance of the trade unions, but the general feeling is that union officials are not actually doing "real work." It is thought that, for those active in it, politics is a means of careerism.

The pros do not have a high regard for those who sit and talk politics—especially if they do not play darts. Here, the skilled workers' concept of their way of succeeding in life is compared to the game. Down at the tavern, they show their value in playing darts; in the same way, they show their value at the workplace through their professional skill. Those who have no skills use politics to get ahead:

Aki: They're the best subjects if you want an argument, religion and politics. And we're not the kind of people who want to spend all our time arguing.
Ossi: Yeah, but the ones who mess around, they're no good. They certainly don't belong to our group. There'll always be a lot of different views in a group like that, when all sorts of guys come together.

The same conflict between leadership and membership that is seen to permeate the trade union movement is also repeated in the darts club, albeit on a smaller scale. The chairman of the club complains that it is hard to lead the group. On the other hand, the men consider leadership to be an essential factor in any kind of activity.

The main difficulty in leading the group derives from the importance that the miniculture of the darts team attaches to independence: the darts players greatly appreciate the opportunity to be free from supervision and control, and to bear their own responsibilities. In working life, too, there must be someone in charge of union matters, but there is a subtle distinction between being "boss" and being "one of the directors." The only kind of collaboration among workmates that meets with everyone's approval and acceptance is based on concrete, mutual solidarity and equality. Honesty is the best way to guarantee the success of this cooperation, both in the workplace and at the tavern.

Shop-floor trade union solidarity also serves as the model for cooperation in the darts players' relationship with the tavern management. Whenever they confront the tavern management, the men present a united front; no one is an individual customer. In a sense, the darts team is the patrons' trade union. The men insist that the tavern respects them as good customers, and they are sharply critical of the proprietor's rather snobbish policy toward customers "She wants to turn this into a place for snobs." Behind this disagreement we find a clash of two cultures and cultural forms.

Family

Family life is not a popular subject of discussion among the darts players, although the men tend to have a pretty good idea of each other's domestic affairs. If there have been problems or rows with the wife at home, these will be related indirectly, often through humorous hints. It is not unusual for the men to have to think up excuses to get away from home, and these raise a good deal of laughter around the darts board. They might have told the wife they were going to take the garbage out, or they could have sneaked in straight from the sauna, leaving their wet towel with the doorman.

For the darts team at Vapaavuoro, the man's independent position in the family and the entire patriarchal family set-up is regarded as somewhat problematic. The men feel their position is rather insecure; they are afraid that it might change. And these fears are indeed justified. Aki is separated from his wife and Pekka is divorced:

> *Pekka:* Aren't they trying to get the old system back—where women are queens and men are slaves—like it used to be some five thousand years ago?
> *Aki:* Or princesses.
> PA: Wouldn't that be great, eh?
> *Ale:* Depends what kind of princesses they are (laughter).
> *Pekka:* It couldn't change all that suddenly, at least not in our case.

PA: So, you're the masters of the house, are you?
Aki: Yeah, we were (laughter). Or what do you think, Pekka?

The darts players' generation is the first to be affected by the rapid increase in female wage employment, which has imposed completely new demands on family life and on the division of household chores. This is experienced as a serious problem; the typical solution is to refer to the fact that men "are not good at it."

Lack of skill is not the only reason for disagreements between husband and wife as to who should do what at home. The general feeling is that household chores are "women's work," totally unsuited to men. This is not only a normative attitude inherited from older generations. The nature of household chores in the typical suburban home differs in significant respects from that of traditional male jobs, which are characterized by action, clearly identifiable individual performances, and a concrete, visible result. Housework, by contrast, is for the most part invisible; the only time it is noticed is when it remains undone.

Household chores represent a serious threat to mens' independence. They are not in charge at home, they are not responsible, and therefore they fail to see the need for this or that "maintenance job." If the wife intends to get help from her husband, she has to keep urging him, she has to give him specific advice. In this situation the husband easily feels that the wife is giving orders.

It is of course no new discovery that men often remain outside family life. According to certain earlier interpretations this significant and continuing trend started when male wage-labor became the family's most important source of income. In Finland this has happened quite recently, and it has brought with it a change in people's ways of living. Large numbers have moved from small detached houses into single-family apartments in suburbs, where men have had great difficulty in finding "meaningful" jobs for themselves around the home. This, according to Matti Kortteinen (1982), has caused considerable frustration among men, it has made them feel totally useless at home, and the problem is made worse when the wives go out to work. As one of Kortteinen's housewives said, "I work my fingers to the bone day in and day out, and he can't think of anything to do." There seems to be good reason for a redrawing of the division of labor at home, but for most men this would be extremely difficult to accept.

The darts players are by no means unaware of the conflicts that are caused within the family by male independence and activity. The group of professional players includes two who are divorced and one who is separated. These conflicts find concrete expression in darts. The tension between visiting the tavern on the one hand and family life on the other must be resolved in some way. One strategy is to interpret a round of darts as a well-deserved evening off, a reward for doing one's share of the household chores.

Another useful strategy is to try to find some rationale, an independence in household chores that supports the male identity, so that you can justify doing it to yourself or to the mates. One of the men, for example, told about the interest he has developed in preparing good meat. Another one justified his doing the dishes by stressing how well it makes greasy, black hands white. Once you have learned how to go about it, you also learn to enjoy it.

The tension between male independence and responsibility is, in the husband's mind, focused on the wife. She is seen often as a representative of social coercions and a guardian of proper moral standards.[2] Some of the dart players are also members of a private pool club, which operates in the basement of a near-by highrise. In the pool room, there are two signs hanging on the wall, both handwritten by one of the club member's wives. The first gives its approval to the common freedom of men:

MAKE YOURSELF AT HOME
—BUT ENJOY YOURSELF

The other serves as a reminder:

BOYS TO BE BACK HOME BY 11

The men must be home early so they can get up in the morning for the day's work. The wives assume part of the responsibility for this by providing reminders and by controlling their husbands' leisure time and especially their drinking. This is a natural extension of the work they do to keep their husbands in "working order" getting meals, washing their clothes, and keeping the house clean and tidy so that the men can have a good rest. The effort they make almost every evening to keep alcohol consumption within limits so that it does not adversely affect the husband's main responsibility—wage-labor—is actually part of the recurrent struggle between, on the one hand, the coercions imposed by society and one's responsibilities toward one's family, and on the other hand, the independence of men. In this battle, women have taken the role of imposing coercion and obligation.

It is paradoxical that the more the wife assumes responsibility for these obligations, the greater the sense of freedom and independence felt by the men. The wife's participation in wage-labor is also seen in this light:

PA: Do you talk about your wives here?
Reke: Very rarely. The wife is all-important in family life.
PA: In what way?
Reke: How important? Well you've got to get more of this somehow (picks his glass up). . . . I already told you that she's really important, the wife is, otherwise we wouldn't get more of this. Get her working three shifts.
Tarmo: Yeah, I'd still like to say on the tape that this was not serious, I mean this is really getting you nowhere with your research, when you start talking about women this way. Just forget it!
Niilo: No, be honest Tarmo, if you had a wife who earned a hell of a lot, you'd drink your life away. You wouldn't do a single day's work all your life. Nor would I.

The joking that goes on about women seems to reflect the pride that men take in their freedom and in the symbol of that freedom, drinking in a group of men. It also gives us an idea of the kind of freedom they appreciate; if there were someone else to take care of their social obligations, their life would be a ball.

But on the reverse side of the coin, it would actually be catastrophic for the men if the wife were responsible both for the home and for earning the family's income. "You'd drink your life away" is at once a proud manifesto of freedom and a threat: if the man became redundant in his breadwinner role, he would be left with nothing but boozing, drowning his sorrows in drink. In the final analysis it is more important for the men's self-respect to hold down their job than it is to have a happy family life.

Class

Even though in Finland the urban working class has no coherent, long-standing and independent cultural tradition, some of the features of the miniculture can be interpreted as class-based attitudes. Not that the men would think that class differences play any role in the suburb or the tavern; especially the professionals, with their relatively good wages, understate class distinctions. But the way the club members think about drinking resembles the way working-class culture has been internationally described.

There are several postwar developments that have somewhat blurred class differences. This applies in particular to the generation that the darts players represent, one described by J.P. Roos (1980) as that of "postwar growth and reconstruction." In economic standard of living terms, they have started their family life from the level that their parents had reached after working their whole life. Furthermore, the close, tight-knit worker communities have gone. In Tampere, many working-class areas were pulled down to make way for new suburbs. Collective forms of leisure that were typical of worker communities also gave way to a more family-centered way of life, which in former times was a distinctively bourgeois phenomenon. There have been significant changes in consumption patterns, indicative of an increasing privatization of leisure time. People are spending less money than before on books, collective entertainment, and cultural activities, and more money on the home and the family. The lion's share of leisure consumption is taken up by the family's private car and other leisure and sports equipment intended for private use.

For the dart players, pub-going is a way of resisting the new, bourgeois consumption patterns. Their protest is directed against the privatized and family-centered bourgeois way of life; it is for collectivity. It is criticism directed against persistent work to achieve a higher social status, against thriftiness, and against a competitive way of life that serves as a facade for the family.

The suburb offers hardly any opportunity for collective activities, and at home the man faces the frustrating choice between masculine idleness and emptiness and feminine concern for everyday cares. Many of the contemporaries of our darts players have solved this problem by getting themselves a house outside the suburb, a detached house where there is a much better chance for them to find something meaningful to do around the home. A summer place is another possibility. However, the darts players feel that the kind of savings required by such investments would make their life empty and meaningless, no matter what advantages the investment would bring. Ale cannot understand the way of life of his parents, who live nearby:

Ale: It's the same thing with our old folks. Both of them are busting their asses at the factory on low pay, and still they've got themselves a house and a car and all those savings and . . . and all they do is sit in their stupid house, they don't even know what liquor is. Or cigarettes.
Aki: It's peaceful and quiet at our place.
Ale: You can keep your quiet. I mean they've lived in that fucking place for twenty years, and the old man he's been to Vapaavuoro once in his whole life (laughter). And all he had was a bottle of pop.

While the men readily admit that darts and beer are an expensive pastime, they are extremely important to them as an alternative to the petty-bourgeois way of life, to the meaningless pursuit of "collecting the pennies." The darts players are perfectly well aware of this difference in terms of way of life.

THE STORYTELLERS OF KATAJANMARJA

In comparison with the darts team at Vapaavuoro, the regulars of Katajanmarja form a looser community. In fact the male community in the tavern used to be more tight-knit, but as it gradually dissolved as a result of a succession of divorces, the social life of the regulars consequently become more diversified. Also, there have been changes in the forms of sociability in recent years as women and couples have started to frequent the establishment, especially during the week. Darts have long gone out of fashion: the board is now hidden in a cupboard, with a pool table brought in to replace it. Most of the time no one plays, and because it is placed in a remote corner, it does not tend to dominate the scene. During the weekends the tone is set by the jukebox and dancing, but normally it is dominated by the rather loud conversation of the regulars sitting at the foremost tables of the tavern. The core clientele consists of the remaining members of the earlier male community of regulars. The women of the group are mainly new partners of the divorced men; unlike most of the ex-regulars, the men who have stayed with the tavern have not radically modified their lifestyle, but rather arranged their life in such a way as to minimize arguments caused by drinking.

Story Lines

There are a few central themes in the constantly ongoing chatting and storytelling of the regulars—the main main activity of the group. Let us take a look at the topics, since they reflect the cultural forms of these people.

The social life of the club revolves around drinking and stories about drinking to a much greater extent than in the case of the darts club. In a sense, drinking serves as a substitute for the excitement and the feeling of action that darts players experience in a good game. The storytellers' club often starts the evening by a recapitulation of what happened the previous night or during the weekend. While the darts players at Vapaavuoro take pride in their self-control, the men at Katajanmarja admire each other's ability to consume vast quantities of liquor. A careful account is therefore kept of the exact quantities consumed during the evening. Sometimes the men will vaunt a certain member's ability to hold his drink. Mattila described one of the older members of the club: "We'd all have passed out and he'd still be swaying around." The story was confirmed by another member: "That guy's really something."

Hangovers are also discussed openly. Indeed, the worse the hangover, the better the story; the more degrading the situation and the more nauseating the descriptions, the more fascination this produces in those who are listening. For example, one man described how he vomited in his mate's toolbox at the construction site after a booze-up the previous evening.

The men at Katajanmarja have a similar attitude to the darts players at Vapaavuoro in that they are careful to avoid all kinds of snobbery. But the regulars at Katajanmarja crystallize their straightforwardness in alcohol, to which they have a very rational and money-conscious attitude. Although they have their own preferences, the only important factor is the price of the drink in relation to its alcohol content. They can even be hostile toward people who show off by drinking wine. On one occasion Sepe thought that a customer, who had complained that his drink was not properly mixed, should be thrown out of the tavern. He has an agreement with the tavern staff that if a customer refuses to take and pay for a drink because it not mixed in the right way, he will buy it for the price of the alcohol that has gone into it.

The regulars not only compete with their tolerance of alcohol. They love all kinds of competition, as long as it is not too serious. For instance, someone may boast that he has been up a high radio tower to do some installation job. However, there is a set of tacit rules as to what kind of skills and achievements are accepted as a basis for bragging.

The club tends to avoid intellectual subjects and anything that is "highbrow"; or at least such topics should not be discussed in a serious or pompous way. A discussion on matters related to various world-views is often in violation of this particular rule.

By means of quizzes, betting, or various kinds of tricks that require manual dexterity, strength, or speed, the club may sometimes try to animate a discussion that has become stale. Repe has demonstrated several times that he can tear a telephone directory into two with his bare hands. One evening he tested everyone's reaction time by snatching a coin from their hand before they could close their palm. He beat them all.

In quizzes and in their debates the men usually favor questions to which there is an unambiguous answer, or at least one that can be checked from some reliable source. A lot of numbers and figures are bandied about. Sports provides an ideal subject. In quizzes the successful competitor has a good memory and this will earn him the unreserved praise of others. By contrast, the kind of knowledge that is accumulated in formal education or the ability to talk seriously are not appreciated.

Humor is ever-present in tavern conversations. It creates a mysterious sense of solidarity, of being involved in the same mischief. Even the most ordinary stories are often seasoned with double meanings, so that the club's conversations tend to flow effortlessly from one subject into another. There appears to be no logic whatsoever in the way the conversation progresses. A drunken listener may interrupt a speaker at such a strange and surprising point that the whole story is dropped in favor of another one through some association. Very often this kind of association leads the story into sex.

The presence of women does not prevent the men from telling dirty stories; in fact it actually encourages talk of sex. Sometimes the stories get really filthy. Indeed, the purpose of the stories seems to be to embarrass the women, to get them absolutely speechless. When they are talking with women whom they know and who are used to their coarse and offensive language, this becomes a kind of role play.

One of the most common of these role plays is the love story, where two regulars, a man and a woman, act the parts of passionate lovers. The other men then compete for the woman's favor:

> Both men were around thirty-five. One of them kissed the woman's hand; she was in her fifties. The other man said: "Stop licking her hand! She'll be so wet she won't be able to get a grip on anything." "What is she supposed to be gripping?" "You and your dirty imagination," the woman said.

Even though many of the regulars have divorced, the conflicts that are caused at home by frequent visits to the tavern tend to surface in different ways in the conversations. One of the popular subjects of tavern talk is the broken marriage, and the reasons for divorce. For many people it is only after they divorce that drinking and frequenting the tavern become an integral part of their way of life. What they are looking for at the tavern is someone to talk to, and perhaps a new partner; drinking offers consolation and, strangely enough, a vehicle for revenge as well—regardless of who the man considers to be the party responsible for the breakup of the marriage.

The couples who visit Katajanmarja form a special group within the storytellers' club in that their lifestyles and life situations are rather similar. They insist that the use of alcohol does not cause disagreements between them:

> *Sepe:* Well we're lucky 'cause we've never had any rows about drinking . . . with a lot of couples, one says they don't like it. We've never had those sorts of problems. Asta's used to it, and she has a beer herself when she feels like it.
> PA: Isn't that the only chance, really? If you can't get used to it, you've had it?
> *Sepe:* Yeah, I suppose so. I remember at the beginning. . . . Asta, she never touched a drop. . . . And it's been a long time since she really had a go at it. She'll often say she don't wanna go, you go if you feel like it.

Working-Class Culture and Drunkenness

Many researchers would no doubt use the term alcoholic when describing the way of life of the storytellers, the core group of the regulars at

Katajanmarja. Their life attitude is characterized by a strange sort of duality. On the one hand there is a sense of fateful submission, an awareness on the part of the men that they could lead their lives in a completely different way—and perhaps with less pain and suffering—but that it is too late to change. They have made their choice; all they can do now is put up with it and live the life they have selected, accepting the drinking and the inconveniences it causes. On the other hand the club members have a high regard for their own ability to carry the weightiest of burdens, their boldness in tackling the problems that destiny brings their way. They act as real men are supposed to act, regardless of the consequences. It is through this duality that we can see how the cultural forms of these men are—quite like those of the regulars of Vapaavuoro—just another variant of working-class culture.

The storytellers are inclined to submit to their fate, and this finds concrete expression in the way they describe their drinking history. They like to tell stories about when and how they started drinking, and when and how it became a central part of their life. In these stories there is always a very strong dramatic element, an event that may have caused a real change in their life such as divorce, bankruptcy, or an accident:

Alpo: I'm an alcoholic, I admit it. My very first drink . . . it was when I was 24; the first time I smoked was when I was 22. Yeah, my first drink. I'll never forget it. I was back in the town I grew up in. They said let's have a bottle of wine. I said I'm not interested, I wanted my life to be different. It was during the war and I knew . . . There were a lot of people getting social assistance, and I had to get out of that town.

PA: Did you drink a lot before you got married?

Alpo: Never touched a drop. None at all. We met at the place where we were working together. I was a teetotaler I was, no liquor, no alcohol, no cigarettes. Nothing. But that's all changed over the years.

PA: Why did things change?

Alpo: There were all sorts of things that influenced me. Society . . . my relatives . . . and especially mates, they made a big difference. Those days I was doing really well, earning a hell of a lot. They were scared I might get somewhere, real envious they were. If somebody tries hard, makes a go of things, eventually they'll make it big and the rest have lost a friend. That was the sort of

problem I had . . . started to drink, showed them that I didn't
wanna get rich. And then I just drank more and more.

Many of the men readily admit that they are alcoholics, even
though it may turn out in subsequent interviews that the actual quantity
they drink—and especially the frequency of their drinking—is not at all
excessive. In any event their ready admissions mean that the club members like to define their identity through drinking.

These men have no difficulty in adopting the AA philosophy
and concept of alcoholism as a disease or a handicap that lies within
the individual, even if they have never been to an AA meeting. They
sincerely believe that they are different, and that this difference is
their destiny rather than the result of their own choices and actions.
Therefore there must also be a specific turning point in their life that
marks the beginning of their present alcoholic career. These men's
stories of their first drink form an integral part of the theories they
have developed to explain their deviance as human beings. They are
personal original myths, essential elements of their personal identity.

The storytellers' submissive attitude toward drinking is related
to the fact that their use of alcohol is not regular. There are only very
few who drink on a daily basis; many of them will stay off the bottle for
quite a long time, or drink in periodic bouts, using alcohol in moderate
quantities. Sometimes, however, they do hit the bottle hard. One spell of
drunkenness can last several days, even weeks. Then they are "on the
bottle" as the men themselves put it.

Sometimes the drinking spell may be triggered by a single, identifiable factor, but this is by no means always the case. It may even
come "like a bolt from the blue":

Timo: I once went six months without touching a drop, and I even
went to AA meetings as well. But then I started going to AA less
often, and one morning when I was on my way to work, I just got
the idea in my head, fuck it, I'm gonna go and have a beer, I'm not
going to work, I'll take the day off. I was going for the seven
o'clock morning shift and I had to hang around till nine before I
could get in for a beer.
PA: Does it really happen like a bolt from the blue, or do you
think about it, afterwards maybe?
Timo: No it happens just like that. When I left that morning I'd

had an argument with my girlfriend and I was a bit cheesed off. Or did I just use that as an excuse, "bloody hell that's it."

There may also be completely "rational" reasons for the extended periods of drinking. The men may feel forced to continue because of a hangover, a sense of guilt and shame, or because they simply cannot stop after a weekend's drinking. But whether or not there are external reasons for the extended bout of drinking, it is a matter of honor that it is carried through to the bitter end. "When you've drunk your ass off anyway, you gotta see the thing through!" as Santtu commented. This is indeed no pleasant experience, and it certainly is not fun. On the contrary, an extended drinking bout is a very taxing experience, both physically and mentally. It is tougher than going to work.

Nonetheless there seems to be something very pleasurable or at least worthwhile in the process of submitting to drunkenness. Although the men feel that the beginning of a drinking bout is a personal misfortune, which luckily occurs only rarely, it is still something that every man must experience at least once in his lifetime. It is a hard experience, but worth every minute of it.

The enjoyable part about submitting to drunkenness is not the happy state of intoxication, because that only lasts for a couple of days at best. Once that has worn off, there is nothing that even the best of the storytellers can do to cheer up the drinking party. The self-confident, loud boasting of the group of men who have been drinking for several days is their way of showing their defiance of the severe hangover that they will soon be suffering, and of the whole outside world, which is all the time threatening to tumble down upon them. "Were in the shit— and we're in really deep," said Tane one evening, telling us how he had been drinking nonstop for more than a week. There is a definite sense of defiance about drinking, even though it is aimed mainly at the drinker himself. It may make things hard for the people who are closest to the drunkard, but he will continue to drink as long as he does no actual harm to anyone except himself.

Indulgence in drinking is not only a subconscious means of self-destruction; it also has its own inherent logic. The defiance we have identified in the drinking of the storytellers' club is obviously aimed not only at the men themselves, but in fact against all the necessities and coercions of everyday life, which require of them a certain degree of self-discipline. A man would not be free if he continuously controlled his own drinking only in order to be able to meet his social obligations. Taking to drink is an expression of freedom.

In general the state of drunkenness is a real realm of freedom for the Finnish man, a realm that offers bleak prospects but perhaps for this very reason is considered to possess an almost religious sanctity. The gates to the most sacrosanct places in this realm are open only to those blessed people who are prepared to sacrifice everything, including their self-discipline, for that freedom. Paradoxically enough, the state of complete freedom is reached only by those who are slaves to drink.

Rejection of self-discipline does not mean that the men, disregarding all risks, will always drink themselves into such a state that they are incapable of doing their job and attending to their other obligations. This would merely translate drinking into a duty and a norm imposed from the outside, like all other duties. The storytellers simply drink when they want to, and they take as much as they want to. In practice this means that they stop drinking when some external factor intervenes—usually the announcement that the tavern is closing, but sometimes they also run out of money.

Since rejection of self-discipline is an indication of male freedom, men who drop in for a quick beer or two are generally scorned by the story-tellers. Because this attitude is common knowledge, the visible signs of male freedom may acquire normative status. Men who leave while the evening is still young feel they are obliged to give some excuse.

Unlike most weekend drinkers, the storytellers do not tend to stress that they know when they have had enough to drink. On the contrary, they leave the whole question to the discretion of the tavern staff and external circumstances. Freed from the responsibility of self-control, the men can celebrate their freedom.

In other words: while the darts players take pride in their ability to control their life by virtue of their own skills and their self-discipline, the storytellers have a high regard for men who have the courage to let go and put themselves at the mercy of life. This is the main difference in the life attitudes of these two groups. Why is that?

The inability and reluctance of the storytellers to control their drinking is not an isolated phenomenon in their life attitude; it cannot be explained away by reference to their physical dependence on alcohol. That giving up is so difficult is due not only to the biological changes caused by alcohol in the metabolism and the central nervous system. True, these biological factors are of consequence in prolonged drinking bouts, as are withdrawal symptoms, but they hardly provide an exhaustive explanation of the normal situation where the men bravely confront their daily drunkenness and daily hangovers. The tendency of the storytellers to delegate all responsibility for control to other people is related not only to alcohol, but constitutes a central element of their class habitus.

For example, in the work place they have never shown any real dedication to the contents of their job; since shop floor workers are not paid for that, it is the responsibility of someone else. It is none of their business to get involved in planning work tasks, because all they are paid for is the mechanical implementation of their given tasks. They have a very similar attitude to money as well. They despise the idea of budgeting and saving:

> *Santtu:* I'm a working man, that's what I am. I do work with my hands, not with my head. Money doesn't mean anything to me— that's the way I'm used to living. And I've never gotten used to putting something away for a rainy day.

In comparison with the darts club, the way in which the storytellers express their freedom from the shackles of self-discipline may seem rather strange. At first glance it might appear as though they were voluntarily submitting to their bosses' arbitrary authority rather than showing real courage. Timo told us about his argument with the boss, who then gave Timo's job as crane driver to a young, unexperienced lad and had Timo transferred to a cleaning job:

> Well the guy tried the crane but he wasn't really up to the job. The lads were laying this floor and they kept having to duck down because he couldn't keep the bucket still, it was swaying like hell. So in the end the guy in charge comes and says, you go up there and work the crane. And I says, what d'you need me for, you got your driver up there, I can stick with me cleaning. . . . And I started to call 'im dad as well. You know, "dad, is this how we're supposed to do it?" Anyway, I got so worked up I started drinking and then they sacked me. So yeah, I guess he succeeded. I sure was shit-faced when I went to get my pay packet. I called a cab to take me home, and the boss had to carry me to the cab.

Refusal to take back a job once one has been busted can still be understood as a protest and as an effective form of passive resistance, but hitting the bottle seems to represent total surrender. Yet there is also a sense of pride in the way this surrender was shown to the building site manager. By his drinking, Timo clearly wanted to tell his boss that he could not care less: he was free to do what is expected of every real man. In normal situations the storytellers do not really mind that they have to do what other people tell them to. This is why they rarely stand up to protect their rights of self-determination even when they meet with arbitrary authority and injustice. In fact, when they feel that they are being properly taken care of, they can conveniently lay aside the self-discipline, which tends to shackle their male nature. If this positive caring relationship becomes transformed into restrictive control, then they will be exchanging one form of care for another. They cannot be ordered about, they can only be taken care of.

The way in which the men allow others to take care of them, thus externalizing their self-control, is in many cases related to their experiences of divorce. During their previous marriage they have had their fill of control. There is no way they will let drinking make a mess of their new relationship; instead they have made more or less conscious agreements with their new partner about drinking. The agreement to guarantee peace and harmony in the new relationship is not based on a voluntary commitment on the part of the men to control their drinking. They will continue to drink as much as they want or "have to." The new partners of the divorced men are well aware that there is no use in trying to stop them. Sometimes they will join the men at the tavern, sometimes they stay at home.

Wives and girlfriends are well-advised not to interfere in their husbands' drinking, but they are required to take care of them, to support them when they play out their role of real man. The storytellers' expectation of a good wife is that she takes care of the man's life, but this she must do with extreme discretion. She must listen out for her husband's conscience, and then give voice to it. Occasionally the wife will refuse to serve as controller:

PA: Do you ever phone home and ask her to come and fetch you?
Sepe: I've phoned her alright, but she won't do it no more. I remember when that guy Humalisto was still the doorman here, there were several times I asked him to phone the wife and tell her to fetch me because I was so drunk.
PA: But Asta doesn't fall for it any more?

Sepe: No, not any more. She says: he can sleep there if he can't get home. She knows I do it on purpose.

However, the most effective strategy for laying aside self-control is different: the tavern staff is assigned the status of trusted professional helper. The men want the waitress to interfere in their drinking without having to argue about any defiance of control. "I told myself that's all I'm gonna be served this time. I told Kirsti not to serve me any more no matter how hard I pester," said Kalle, returning to the table from the bar.

Money is also a silent and neutral, but uncompromising, opponent. Even when spouses are dependent on each other's income, it is possible for them to work out an arrangement that causes no quarrels about drinking. For instance, the couple may agree on a fixed sum that the husband automatically pays his wife out of his pay packet so she can get the food and pay the bills, and the husband then keeps the rest to spend as he wishes.

In the case of the storytellers, the wife rarely acts as a controller of her husband's drinking, but she does often serve as a "caretaker." For the man there is nothing shameful or submissive in being the target of a woman's caring. On the contrary, it is a tribute to the nature of man; indeed, it is so valuable that it is worth accepting even if it leads to a regression in the relationship, to the woman/man relationship being reduced to a woman/child relationship. Women and liquor become homologous as objects of pleasurable submission. They have the power and security to control the man, but at the same time they afford him a sense of complete freedom. They are like death:

> I won't be around for long, I'm on the way out. There's a lot of drunks here at Katajanmarja, but you're the one I want to come to my grave sometimes. But don't bring anyone with you, come alone. And I don't want no flowers, either! Bring some juniper twigs. The ones they make gin from. Bring a bottle and take a good long swig while you're at my grave. Yeah, don't forget the juniper twigs . . . with berries on . . . they smell just like gin.

The main factor controlling the storytellers' drinking is their financial position. And this same factor keeps them at work. For them the idea of work as a way of enriching one's life is completely unknown. The members of the darts team actually value the pleasure they get from knowing how to do things, from being "on top of the job" both at work and in life generally. But for the storytellers, work in itself is a meaningless toil. When the storytellers define work as a meaningless toil, it expresses to them the masculine stamina and endurance of those who have to do the work. In the same way as they have a high regard for men who can hold their liquor, they also appreciate the ability to take the stress of hard work. An evening out at the tavern is like a second shift, at least as hard as the first one, especially if the drinker concerned is "having a hard session." But a real man can cope with it, just as he can cope with the hangover the following morning.

The storytellers' high regard for physical endurance often comes out in their conversations. They frequently talk quite openly about sex, or at least are openly ambiguous. These stories easily give the impression that the men's sexual appetites are totally insatiable. In this they see a positive identity; virility equals vitality. Male sexuality is an inevitable natural law; it is similar in nature to the craving for liquor. However, the satisfaction of sexual desire requires physical performance, a form of toil. Yet this is precisely the way in which the man must prove his masculine competence.

In these stories women no longer play their caring role; their status has now been relegated to that of the passive objects of the men's physical performance. This is the other side of the male image of women, the side that is compared to nature:

> Sepe is telling a story about one of his friends who claims he hasn't stopped thinking about "it" for more than two minutes at any time since his fifteenth birthday. "Once I was walking across a frozen lake, and I fell through the ice and almost drowned. I did stop thinking about it then, but as soon as I managed to clamber back up . . . I started thinking of it again."

As a measure of male endurance, the female object of sexual performance can be compared to the object of the men's work, to the machines and equipment that they use. Successful performance requires more than physical stamina; it also requires a certain measure of skill.

All in all, heavy drinking derives its meaning from the storytellers' living conditions and from their way of life. On the one hand, hitting the bottle is an act of pleasurable subjugation expressing a particular view of freedom: one is not really free unless one gets rid of self-control. On the other hand, a drinking bout is hard work: carrying on with one's drinking, without any feelings of pity for oneself, is an expression of a man's masculine guts. Both of these ways of relating to drinking have their counterparts in the manual workers' attitude toward their labor. On the one hand, it is perceived as per se meaningless toil that gains its positive meaning as an expression of masculine strength and mastery. On the other hand, manual wage-labor is appreciated because it leaves intact a measure of freedom: the work only requires one's muscles, not one's thoughts or—unlike sales personnel, for instance—one's personal appearance.

DISCUSSION

The Cultural Construction of Desire

As unique and singular as the two case studies are, they nonetheless show that people's "need for a drink" can and must be understood in terms of their living conditions and cultural traditions. One's relation to alcoholic beverages cannot be reduced to, or even properly understood as, the relation of an organism to a chemical substance. Alcohol does generate effects within the human metabolism, but it does not convey meanings to the human consciousness. The pharmacological effects of alcohol—like disturbances in the functioning of the central nervous system—are always experienced, interpreted, and responded to by an individual human being, and it is this totality that we call drunkenness. Unlike a causal effect studied by natural sciences, meaning is a product of the human mind.

Analytically, we can distinguish two aspects of the concept of meaning. First, the form of the alcoholic effect on human metabolism, when transformed into contents of consciousness, depends on the way an individual as a culture member has learned to classify sensory experience and to give it meaning. Second, we cannot have an adequate understanding of drinking if it is considered as mere ingestion of alcohol, regardless of the position and role drinking has in the practices of everyday life. Or one might put it more strongly by saying that social meanings arise as responses to social situations; they are "incarnated" and "accountable" social practices (Garfinkel 1984).

However, as creative as people are in the cultural production of their own reality, social meanings are never totally produced on the spot or from scratch. "Social practices" rely on intersubjectivity—that is, on a number of shared presumptions about the world, only a few of which are negotiated between the parties of an interactive situation.

In the two cases, the pleasure the men get from the habit of pub-going is related both to the historically given living conditions of sub-urban, working-class life, and to the way various situations and condi-tions are interpreted in Finnish cultural tradition as well as by the grass-roots actors themselves. First, the cultural position of the tavern must be understood in terms of the gender division of labor and of the gendered spheres of life. As was pointed out throughout our local tav-ern research project (Sulkunen, Alasuutari, Nätkin, and Kinnunen 1985), the tavern is mainly a male preserve. From this point of view, it is a hide-out and a refuge for the husbands who—in terms of the tradi-tional division of household tasks—have "nothing to do" at home, while the wife will be working outside the home, and taking care of all the housework, too.[3] Second, by their drinking the men of the two case studies make and express their difference from other suburbanites and from their parents' generation: drinking is a protest against out-dated Protestant consumer ethics, where a man always saves in order to get a one-family house or something, and never really enjoys life. And finally, as informal, cultural groups the men are involved in the cultural pro-duction of their identities in an on-going attempt to impose order on disorder, to develop a meaningful account of the world, and to gain a measure of self-respect through the symbolic ordering of their envi-ronment (Willis 1977). The men's relation to their work, and to their own role as manual laborers, is at stake in this respect. In conclusion, one might say that the men's desire for drinking and pub-going stems from the meaning of tavern as a realm of male freedom.

The details of the two cases are of course specific to the particular groups, but other literature dealing with the position and meaning of male drinking[4] seems to suggest that even on the level of social mean-ings, the cases are only variants of a more general theme in the cultural forms of modern, Western societies.

Phases of Alcoholization or Variants of a Culture

What conclusions can be drawn from a comparison of the two cases? Let me first give two main hypotheses I have myself considered, present the evidence supporting them, and then discuss what conceptions of the nature of alcoholism they imply.

The comparison seems to give grounds to at least two main hypotheses. The storytellers of Katajanmarja could be interpreted as a group who represents the next stage after that exemplified by the darts club in a process of alcoholization (the "stage hypothesis"). That was the initial hypothesis behind the idea of choosing a "lower level" tavern as the object of another case study. The other main hypothesis would be to treat the cultural forms of the storytellers as just another variant of working-class culture (the "variant hypothesis").

Let us first discuss the observations speaking for the "stage hypothesis." First, it seems that the Katajanmarja's group of regulars has a history that reminds us of the darts club. The regulars used to be married, and they even played darts, until the group dissolved mainly as a result of a succession of divorces. Consequently, drinking has become the main activity for those who are left. In other words, it could be reasoned that Katajanmarja represents a lower class place, a "second station" in a process of "moving down" as one becomes an alcoholic. LeMasters (1975, 156-57) describes a local system of bars and taverns as a route down to the bottom; while a typical white-collar type, for whom it had become difficult or embarrassing to drink in his former middle-class bars, was a refugee from the middle-class world, the blue-collar "drunks" would disappear from the tavern and "gravitate to skid-row type bars where they do not have to face their former colleagues."

The storytellers are not refugees from another, "higher-level" bar, but it could be argued that they were the ones who were left with the tavern after it had gone through a phase of "social aging." By this I refer to the observation we made during the local tavern research: in Finland every bar and tavern seems to experience a developmental process from its founding or renewal to its next renovation. During this time, which in the city centers is often less than five years, the regular patrons selected out of its clientele more or less mess up their lives, become alcoholics or at least begin to look shabby and worn out, just like the sofas and decorations of the place. Consequently, in the renovations of bars and taverns that have been carried out during the 1980s, the regular patrons are often denied access to a renewed place. The reason for this is stated explicitly in press releases and interviews: "alcoholized" patrons lower the "level" and worsen the reputation of a restaurant. As one of the consultants in the restaurants' image renewal business put it in a private conversation, there is an iron law that governs management: individuals will consider going to a place, the "level" of which they judge to be equal to or "above" their social status, but not to a restaurant that is "below" their own "level." Consequently, the higher the level of a restaurant, the bigger the potential population that it may appeal to. Since the Katajanmarja case study was done, the place has been renewed twice, and the second time they even changed its name. Thus, it may be reasoned that the storytellers represent a group of regular patrons on their way "down;" the next "station" might be a detoxification center or some other treatment institution.

According to the "variant hypothesis," the storytellers' heavy drinking habits and attitudes toward drinking simply stem from their typical occupational position as manual workers—that is, the storytellers would be interpreted as a variant of working-class culture. Quite like the darts players, their drinking habits are a symbolic expression and realization of their view of life as laborers under strict supervision and control.

In terms of this interpretation, it could also be thought that the two case studies illustrate aspects of Finnish blue-collar drinking, inherent logics or frames of mind that guide drinking situations and thinking about drinking. The darts club illustrates the logic and cultural sense of control and mastery of one's life and drinking, whereas the storytellers' case illustrates pleasurable subjugation. One would reason that the two logics exist in any one drinking situation or with any individual drinker. Take, for instance, the darts players. When they emphasize and value self-control, they anticipate the possibility and temptation of not being able to control themselves. And heavy drinking for the darts players is not an "accident"; during the weekends they sometimes drink the more traditional heavy way.

Let us now discuss the implications of these main hypotheses. First, there is the question as to whether they are mutually exclusive.

The conviction that two main hypotheses are not exclusive would lead to a conception that could be crystallized by the thesis "blue-collar workers are more alcoholic than the middle class." This is quite near to what LeMasters (1975) implies. According to his interpretation, blue-collar drinking habits are—at least from the middle-class point of view—at the onset "alcoholic"; men may engage in heavy drinking bouts, and voluntarily lose their self-control. That is why a white-collar alcoholic does not attract annoying attention in a blue-collar bar. In the Katajanmarja case this thesis would have to be turned upside down by saying: "drunkards become workers." One would have to assume that, along with their increased alcohol consumption, Katajanmarja's regulars have maybe lost their previous jobs, and have therefore a less independent position in their work. Or along with their increased drinking, they have taken a more submissive stand toward work.

As a whole, this would lead to the thesis that "alcoholism is an indicator or reflection of social conditions." In other words, one would relativize the whole concept of "alcoholism," and conclude that it is just a label people use. Such an interpretation would explain the findings, discussed in chapter 4, according to which there is a higher prevalence of "gamma alcoholism" found among blue-collar populations. This would be explained as being due to a middle-class bias. It would be reasoned that "alcoholism" is just a bourgeois name given to working-class drinking habits, with the intention of deeming them unacceptable and pathological.

A "social problem" variant of the same interpretation would reason that hard drinking allows men to express their unhappiness and relieve their distress. From this point of view, the Katajanmarja regulars' drinking habits would be interpreted as a reflection of their worsened social conditions, caused by divorce, unemployment, problems in adjusting to technological changes in their workplace, or by other factors.

The other alternative, considering the two main hypotheses as mutually exclusive, implies at least two premises. *First*, the opposition between the main hypotheses implies that alcoholism is somehow beyond or outside reason; that alcoholic drinking and behavior is irrational. This can be interpreted in two ways: either alcoholism is thought to be a physical phenomenon, therefore belonging to the sphere of "nature," or alcoholic drinking is deemed "pathological," which cannot be accounted for in terms of meaningful action. *Second*, there is a preconceived idea of the process of becoming an alcoholic, with distinctive phases on the way. It is of course quite natural to make such an assumption, since even if one believes in hereditary traits or alcoholic personalities, one has to assume that people are not literally born alcoholic. The premise here is that "alcoholism" is a persistent, personal characteristic, not a passing ailment. It is taken for granted that there is a process that leads to alcoholism, that some day we will know what it is.

If one thinks that the main hypotheses are mutually exclusive, the implications of the "stage hypothesis" have been pretty much discussed in the previous pages. There are of course different criteria, which lead one to think that the storytellers are more alcoholic than the darts players. But is it the amount drunk, the drinking habits, or maybe the "loss of control" that counts? The "variant hypothesis" in this case implies the premise that "alcoholism" cannot be equated simply with culturally prevalent drinking habits; that manual workers are not alcoholics even though it is typical of them to drink more heavily. This further implies the idea that on the same consumption level, some individuals could be defined as alcoholics, others not.

Alcoholism as a Modern Myth

It is quite obvious that to put the hypotheses presented above to an empirical test would be quite difficult. An especially confusing thing is that several of the conflicting views on alcoholism outlined above seem to make sense. Many of them have indeed been defended. So, instead of making a choice between the alternatives presented above, let me suggest a view of alcoholism that is in accordance with many of the theses.

I suggest that alcoholism is most of all a Western myth, a shared concept of the meaning of heavy drinking, associated with an individual biography. It seems to be a persistent myth of the Western culture, a story told in a number of ways in lay and professional theories of alcoholism. The presumption of the "alcoholization process" is a myth in the sense that "alcoholism" is assumed to be a personal characteristic.

A story format is, according to many definitions, most central to a myth, because the mythic elements do not reside in the separate concepts or symbols of a myth but rather in the narrative as a whole. "Myth is language, functioning on an especially high level where meaning succeeds practically at 'taking off' from the linguistic ground on which it keeps on rolling," as Lévi-Strauss (1969, 210) puts it. It is the structure of the story through which its elements have meaning; and the whole synthesizes our experience, it organizes and models it (Wright 1977, 4-15).

In the case of alcoholism this means that there are certainly numerous conceptions and theories about how people become alcoholics, and how they recover from it. The ingredients of the myth are hiding in the presumption that there is a way down, and another one up, or that there is a limited number of ways, for that matter. There are many shared features in the way individual stories of "hitting bottom" and recovering are told, "Jellinek's horseshoe" being one of the classic formulations of the myth. Even if all storytellers do not share the view that, say, one has to hit bottom as a necessary precondition to the path to recovery, the elements of the myth of alcoholization nonetheless synthesize experience. The dissidents have to take a stand, they have to present their own versions in terms of the discourse that is structured by the old story. There is, however, a more fundamental level at which one could talk about the "alcoholization process" as a myth; the story format makes one think of alcoholism in the form of an individual biography. The myth is a reflection of the prevalent Western view that drinking is—at least when it is problematic—an essential and integral part of one's whole life, past, present and future, not just a passing ailment.

In the sense defined above, a myth is not a "false belief." Neither is it an "accurate belief." A myth organizes experience, provides a story-teller with a narrative form, and guides behavior.

In that sense it can be said that the alcoholization process does exist; there is the shared *alcoholism frame* that structures individual experience and channels the expressions of unhappiness or discontent. The alcoholism frame has to do with an automated working of self-control, with an alienation from one's desires. Since those doing mental work are more in need of self-control, blue-collar drinking habits appear to be more alcoholic from their point of view. On the other hand, for middle-class people, a slight loosening of self-control may already create a crisis, which makes individuals or their significant others apply the alcoholism frame.

If we assume that alcoholism—produced and reproduced by the alcoholism frame—is a myth in the sense presented above, it follows that empirical hypothesis testing is a tricky task. To study the process through which people actually become alcoholics requires that the researcher uses certain criteria for defining "alcoholism" or determining a "degree" of alcoholism: "consumption level," "loss of control," "increased tolerance" or some other measure. The problem is not only that the results depend on the criteria used. Rather, the same criteria or symptoms are used by drinkers or their significant others in their attempts to make sense of their lived experience. And what is more, the public results of the studies join in with other information to reproduce or modify alcoholism. The measures cannot show us the dynamics of cultural production.

Loss of Control as a Cultural Construct

The assumption that alcoholic drinking has its inner (even if odd or unacceptable) logic, leads us to look for the methods and criteria we use in defining it and distinguishing it from "normal drinking." In several theories and official definitions of alcoholism, "loss of control" has been the key concept. So, what are the criteria in defining, or methods in recognizing loss of control?

From an ethnomethodologically informed vantage point, it would be a routine procedure to bracket "loss of control" as an actual behavioral phenomenon, and to concentrate, instead, on the way loss of control is defined and recognized. The opposition of accounts and behavior is needless, however, if "loss of control" is treated as part of the modern myth of alcoholism, as a frame that guides both behavior and its interpretation. What are the dimensions of this modern myth?

The storytellers' case gives us a clue here, too. It is part of their culture to actively delegate all self-control to others or outer conditions, because they reason that they are more free that way. This tells us that there may be an inherent logic in the loss of self-control, and that the negative connotations of "loss of control" are due to certain presuppositions of the modern individual, one of them being a strong belief in independence from others or outer conditions. What is missing in the storytellers' case is the men's personal experience or acknowledgment of loss of control. A group of men with that characteristic will be studied in the next chapter.

Chapter 4

BLUE-COLLAR MEN'S
LIFE STORIES AND ALCOHOLISM

LIFE STORIES AS RESEARCH MATERIAL

Consider this summary of a life story, told by a Finnish metal worker in his mid-thirties:

> My childhood was peaceful from birth till I went to school. We were poor. We were short of everything, and there were many children. When my grandmother came to live with us, the discipline changed since she was very severe in her upbringing. Going to school was a highpoint. At school I got more friends and hobbies. I was a lively child, and did not concentrate much. When I was fifteen we moved to Sweden, and our home farm was sold. It was quite a shock. In Sweden I worked with my father as a lumberjack. Life started to feel better before the army. They were happy times; I had a car and I used to go to Finland on my holidays, and go to dances there. And to a young man, there were no worries in life. In the army life was steady, but after that there was a drop. The money was spent during the army, and the car broke down. I got married right after the army. My parents helped

me to get started in Sweden. I got the money for a new car, and
came back to Finland. I went to occupational training in the metal
industry. After that I worked in a metal industry firm for five
years. For the first two or three years it went fine. I had a new
job, my children were born, and the surroundings were new. But
then I began to feel rootless, and working in three shifts began to
oppress me. I went to work as a hired hand to my brother-in-law's
farm. In the beginning it went all right, but the relatives are the
worst. I gave my notice, and took several courses in the metal
industry. They were peaceful and nice times. For nine months I
was unemployed, and then I got a job in a small firm. My life was
smooth till the firm went bankrupt. At the same time, I was building a house for myself, and the building contractor also went
bankrupt. That was a low point. Then I got a job in another firm in
the metal industry. I had been unemployed for less than two
weeks. About the future I think that my life is going upward, the
worst is behind.

That is one of the stories I got by using the method of unstructured life story interview. The interview was open-ended but not an
in-depth interview—it usually lasted less than 45 minutes per interviewee. All interviewees were men; some of them were metal workers, some were men who had drinking problems. The men were
asked to tell their life story in their own words, and the interviewer's task was only to ask for more details by posing further
questions about the episodes already taken up by the interviewee.[1]
As was said, the story presented above is a shortened version, and
of course a life story told in an interview has to be edited. But the
words are those used by the men, not by the interviewer or the
researcher.

The main data consists of fifty-four life stories told by married or
divorced male manual workers. Of them, twelve have come to search
for help with their alcohol problems at an A-clinic and seven at a detoxification clinic operating as a part of the clinic.[2] Five of the men are
members of an A-guild, a society founded by recovering and ex-alco-
holics. The remaining thirty interviewees are metal workers, recruited
for the study at their labor union's training center. The study was conducted in Tampere, Finland.[3]

Now consider another story, told by a man who has come to
search for help with his alcohol problems at the Tampere A-clinic:

When I was a child, the discipline was very strict. I still remember when my younger brother broke a sugar cup, and the two other brothers had it so that I got the spanks. When my father died, my mother remarried. The new husband did not accept my youngest brother, which still shows. The youngest brother went to prison several times, and he has really gone down now in Sweden. I did not join my brother's businesses, even though it was close. When I was in the army, my wife had been unfaithful to me. After leaving the army I didn't come home for two days. I started to drink. Previously, I had brought my paycheck home 'cause my wife took care of the household. Now, when I started to drink I left straight from work and drank the money. And I began to use other women (sexually). I drank and brawled, because I was pissed off and because her treacherousness was in my mind. This is how the fall began. When I came to the A-clinic, it made me think. I abstained for a year. There was some progress, but also bad times. I grew up somewhat. When the therapist changed, I was pissed off and gave it all up. I left the A-clinic, and started drinking. When I got divorced, I was pissed. But my drinking was not as hard as it used to be. In occupational training in Pori I got into drinking. I went to the A-clinic, because I was afraid that I go to the dogs and wouldn't get any occupation. The rest of the course went okay. I was divorced because of my drinking. My old lady got mad at me if only I had some beer, even though we did not fight any more. I am a jealous guy, and most of the quarrels and drinking were because of that. My wife divorced me, and her unfaithfulness was reported as the reason, so the children stayed with me. After the divorce I was going steady with a woman, and a year ago I got engaged with a woman I met at a dance. The spring was a nice time. I persuaded her to get a driver's license and bought a car, even though I don't have a license myself. When we got engaged, I gave her freedom to take care of my bank account, so that we could save some money. I started to drink in the fall as revenge, because she did not give me any loving. Life had changed by and by after we had become engaged. The woman left all of a sudden without leaving any note. The downturn started from small quarrels, bedroom affairs. I have a grudge against that person.

These life stories could be used as research material in many ways. They, for instance, give us information about typical incidents in alcoholic and nonalcoholic blue-collar men's lives. Provided that the sample would be statistically representative, one could compare their life histories, and maybe find factors that later cause alcohol problems. However, that was not what I had in mind when gathering these stories. I do not treat them as stories that give us information about the causal relations that predict later alcohol problems, but as narratives that reflect the storytellers' worldview and self-concept. In that respect my approach could be likened to, say, Will Wright's (1977) study of American Western movies. He treated them as narratives that reflect the cultural structure of American society; not as myths—in the sense of false beliefs—about American history, but as cultural products that reflect the way Americans think about, say, the individual's relation to society at the time a movie is released.

The same approach can be applied to life stories. By selecting past incidents and arranging them into a narrative, storytellers are engaged in biographical reasoning, in articulating their present worldview and self-concept. These stories are not only views of the past; the picture of the life history an individual translates into speaking terms, into a story, reflects his present way of thinking and behaving. "Suddenly and momentarily to see oneself as 'aggressive,' 'poetic,' or 'male,' for example, might seem mere whimsy unless such concepts could be secured to a series of earlier events" (Gergen and Gergen 1984, 173). But the selection of particular past events to be told is not the main thing in this respect; it is the way they are connected to each other to compose the narrative. The structure of reality as it is perceived by people in a culture is reflected in the overall format of the story.

Since the material consists of stories told by men either with or without alcohol problems, should we divide the stories into two groups—that is, "alcoholic" and "nonalcoholic" stories—and then compare these two groups? Such a research setting would, at the onset, reproduce the culturally prevalent division into "normal" and "pathological." Yet the whole idea was to relate the worldview and self-concept of the men with alcohol problems to that of other men. Or to put it in other words, the idea was to study the everyday-life frame that provides drinking—heavy or moderate—with its social and cultural meaning; to analyze what the accounts of drinking signify in the plots of the life stories. In this sense the case study could be likened to the research showing that attitudes toward, as well as meanings of, drinking, reflect people's way of life and their overall view of life (P. Sulkunen et al. 1985; Kortteinen 1983; P. Sulkunen 1979; Mäkelä 1976). One cannot simply assume that problem drinkers are a separate case on this level of abstraction. If no differences between problem drinkers and other men would be found, it would be a result in itself. Therefore, I studied the *narrative structures* of these stories irrespective of the backgrounds of the storytellers. The general idea was that there would be as many groups of men with different worldviews and self-concepts—or, in one word, *collective subjectivities* (Willis 1977) or *habitus*[4]—in the sample, as I would find different types of narratives. Let me now introduce the method of narrative analysis and present the results.

THE NARRATIVE STRUCTURE

From the mid-1970s onward a great deal of research appeared dealing at first with story grammars (Prince 1973; Rumelhart 1975) and later with cognitive structures that guide one's perception and under-standing of texts, episodes, and scenes, as well as structure one's speech and behavior (for an overview, see Mandler 1984; Beaugrande 1980; van Dijk 1980). The careful, empirical research in "schema-theory" sup-ports the argument made above that there is indeed a linkage between the narrative structure of a life story and the cognitive structure guiding one's perception of the world. However, most of the research has been focused on abstract intracultural features of cognitive structures, neglecting their social and cultural boundedness in the name of the psychologists' search for universal human characteristics.[5] This is why the method applied in this study draws on that of Vladimir Propp (1975, originally 1928). As an important inspiration for later students, his treat-ment of the structure of a plot is in essence shared by later researchers and supported by their findings. But the task fulfilled by his study, the classification of tales into types in a more precise way, makes his approach particularly appropriate for the purposes of this study. In classifying the tales, he paid much attention to the content of the stories.[6]

In the present study, explanations were based on a common form or structure inherent in several otherwise unique stories. This kind of approach is usually employed in case studies dealing with a group whose members are known to share the same worldview and view of life. As informants they are then asked to tell about their culture. But because the interviewees of this study do not belong to one particular cultural group or collective, such a procedure was not satisfactory. Even though the interviewees can be classified as belonging to the same social class—manual workers—it cannot be simply assumed that their life stories are structured by the same narrative structure, reflecting a shared collective subjectivity. Neither could the stories be classified into types according to an impression of the main "theme" in them.[7] Some kind of coding according to words, symbols, or phrases used in a story would not work either. For people not belonging to a local group the same signs may carry different meanings even if the overall pattern of their thinking and behavior is similar. Propp shows a way out of these problems of classification by focusing on the overall pattern or "morphological" form of a story, studying its plot at a level abstracted from its particular content. In analyzing the tales, he paid attention to the chronological order of the sequences—events—in a story. According to Propp, the component unit of a story, a function, must be defined from the point of view of its significance for the course of action. If several stories are composed of the same functions in the same chronological order, they belong to the same type.

A thorough report of the way narrative analysis is in practice done would be the topic of another writing. Besides, a reader interested in research methods can consult for instance van Dijk (1980) and Propp (1975). Let me just say that the general idea in narrative analysis is to attempt to write a shortest possible summary of a narrative; a summary that still includes everything that—as Propp says—has "significance for the course of action." Such a task leads one into questioning what makes a narrative narrative, and what these "component units" or functions—as Propp called them—are like. In this study, I applied also Prince's (1973) ideas about the grammar of stories. According to him, any story recognized as a story necessarily consists of consecutive *stative events*, sentences describing a state of affairs, and *active events*, which change that state of affairs. When such summaries of different stories are then compared with each other, the parts that in different stories describe a phase—a stative or active event—that has the same significance for the unfolding of the plot, are grouped together, and given a name that describes the phase's function in the story. Following Propp's idea, the stories may be then said to belong to the same type when their plot structure consists of the same phases in the same chronological order. In accordance with a general methodic rule in qualitative analysis (Alasuutari 1989a; 1989b), a story type described in this way has to account for *everything* a story classified according to type consists in; no exceptions to the rule can be allowed.

When the life stories were analyzed, it turned out that the narratives could be divided into two types. The great majority of the stories, fifty-three out of fifty-four, represented the same narrative structure, which will be analyzed here. The divergent type will be discussed later in this chapter.

The dominant story type consists of nine phases of the narrative, which by turns describe a life situation—or, to use Prince's (1973) terminology, a *stative event*—and an (active) event that changes the situation (see Prince 1973; Brémond 1970; Dundes 1964). I have given every phase a name that reflects the way men characterize it in their stories. The phases are:

a) childhood
b) the man becomes independent
c) wild youth
d) the man settles down
e) settled life
f) the man breaks the rules of decent life
g) crisis
h) the man mends his ways
i) the man is divorced

The narrative structure characterized in this way does not describe any "typical" or average story. Rather, it takes into account all the stories of the type and the details within any story. All the men did not, naturally, tell about a divorce and neither does a divorced man necessarily *end* his story after telling he has had one. Men do remarry or cohabitate, for instance, or experience other things that are worth telling in a life story. But these kinds of differences are allowed in terms of the method. The general idea is that the list of phases includes all incidents mentioned in any story. Not all stories show evidence of all phases, but those mentioned always appear in the same order (see Propp 1975).[8] If, for instance, a man does not give any description about his youth as a meaningful phase of life, the story will in any case continue with a description of settling down. On the other hand, some phases may appear many times in a story. After a divorce, say, the story may reiterate and continue from phase, wild youth, onward. The reason for this lies in the way the narrative structure and its component parts— the phases as I call them here[9]—are defined. A phase of a story is defined from the point of view of its significance for the course of action (see Propp 1975). When, for instance, a man says "Well I think it was in the army that it became clear to me that I'll make up my mind and leave [home] as well" it is obvious that the story moves over to the next phase, wild youth. Before the decision, the man is at home, dependent on his parents, but afterward he is independent both mentally and economically. The phases in different stories are of course not characterized in the same way. Rather, the differences between the ways the same phase is expressed in particular stories are often remarkable. This can be illustrated by excerpts from the life stories of two men:

> At the age of sixteen the curve took a downturn. I left school for music. First we did a few gigs, and then we were hired by a restaurant for a couple of months. And that's what I've done since.

Another man said:

> I had a fight with my father on Christmas eve. . . . I finished my school all right but then I left and didn't see my parents for many years. My mother did come to see me.

In terms of the common narrative structure, stories differ from each other in their overall contents and emphasis. Grossly characterized, it can be said that the men who had alcohol problems described the key events in their lives by speaking about the human relations, while others—having the same structural component parts in their story—paid attention to the changes in living conditions.

To translate his life history into a story, a typical man without alcohol problems continues by describing how he got along in his life, managing to acquire some property as well as a family of his own: "I bought an old car and got married—and we have three boys." In this kind of a story the man might mention some occasional hardships, like illnesses or unemployment, but usually the stories of these men—who were born during or shortly after World War II—end up in a description of the settled life:

> We got married in 1978. I got a job and I have stayed there for seven years. A room with a kitchen has changed into two rooms and then into a house of our own, which I built by myself. A couple of sons were born.

A typical story told by a man having alcohol problems is a bit different. When describing his childhood he might pay attention to hap-

piness and factors that have an effect on it: "Childhood was the happi-
est time of my whole life; I never had more fun, even with alcohol."
Similarly, another man paid attention to the atmosphere at home: "My
father abused alcohol, and the discipline was too strict."

The alcoholics' stories emphasize the dimension of independence
in the phase of "wild youth," when they got rid of parental control.
But "wild youth" typically turns out to be a "downturn" because of
inordinate freedom. Finding a wife and settling down in this perspective suggests the meaning of finding a new safe harbor:

> My drinking had become what you call excessive. I noticed that
> the only way [to get it under control] was to get a very bitchy
> wife, otherwise I was just as good as dead. It was the only possi-
> bility.

But the hardships do not end here. Even though the wife is useful
in keeping order, she is restrictive. The man does not have composure
enough to lead a decent life; rather, he breaks its rules. Many crises
might be solved by his mending his ways, but in the end divorce is
inevitable. As a result he again achieves freedom and independence—
with the old problems:

> *Interviewer:* You have marked the divorce as a downturn?
> Well that's what it was—or after it I began to drink like hell
> because I felt free, I kind of thought I could drink more.

In order to regain control over his overt drinking a divorced alcoholic typically gets himself a woman as a controller—whom he opposes
by drinking when life has returned to its everyday trails. Some men
have been involved with several women in the course of these cycles.
This is why successive relations and separations do not deserve to be
called separate phases of the narrative structure. There is nothing new
in them, compared to the first marriage. Naturally, this does not mean
that the story cannot have a happy ending.

The story variants characterized here cannot be neatly separated
from each other; rather, they are caricatures created by the researcher,
metaempirical ideal types that cannot be found in any of the stories in a
pure form. Most stories are more or less mixed, including features of
both ideal types.

How should one, then, explain the meaning of such variants? A special feature of the stories that most clearly violates the overall rule stated above—those concentrated on human relations even though told by nonalcoholics—suggested an interpretation. All these workers report some problems in human relations, either during their childhood, youth, or marriage. Now it can be concluded that a shocking experience is enough to shift the emphasis of the whole story toward human relations. It can for instance deal with a girl during the years of youth: "A girl wanted to get married to me, and got herself pregnant. I left for Sweden and from there went to sea as a sailor." But when the hardships are over and the man gets happily married, the interest in the story shifts to changes and goals in the living conditions.

Another man, who told about personal problems connected with his parents' continuous quarrels, put it this way:

> The age of eighteen was a turning point. I met my wife-to-be. From then on, it has gone for the better.
> *Interviewer:* What are the expectations and plans for the future?
> Normal life, enlarging the apartment and the family.

Problems in human relationships seem to motivate the men to reflect on the role of human relations in general. Heavy drinking is one example of reasons for such problems. The fact that overcoming problems in human relations returns the focus of a life story to economic affairs, enables us to study the interrelatedness of different spheres of everyday life in the men's collective subjectivity. Moreover—because the overall narrative structure of the life stories was the same, despite the differences in content—it can be argued that the narrative structure reflects profound cultural patterns shared by all the men. It reflects their collective subjectivity, as will be shown.

THE COLLECTIVE SUBJECTIVITY

In order to analyze the narrative structure as an expression of the men's worldview and self-concept in a systematic fashion, a method "translating" the general plot into a picture of the men's collective subjectivity had to be developed. This will be presented first before a discussion of the results of the analysis.

There was no ready way from the narrative structure to the analysis of a worldview and self-concept, even though many solutions have been suggested (Dundes 1964; Wright 1977). Still, the connection between narrative structure and collective subjectivity seems to be quite obvious: the relations outlined above between the story variants and the common plot that structures them gives a hint of the way that different spheres of life are connected to each other in the men's thinking and living. As a preliminary, it can be suggested that as soon as human relations are in good condition, the men willingly take care of the family economy. The story is accordingly made logical by referring to the changes and goals related to it. The methodological principle to follow is to study the relations of the contents of excerpts from different stories that serve the same function for the course of the plot. This kind of method is in a systematic vein developed by Turner (1977). According to him, the ability to understand a text as a narrative is based on the fact that one distinguishes the interrelated dimensions of opposition, the transformations of which make up the plot. We can reinterpret the concept of narrative structure from this point of view: a shift from a "phase" of the plot to another one means that a transformation in the structure of oppositions has taken place. The fact that we were able to equate the overall narrative structure of a life story with another one was possible because the stories are composed of the same *dimensions of meaning*. These dimensions are interrelated, and the structure embedded in them can be seen in any phase of the narrative. This structure of the dimensions of meaning is the men's *collective subjectivity* in the sense that it provides the men with lenses through which concrete phenomena or events are perceived and interpreted. Analytically, there can be distinguished two aspects, the *worldview* and the *self-concept*, in the collective subjectivity.

By the concepts *worldview* and *self-concept* I refer to two aspects in the conceptual grid within which people perceive and interpret phenomena or events. On the one hand, the *collective subjectivity* provides people with a shared conception of the way the world is organized, the *worldview*. On the other hand, culture's members have a shared conception of the self, *self-concept*, within which they conceive of themselves as actors in the world perceived in a particular way. Let us now discuss the men's worldview.

Even the name given to the first active event in the plot, "the man becomes independent," has to do with achieving personal freedom and independence. The economic independence that going to work enables is a precondition to it. In this way the authority of the family and especially of the father loses ground. The wild youth means that the man leaves home mentally also:

I had a job during the summers and leisure time from when I was twelve until fifteen when I finished my school. My upbringing was very religious on my father's side and I bought it until age fourteen, which was the time I began to go to dances secretly.
Interviewer: How would you describe your childhood?
I would have to say that I experienced my father as a very strong personality and authority. I have realized that I joined the labor movement so late because I had to grow free from my religious rearing. It was only through work that I became conscious of my position.

This dimension of meaning, here entitled *dependence*, articulates the whole plot. From this point of view, the whole narrative consists of consecutive changes from dependence to independence and back again. To take an example, phase (b), the man becomes independent, can be equated with phase (i), the man is divorced, while the settled life can be equated with childhood: "At first my mother carried the responsibility, then my wife. Only little by little has it been turned over to me.

But the dynamics inherent in the stories, the alternation between the valuable freedom and its voluntary restriction or abdication, makes sense only after taking into account another interrelated dimension of meaning inherent in the stories: the dimension of *social bond*. This refers to one's relation both to society and to significant others. It is the social, emotional bond that the men seek from the marital relation and makes it a desirable thing in their life:

At age eighteen there was a turning point. I met my wife. It was an upturn.
Interviewer: What was changed?
You feel that you have a person whom you care for and who cares for you. I felt that I have reason to live. Before that I had a depressing period.

These two dimensions are interrelated in the sense that a man has difficulty in achieving total personal freedom and at the same time preserving a peaceable social bond to a wife or girlfriend and to society. The life stories express different models of balance and compromise between these two contradictory desires. When the man in his youth acquires more freedom he simultaneously has to give up the close relation to his parents. By getting married he regains a close social bond, but at the same time loses some of his personal freedom.

In addition to joining the phases of the narrative, the structure of the men's worldview is built into the descriptions of the consecutive phases of the plot. Take, for example, the individual descriptions of "the settled life." The contradiction between the desire for a measure of personal freedom and duties toward the family and society can be seen in them:

> *Interviewer:* What do you usually quarrel about?
> Well, I'm active in the labor movement and often away from home. That is usually what causes our fights. And I admit that I'm away quite often.

An alcoholic, whose story is sliding into open conflict, describes the same phase in a similar, even though a rougher way:

> When I was twenty-five I began to drink more. I was working temporarily in another town, I was away from the family and got more money. Every spare moment, I went for a drink.

Thus, the structure of interrelated dimensions of meaning is not tied to the relations between consecutive phases of the plot. It is a frame that organizes the perception and interpretation of any event or action. Its very kernel is deeply rooted to men's notion of the tension between individual and society.[10]

In everyday life, the tension is lived out primarily as that occurring between family life and life outside. That is, the men's stories imply at first a feeling of dependence when the man is still living at home, and later while living with his own family. Both spheres can be equated and generally called the *family sphere*. In a similar vein, the time out of the family sphere, either as a specific phase of the story called "wild youth" or the time spent outside the family during marital life, has a meaning of personal freedom as well as a lack of satisfactory human relationships. This is called the *public sphere*. Interestingly, only the alcoholics, when facing conflicts with employers because of their drinking, pay attention to the limits the world of work places on an individual:

> At the beginning of the 70s I had conflicts at work because of alcohol. The engineer said that he observed that I have serious problems with alcohol since I have to drink on the job. Well, I didn't

give him the old explanation that I had a quarrel with my wife and that is why I had to move my drinking to the work place 'cause I couldn't drink at home.

That the tension between individual desires and social constraints is primarily articulated as that between the public sphere and the family sphere transforms it into an issue of human relations, of the relation between man and woman. The tension between the two spheres defines and reproduces gender conflicts over the roles of the sexes. In the men's stories, the family sphere is defined as the *female*, and the public sphere as the *male* domain. This, in turn, implies the division of domestic labor where the husband is the primary family breadwinner, whereas the wife takes care of the household and children. Since she also has the role of her husband's controller, as the one who takes care that he does not neglect his duties, she is the nearest representative of society.[11] The alcoholics especially perceive their wife as the one who should take care of their working:

It was largely because of my wife that I was away from work.
Interviewer: In what way?
In the evening when we had a quarrel, my wife threw the alarm clock at the wall. I didn't wake [in time] for work in the morning. I got angry at her and went to the railway station. I went to a restaurant, bought a bottle in a drugstore near the railway station, and jumped on the first train that was leaving.

The organization of spheres and practices, and their meanings described above is not an exclusively Finnish phenomenon. Rather, it seems to have a lot in common with all descriptions of Western "working-class culture," which in England and the United States was fully shaped by the turn of the twentieth century.[12] Recent research on blue-collar people also shows a similar patterning of the everyday life and the role of alcohol in it. While the home as a female domain has an effect in restricting men's drinking, the drinking takes place almost completely outside the family sphere, in all-male groups on the job, during lunch breaks, and after work in parking lots, or nearby bars (Ames and Janes 1987; Klee and Ames 1986). Ethnic differences would, of course, change and complicate such an overall picture, but it is nevertheless interesting to find how widespread certain patterns of everyday life are.

Before discussing the reason for these patterns of behavior among blue-collar populations we must first pay attention to another aspect of the concept of collective subjectivity, the men's self-concept, which is also built into the plot of the life stories. In addition to reflecting the men's way of perceiving the reality they encounter, the life stories also express their conception of themselves as human beings, as subjects behaving in the environment.

The central feature of their *self-concept* is expressed in the way men tell about their schooling. For some, leaving school is a totally positive turn, but many stories include a certain ambivalence in this respect:

> *Interviewer:* I understand you were held back a year, what was it like?
> Actually there was a lot happening that year. I was sixteen and it was the last year of my schooling. I, for example, had an affair with my teacher. It was a wild experience.
> *Interviewer:* Was it an upturn in life?
> I suppose I was held back as a consequence of all this. So it really can't be perceived as a high point.

The ambivalence about schooling comes from the fact that this phase of life can be evaluated from two points of view. If the men pay attention to what they liked and wanted themselves at the time, schooling was boring and ending it was a relief, a liberation from the straitjacket of school. From this perspective, having fun during school hours was the positive part of that phase. If, on the other hand, they consider how they got on at school and the usefulness of conscientious schooling for a future life, the values turn upside down:

> I wish I had gone on with my schooling. Not then but now, afterwards. I sure would have handled it, even though I wouldn't have liked it then. Father should have forced me, but it was a question of money and the fact that I didn't like school. At that time people said that those who were good at school were pansies and that's something I didn't want to be. I guess it's some kind of timidity, you go along with the group.

The contradiction between the two points of view reflects the tension between future-oriented, purposive rationality and behaving according to one's own desires. In the stories, the men's desire was to leave school as soon as possible. School was, indeed, seen as instrumentally useful, but as a disgusting place. Even though many men have changed their mind since their school years, the articulation itself has not changed; they say that their parents should have forced them to stay at school, or that they should have forced themselves. They should have practiced self-discipline. In the stories, the men differentiate this part of themselves from what is being disciplined, their own desire. Such a division between *self-discipline* and *desire* is inherent in the men's self-conception; it is built into the narrative structure. The tension between man's desires and self-discipline is often expressed in descriptions of drinking. Among the alcoholics of the sample, the drinking, which in all the stories expresses and emphasizes freedom and personal independence, becomes an uncontrolled craving, alien from the man himself: "It was a highpoint when I got a job and became a sailor, although I drank a lot. Before I went to the army it got out of control really, I couldn't hold back."

The common and self-evident concept of self-discipline is indeed of central importance for understanding the social and psychological problem called alcoholism, often characterized by the concept of "loss of control." That it actually seems to be a "culture-bound syndrome" (Room 1984a), implies that the whole tension between "desire" and "self-discipline" is of social origin, deeply rooted to the existence of the exchange economy. Accordingly, it has been argued that "alcoholism," defined by using "loss of control" as one of the criteria, only exists in countries where the division of labor is predominantly based on an exchange economy, which has thus become the main organizing principle of the society.[13] That is in accordance with the way the form of alcoholism found among the workers studied here is intertwined with their interpretation of their social position as manual workers. Why this is the case could be explained at the level of identity. I will first discuss the concept and the method employed in studying it, and thereafter present the results of the analysis.

IDENTITY

Thus far, the analysis of the life stories has been concerned with the dimensions of meaning that provide the men with lenses through which they perceive and interpret concrete, practical issues of everyday life. I have called this aspect of the consciousness the collective subjectivity. In the same vein Bourdieu (1977, chapter 4) talks about *doxa*, the universe of undiscussed and undisputed knowledge, on the basis of which people's discourse, arguments, and attitudes arise:

> Because the subjective necessity and self-evidence of the com-monsense world are validated by the objective consensus on the sense of the world, what is essential *goes without saying because it comes without saying*. [p. 167]

Even though they are here analytically separated, the level of col-lective subjectivity can never be treated as autonomously distinct from the forms of *identity*. We are never only condensations or products of social and cultural structures, forever doomed to blindly manufacture society behind our backs, either in a Levi-Straussian or a Marxian sense. One has, somehow, to "make sense" of his view of life, impose order on the distorted and contradictory disorder of symbols, articulations, and practices of social reality. It is the very basis of identity formation—which, in turn, while consisting of an active process of interpretations and symbolic constructions of the social reality, reproduces and trans-forms the collective subjectivity. This kind of cultural production, aimed at the construction and preservation of identity—of self-esteem—is a form of inventive creativeness within the structured and structuring limits of *doxa*, as Bourdieu (1977) puts it, and it is constantly redefining the boundary between the universes of the conscious and the subcon-scious.

To further illustrate the difference between the levels of collective subjectivity and identity, let us consider the parallel difference between the concepts of meaning and sense in the case of drinking. A collective *meaning* of drinking could already be found by analyzing the narrative structure of the life stories. In the plot, drinking always expressed the desire for personal freedom; it always took place outside the family sphere, either during "wild youth"—expressing independence from home—or outside the men's own family. Drinking at home did not seem to be significant enough to be voluntarily mentioned in the story. When comparing excerpts from different stories, it turned out that men's traditional vices—smoking and other women—in addition to hobbies like volleyball or labor union activities, could be equated with drinking as serving the same function as expressions of "time out" from the family.[14] But, even though the inner logic of such a patterning of everyday life and the meaning of drinking in it can be intuitively understood, the plot does not in fact explain the *sense* of drinking or the sense of "freedom" that it expresses. Or rather, the patterning of life and the motivation for drinking can be rendered sensible in a number of ways in terms of the collective subjectivity. As stated earlier, particular stories did indeed differ from each other in their content in terms of the common plot structure. While, say, getting a wife was, for a youngster with alcohol problems, a means of regaining control over his life, for another it marked the end of an interesting period and was a way of finding a new meaning in life. These variants reflect different ways or aspects of making sense of one's way of life at the level of identity, and illustrate the analytical distinction between the concepts of meaning and sense. Whereas the meaning of an act, object, or artifact is a shared, taken for granted way to perceive it, for an individual it has a sense in the context of his or her view of life. From this perspective, the differences in content and emphasis of the narratives give "clues" about the forms of identity among the men.[15]

The forms of identity in the men studied can also be seen in the men's evaluations of the reasons and rationales for their drinking or abstinence. Altogether, five modes of speech could be found in the data. Men say that they *control* their drinking; it can be explained as a form of *revenge*; one can present oneself as a *self-conscious drunkard*; drinking can be explained by the fact that *restraints were missing*; and finally, one can express his *unawareness* of the main reasons for his problematic drinking. These modes of speech—along with the variants in the narrative structure—will be regarded as clues in the task of reconstructing the forms of identity. A methodological device employed in grasping the inherent logic of the men's life styles was the homological analysis of the men's modes of speech dealing with different spheres or aspects of their life. Essentially it is concerned with how far, in their structure and content, particular items parallel and reflect the style, typical concerns, attitudes, and feelings of the men (Willis 1978, 191-93). In this way, homologies between the men's attitudes toward, say, drinking, family life, and work are found. There is nothing mysterious about it; it is only natural that an organizing principle used in making sense of one's life is reflected in the accounts of any acts or habits that express one's identity.[16] Because particular accounts are not taken at their face value, the approach differs from that of "accounts theory," which is mainly concentrated in classifying accounts into types.[17]

The mode of speech where the man reports an *unawareness* and confusion concerning the reasons for drinking—or unwillingness to explain them—is not of much help here. It is not that we could ignore this mode of speech, used by men who have said they developed their drinking problems only after marriage. The problem is that these men— despite the fact that drinking is first introduced in "wild youth" and in this sense associated with a desire for independence—do not give accounts of particular events or situations where drinking occurs. They only express an overall "loss of control": "The drinking increased when I was at about thirty. It became a problem. I was not aware of it. I don't remember when I began to take a drink for a hangover.

Because this kind of utterances state the very problem of "loss of control" to be discussed in the next section, they deserve to be treated separately there, after first analyzing the forms of identity on the basis of other modes of speech.

The next mode to be discussed, only appearing in the life stories of nonalcoholics, emphasizes the overall *control* over all aspects of life, including drinking. Should a man report a previous drinking problem, the recovery is presented as the result of his own sovereign decision:

> Finding my wife was the most decisive factor in giving up [drinking].
> *Interviewer:* Why was that?
> If I went on, it would have been a disaster.
> *Interviewer:* Did your spouse say that?
> No, I figured it out by myself. Or it came to my mind when it became obvious that this is gonna be real bad. . . .

> *Interviewer:* Would there have been any other principle in telling your story?
> No, it would have become similar in any case. Maybe I have had a peculiar life, a result of my own struggle. I've had to keep my head above water.

The same emphasis on mastery is also reflected in the fact, noted earlier, that the nonalcoholics paid more attention in their life stories to changes in living conditions. By doing so, they presented themselves as the sovereign subjects of their life. These men, in other words, placed great value on their ability to handle their life situations. However, the satisfaction and pride deriving from this form of identity formation, which is here called the *logic of mastery*, implies that such a control is not an easy matter to preserve. It presupposes a conflicting desire for something else, for freedom, which drinking expresses. In a sense, the logic of mastery is only an instrumental device to regain a measure of personal freedom, a way of negotiating the tension between social constraints and one's own desires. When men take care of their responsibilities and use their self-discipline to control their desires, they think they, in turn, have the right to a measure of personal freedom. In practice, the terms of this symbolic exchange are the topic of a continual family discussion. The ability, strength, and self-discipline needed in handling the situations one faces in everyday life are more than just an instrumental means for presenting independence. This kind of mastery has been given a tone of masculinity. It derives this meaning from the world of work, where the workers' view of manual labor is similar to their view of drinking. As a means of livelihood, manual labor has only an instrumental role, but as an expression of a masculine mastery—the skill and strength needed in performing tasks—it is rendered attractive per se.[18] Often, the masculine tone in accounts of male drinking is associated with the ability to withstand large amounts of alcohol, but it nevertheless expresses a form of mastery. The men show that they are able to handle it, and that they are free to set their limits by themselves.[19]

These accounts of problematic drinking can, in fact, be explained and understood in terms of the rationale behind "normal" drinking. The second mode of account, for example, which presents heavy drinking as a form of *revenge*, can be understood on the basis of the symbolic exchange discussed above. If the wife, in the husband's view, has violated the terms of the "deal," he, as a reaction, gives up his self-discipline and begins to drink in an uncontrolled fashion:

> I was kept eight weeks in the army, without a break. My wife had been unfaithful during that time. After leaving the army I didn't come home for two days. I drank. I had never been unfaithful or used alcohol since we had married, I had consciously tried to avoid it. I had brought my paycheck home 'cause my wife took care of the household. Now, when I began to drink I left straight from work and drank the money. I did it five or six times a year. And I began to use other women [sexually].

The mode of speech, where the man declares himself to be a *self-conscious drunkard*, is pretty similar to the revenge mode. In this case a man is bitter and disappointed in life, and careless of the consequences caused to himself by his drinking:

Interviewer: What would you emphasize?
I have no sustenance.
Interviewer: What about the treatment systems?
I've been disappointed in them. They are of no use. It's all the same brainwash that you should not drink. It's been all right. What I've spoiled it's been because of booze. I regret nothing. Drinking is up to yourself.

Such a rationale for self-destructive drinking does not help us to understand the sense of revenge or an expression of disappointment that primarily hurts oneself. Stated differently, how is it possible to "make sense" of a way of life that leads into humiliating situations, into a loss of control and loss of mastery over one's own life? The mode in which drinking is explained only by the fact that *restraints were missing* made it possible to analyze the inherent logic of heavy, uncontrolled drinking. It implies "loss of control" as a taken for granted point of departure, whereupon everyday life has to be organized and made sensible. A man who has self-consciously or anxiously confessed the inability to control his drinking, has turned his failure into a victory—or, as Bourdieu (1977) puts it, has made a virtue of necessity—by redefining the meanings of freedom or independence. If a person does not control or master things like drinking as a sovereign individual, he can base his self-esteem on voluntary submission. One organizes his life by externalizing his self-discipline, replaces self-control with outer control or restricting conditions. In this way, the wife, for example, has been given the role of a controller and caretaker. This could be seen in the story variant mainly told by alcoholics; when the men were separated, they said they started to drink more because of an increased freedom. When the whole life story is articulated with this orientation in mind, all events are evaluated from this point of view: "During the years of my youth I didn't drink too much, only every two weekends on paydays. Also my girlfriend restricted me some."

Total personal freedom is achieved, paradoxically, only when every kind of self-control and self-discipline is delegated to other people or externalized to outer constraints. All that is left over belongs to the realm of freedom. I call this orientation the *logic of freedom*. It is by no means a distinct form of identity possessed only by alcoholics. Rather, it is an alternative route cut through the articulations and symbolic systems that threaten to humiliate a man in repressive social conditions, found with the help of the map and compass provided by the collective

subjectivity of the blue-collar men. It also has its homologous counterpart in the working-class shop-floor culture. When a worker under
close supervision and control cannot control or plan his work, the situation can be rendered positive by a rejection of the mental work
involved. The separation of planning from the actual manual performance of tasks can in this way be turned into the profane form in which
resistance to supervision manifests itself. A worker will hold on to his
role in the division of labor even when he knows the instructions he has
been given are in error (Corrigan and Willis 1980, Alasuutari and Siltari
1983).

Although the logic of freedom seems to be especially characteristic of the forms of identity of the alcoholics, it is not confined to the
issue of alcoholism, defined in terms of "loss of control." All these men,
as blue-collar workers, need both the logic of control and the logic of
freedom in their daily life in order to preserve their self-respect. While
being forced to do their job to earn money, they cannot claim to be completely free. In addition to being proud of their ability to withstand
"the daily grind," they willingly leave the control and planning to the
foreman, taking pains to relieve themselves of responsibility. If the wife,
in addition, sees that her husband maintains his work habits—wakes
him up in the morning, say—it only lightens his burden and enlarges
his freedom. This overall view of life is then expressed and reconfirmed
in the traditional habit of heavy drinking. Not to use one's self-control
when drinking expresses one's personal freedom.[20]

The recognition of these two supplementary logics inherent in
the cultural forms of manual workers also offers, at the level of identity,
the linkage between the other men and the one who used a different
plot in telling his story. At first hearing, his story seemed to be a collection of incidents in a chronological order. There seemed to be no
plot. He had a "usual" childhood, a "usual" youth, got married, and
had children, and that was it. However, upon closer study of the structural dimensions of the events, there is a striking homology between all
the events. He finds an external reason for everything that happened.
He went to work as a forest worker at age thirteen because his brother
brought him there. One day in the worker's cabin they started to drink,
and on the third day they stopped because the foreman told them to.
He got married because his girlfriend was pregnant. In the evening he
may have a beer or two if there happens to be some in the fridge. In
other words, he does not present himself as a sovereign hero of his
own story, but as an object of external factors—which he is actively

manipulating. He is an excellent example of a way of life dominated by the logic of freedom, but nevertheless he is leading a stable life.

THE CHANGE IN THE FAMILY SYSTEM

Thus far the analysis of the stories has shown the way heavy and even alcoholic drinking derives its meaning and sense from the collective subjectivity and the forms of identity shared by both alcoholic and nonalcoholic manual workers. The last task of the study is to explain how drinking becomes a problem, an overwhelmingly compulsive and uncontrollable form of behavior. In order to explain the reason for "loss of control" in its culture-bound context, we need to reconstruct the process through which drinking becomes uncontrolled at the same time its meaning and sense become obscure for a drinker. It is doubtful that any universal model of such a process could be constructed, not even in a specific case such as male workers. All that can be said is that in all the cases in the present study, drinking reflects the tension between the individual and society, revealed in the conflicting relations between the sexes and often crystallized in marriage. The case of men who became alcoholics while married serves as an illuminating example, even though many other men in the sample became alcoholics before any marriage.

As already stated, it is characteristic of the stories told by these men that they express their total confusion about the reasons and process of alcoholism. Somewhere along the way, they say, they found themselves in the habit of taking a drink to relieve a hangover. But they cannot say when it was.

To make taking a drink for a hangover a first sign of alcoholism, as the men do, means that it is interpreted that way by them. In such a case it is made a part of the definition of the concept of alcoholism. In the context of the everyday life, frequent and heavy drinking only expresses that the man is not satisfied with his life, that he for some reason has too limited personal freedom, or that he pursues personal freedom more intensely. He wants to relax. In the family context a heavy drinker violates the rules of a decent life, and insults the wife. If drinking is heavy, it does not symbolize conjugal togetherness (see Haavio-Mannila and Holmila 1986). It belongs outside the family sphere: "When I began to drink on the second day, even only one drink, my wife couldn't stand it at all. . . . Earlier we did drink together, had a certain company of people. But no more since I began to drink on the second day."

When drinking becomes an object of mutual concern and control, the family life takes on a rhythm of dry and wet periods:

> *Interviewer:* The drinking has had different phases?
> *Wife:* Yes it has. First we drank together. Then my husband drank alone. And the dry periods have appeared.

It is not only that drinking is redefined and that family life gets a new rhythm. As a result of a dialectical process, the logic of freedom also becomes more dominant in the man's form of identity. When the wife tries to hold back the man's drinking, it becomes an arena where the spouses battle over power and over the man's independence. The vicious circle is completed. When resisting the constraints on his freedom, the man drinks in the way that was the reason for the wife's control in the first place.

When the man cannot anymore be trusted in everyday life, the wife has to go on controlling her husband. And when he discovers himself helplessly under control and supervision, in order to regain his self-esteem, he has to turn his situation into a virtue, a positive state of affairs. The more others take responsibility, the more he is free from all duties. He gains the desired independence another way around; not by showing he is entitled to it by employing self-discipline, but rather by actively delegating all the responsibility to others, especially to his wife:

> Right in the beginning my husband took care of the payments. Except that when we were tenants I took care of the rent. At first he took care of the payments, then he began to forget about it. We got many overdue notices of unpaid bills. Then I began to check and take care of them. At that time, alcohol already played a part in our life.

The new situation poses the problem that if she interprets his drinking as a purposeful protest or violation of norms, the logical response would be to put an end to the relation. The women say indeed that they put up with the situation either because of a child or because of the dry periods. During them he tries to make it up to her, to be an exemplary husband.

It is precisely because a wife is the mainstay in the men's life that the men seriously try to mend their ways over and over again. Drinking, when primarily interpreted as expressing the desire to cut loose and be personally free, is contradictory to the men's will to preserve their marriage. To overcome this cognitive dissonance, drinking must be redefined. It is no longer defined as an expression of a desire to cut loose from a constraining marital relation and position, but rather as a proof of the man's physical, uncontrolled, and senseless craving for alcohol. It is redefined in terms of the alcoholism frame. The man's desire is redefined as a "natural" craving beyond the realm of culture. It is no longer explained in terms of any kind of sensible or meaningful human behavior.[21]

DISCUSSION

To sum up, let us first tackle the issue of validity as well as the overall nature of the cultural approach employed in this study, and then discuss the levels at which generalizations can be made of the results.

The chapter consisted mainly of an analysis of the way that life stories reflect the men's collective subjectivity and identity. One could ask whether the format men used in telling their life stories was adopted from, or influenced by, the treatment ideologies prevailing in the A-clinic or in the A-guild self-help group. In other words, could it be presumed that the results are biased by the differences between the interview and life situations of the interviewees?

Such a possibility seems unlikely for two reasons. The first has to do with the research design, while the second is connected to the overall nature of the approach.

On the one hand, the fact that both the alcoholic and nonalcoholic men used the same narrative structure, reflecting the shared collective subjectivity, shows that the results are not, on this level of analysis, determined by the situations of interaction. Accordingly, because the analysis at the level of identity was based on the results of the previous phase, and because I was able to give a consistent explanation of the meaning and sense of drinking in the case of both alcoholics and nonalcoholics, it is hard to see how the result of this phase of analysis should be "biased" by the nature of the data.[22]

On the other hand, the whole issue of "influence" or "effect" of ideologies must be rethought when one is dealing with an approach that expressly analyzes the role of meanings, articulations, and ideologies in the emergence of alcoholism. One must bear in mind that we are always making use of a range of articulations and symbolic systems in reach, when trying to make sense of our environment and our place within it. These structures of meaning appear, in turn, in the way we translate our personal experience into speaking terms, into a story. This is why there can never be any "virgin," "uninfluenced" life story. But then again, as Thune (1977) pointed out in the case of AA life stories, a stereotypic quality of a life story is not merely a sign that an individual is seeking group acceptance. A search for group acceptance is only secondary, and as such a sign of the individual's belief that seeking group acceptance is worthwhile. Primarily, the adoption of the story format is a sign of the individual's effort to make sense of his life in a new way, to adopt an identity that preserves his self-respect and keeps him sober. Finally, ideologies just do not come out of thin air. The pattern of telling life stories that reflect the ideology of the AA movement in a nutshell, for instance, had its predecessors in the Washingtonian movement—the first American self-help association involved in rehabilitating alcoholics (Maxwell 1950)—and the antiliquour fiction of the late nineteenth and early twentieth centuries (Lender and Karnchanapee 1977; Silverman 1980). The similarities between the ideologies of these movements, I suggest, cannot be explained primarily by influences. They are due to the particular location alcohol was to take in the cultural structures of the emergent, industrial Western societies. It leaves only a limited range of options for a culturally "sensible" and successful ideology. Whatever should be the ideology in the background of a treatment program—derived for example either from medical science or from religion—an alcoholic and those close to him understand and interpret it in terms of their own cultural patterns. Alcoholism, then, as a concrete phenomenon, is always—whether in its "active" or "recovering" phase—a result of the endless interplay between lay or professional explanations and the application of these in the face of changing living conditions.

Thus, drinking habits and the phenomenon called alcoholism must always be explained in their cultural context. In the case of blue-collar workers studied here, drinking appeared to reflect the tension between individual desires and societal restraints. To achieve a sense of personal freedom, the man has externalized some of his self-discipline to the wife, who thus becomes—along with foreman at work—a representative of societal constraints. Drinking, as expressive of the man's desire for freedom, is controlled by the wife, and provides the concrete issue around which the limits of male freedom are being negotiated. The alcoholism frame and "loss of control," then, becomes a way of making peace; when drinking is perceived as a craving beyond the man's willpower, it is no longer interpreted as an offensive form of behavior. To put the explanatory model in other words, uncontrolled drinking comes about as a way of solving the cognitive dissonance caused by an individual's effort to preserve simultaneously his social bond and his individual independence. Marital relations have been offered as one example, but they are by no means the only arena where such a dissonance may become acute and needs to be solved.

Other research suggests that there are striking similarities between the patterns found in this study and those in blue-collar populations of different countries. The collective subjectivity and the forms of identity of the workers studied here, for instance, parallel the structure of meanings suggested by historical and recent research on working-class culture. The form alcohol problems have shown to take among the blue-collar workers studied here also seems to be in accordance with studies of drinking habits and types of alcoholism among different social strata (Casswell and Gordon 1984; Öjesjö 1983). In these studies, the researchers have interpreted the typical working-class pattern of binge drinking as proof of gamma alcoholism. Similarly, the therapists with their middle-class bias have, in the case of blue-collar patients, preferred medication to psychotherapy (Schmidt et al. 1968).

Such a preference may well be in concert with the blue-collar workers themselves. As will be discussed in chapter 6, they may reject psychotherapy as "idle talk," because they eschew its middle-class biases and are more often in need of the basic services; they want to relieve their hangover, or they simply need a roof over their head. The researchers' conclusion that blue-collar alcoholics have an especially strong psychological and physical addiction to alcohol may be due to the working-class cultural forms. It may be because of the particular logic of freedom, discussed in this chapter, that in the psychological tests using the Drinking Related Locus of Control Scale (DRIE), middle-class people are usually more internal in the general locus of control scores (Rotter 1966; Joe 1971). That Finnish alcoholics seem to be more external than alcoholics from other countries (Koski-Jännes and Johansson 1989; Kallio 1989) does not change the general picture. The more external locus of control among manual workers is, I suggest, rooted to their cultural resistance to supervision. There is a homological relation between the attitude toward hard work and the sense of heavy drinking; they both reflect a similar way of making sense of one's living conditions, preserving a measure of self-respect.

But the similar forms of identity are not mechanically determined by living conditions, a fact that can be seen in the differences and variations between different ethnic groups. The striking similarities in the way of making sense of reality, and of one's position in it, are made possible by the fact that the materials used in the production of identities—meanings, articulations, symbolic systems—are so similar in the Western countries. There is, throughout the Western world, a distinctive organization of everyday life, as well as a self-concept that is structured by a duality between the desires and the self-discipline in an individual.

At this level, it cannot be argued that the results of this study are valid in the case of male manual workers only. It must be remembered that there is no comparative aspect in the research design. In the case of Finland, one cannot really speak about distinctive cultural histories of social classes. Many characteristics of our drinking habits probably date back to the roots of the general Finnish way of life in peasant society. And the same is true of the Western world in general. Addiction, both as a concept and as an existential experience of loss of control, is a historical creation of the epoch of industrialization. In the particular case of drinking, Levine (1978b) relates its discovery to the emergence of the individualistic middle-class worldview. One might suppose that the similarities between types of alcohol problems between social classes are greater than the differences. To grasp the inner logics of various variants of the alcoholism frame, studies of different socio-cultural groups would be needed. Addictive drinking in, for instance, "wine cultures," where drinking is associated with regular meals in the family, is probably based on a distinct structure of meanings.

Even though "loss of control" can be explained as a product of the use of the alcoholism frame, as arising from the interplay of particular situations and behaviors, it is by no means unreal, mere imagination or personal self-deception. As a part of the family structure and of the wider cultural structures through which the men perceive their living conditions and themselves, it is a solid and difficult social fact.

Chapter 5

THE A-CLINIC:
A STUDY OF EXPLANATORY
MODELS IN PRACTICE

This chapter focuses on the role of explanatory models (EMs) in the functioning of professional alcoholism treatment. The A-Clinic Foundation, a Finnish nationwide alcoholism treatment institution, and the A-clinic in Tampere, a town of 160,000 inhabitants, are used as illustrative examples. Views of alcohol-related problems by different parties evidenced in the A-clinic are studied as holistic models with an explicit or underlying theory of the etiology and nature of the common cultural construct labeled alcoholism. EMs guide choices among therapies and therapists, and cast personal and social meaning on the experience of "alcoholism" (Helman 1984, 72-73; see Kleinman 1980, 105).[1] The EMs of both therapists and clients are shown to be rooted in, and shaped by, larger cultural contexts and by the exigencies of social life.

This far, the role of EMs, regarded as expressions of worldviews, in determining the effectiveness of a treatment model has been analyzed in some studies of indigenous treatment of alcoholism (Gordon 1981; Hall 1986; Jilek-Aall 1981; Kunitz and Levy 1974; Pascarosa and Futterman 1976; Singer and Borerro 1984; Steinbring 1980; Stevens

1981). Because these modes of treatment are not designed by professionals and developed with the help of evaluation research, it has been natural to assume that positive outcomes must be due to the fact that the offered explanations of the etiology of alcohol problems make sense in the worldview of the "clientele" belonging to a particular ethnic group.

In this chapter, a similar viewpoint is taken toward a professional treatment institution. As an illustrative example the study shows how EMs of alcoholism are a means of making sense of the lived experience of both clients and therapists. The approach could be likened to that of the sociology of knowledge. Not only errors and unauthenticated beliefs can be rooted to the conditions where they emerge; even the discovery of truth is socially and historically conditioned (Merton 1973). The purpose of this article is not to prove the superiority of one treatment model over another one. Rather, the inherent logic of the views of alcoholism and its proper treatment held by the parties of a treatment modality are related to their social conditions.

In the light of this viewpoint, the shift from a "psychodynamic" view to a "family systems" approach in the A-clinic institution, a shift that took place at the end of the 1970s, is analyzed as an illustrative case. It is shown to be motivated by the changes in the demographic structure of the clientele, which have affected the working conditions of the therapists. In other words, the shift in the prevailing attitude and treatment approach taken toward the clients' drinking problems is shown to be due to the changes in the typical features of the clinic personnel's practical activity as therapists. And one must bear in mind that treatment modalities, and the scientific tests by which they are evaluated, are always praxis-mediated.

It is therefore obvious that there are no "pure" scientific theories of alcoholism simply put into use in treatment. A treatment modality takes its shape at the crossroads of the therapists' and clients' practical knowledge, and the lay and professional EMs that structure it, the guiding line being that the way clients' problems are tackled in treatment makes sense to all parties. Consequently, section two of this study is an analysis of the EMs of the clientele, and section three is an ethnography of the way family systems' approach is made use of in a family treatment group at the Tampere A-clinic. The last section then discusses the role of EMs in the professional alcoholism treatment on the basis of the results.

From a Psychodynamic View to a Family Systems Approach

To argue that the explanatory model of an illness is rooted in the living conditions of an individual does not mean that the relation between social conditions and explanatory models is a causal one. The experience of the individual is already structured by a previous conceptual framework in terms of which the individual perceives the world, behaves, and communicates with others. That is why the relation between explanatory models and material conditions can be adequately grasped only with the structuring impact of tradition in mind; a new explanatory model is perceived at the interface of tradition and social change. Since the new framework is judged in terms of the older one, it is a transformation of it. Let me therefore outline the history of the Finnish alcoholism treatment systems before turning to the present situation.

In the treatment of alcohol-related problems in Finland, Kettil Bruun (1971) distinguishes four historical periods with different dominant models of treatment. Until 1918, the dominant model was *deterrent*: excessive drinking was perceived as a crime, and the goal in handling the alcoholic, carried out by prisons and hospitals, was to eliminate the problem by punishing the excessive drinker. He calls the dominant model of the prohibition era 1919-1931 *preventive*. Drinking in this second era was perceived either as a crime or a sin, and the goal of saving the drinker was approached by means of an inner awakening. After prohibition a *rehabilitative* model became dominant; excessive drinking was perceived as a bad habit. In addition to prisons and hospitals, special institutions for alcoholics were established. During that era, compulsory treatment was used as a means of changing alcoholics' behavior. Finally, ever since the founding of the first A-clinics, that is from 1953 onward, excessive drinking has been perceived mainly as a symptom of underlying personality problems, or a disease. In addition to compulsory, inpatient institutions, outpatient services were set up, in the form of A-clinics, for people voluntarily seeking help for their alcohol problems.

In many respects, the founding of the first A-clinics marked a break with the past. In the A-clinics, the alcoholics were no longer treated as criminals or even sinners. Rather, they were regarded as clients who had voluntarily come to seek help for their alcohol problems.

However, the A-Clinic Foundation did not entirely or abruptly replace the old institutions or the concomitant treatment models. In 1983, the A-clinics' proportion of all the clients of alcoholism treatment institutions listed in the official statistics (Sosiaalihallitus: Statistical report 1986:2) was 53.8 percent. The other clients were treated in special youth stations (4.9 %), detoxification stations (13.9 %), asylums meant for temporary inpatient care (5.7 %), guardian homes meant for retired problem drinkers or addicts (3.2 %), first shelters meant for clients to be directed to further treatment and care (6.1 %), and havens for problem drinkers or addicts where outpatient services are not sufficient or adequate (12.4 %). In addition to these institutions, which are run by the A-Clinic Foundation, the Finnish government or local communes, there are asylums and havens run by Christian organizations; in 1983, according to Niemelä (1983), they comprised 40.2 percent of the total capacity of treatment in Finland. Finally, there are self-help groups, such as AA-groups, Al-Anon and A-guilds.

Altogether, there were fifty-four A-clinics operating throughout the country in 1985. The staff of such an outpatient clinic consists of therapists, nurses, and a doctor. In addition to the outpatient clinics, which primarily take care of the counseling, there were twenty-two detoxification stations and sixty-one residential facilities operating in connection and cooperation with the clinics. The detoxification stations are places where one can stay for a week to sober up after a binge, and the residential facilities are halfway houses for homeless, recovering alcoholics, where one stays approximately two months (A-klinikkasäätiön, 1985).

From the founding of the first A-clinics until the early 1970s, a psychodynamic model of alcoholism had a dominant position in the A-Clinic Foundation. Then, in the mid-1970s, it was challenged by a new model inspired by family systems theory and brief therapy. Though the new framework has not attained an indisputable dominance among all social workers, let alone psychiatrists or nurses, it has nevertheless been officially recognized and institutionalized as a special area of emphasis in the in-service training of social workers (A-klinikkasäätiön, 1985). The rationale by which the new model was defended demonstrated how the professional explanatory models are rooted in changing social conditions.

The thing that appealed to the proponents of this new approach was that it concentrates on changing the client's present harmful situation, not so much on tracing its idiosyncratic past. The family systems theory views the family as a system with its own structure, interactive behavioral patterns, and homeostatic mechanisms (Jackson 1957; for an overview, see Hoffman 1981). In the case of alcohol problems, it is the system, not the "identified patient" (Steinglass 1980, 152), which is seen as the object of therapy (Bowen 1974; Davis et al. 1974; Steinglass, Weiner and Mendelson 1971). The brief therapy, which is closely related to family systems theory, shares the same vantage point. While its intention is to change the system by working with an individual client, the one who complains the most is often chosen for therapy, rather than the "identified patient" (Watzlawick, Weakland, and Fish 1974). Both of these models seek to intervene with the pathological social system that maintains the symptom, to push the system into curing motion.

The new approach was first introduced in the late 1970s by proposing that the traditional question, "Why does a person drink," should be changed to read: "Why does a person go on with his drinking?" (Aalto 1976; Silvennoinen 1979). Although information about the chains of causal relations leading an individual into alcoholism may be useful in the planning of preventive measures, it does not help the client, Silvennoinen argued. The goal of all forms of treatment should, in his opinion, be to influence the issues and incidents that have significance for the client's life today, rather than to dwell in the irreversible past. According to him, the methods of brief therapy are better than the psychotherapy of the analytic tradition. All types of clients can be, he argued, treated in terms of the new approach, and that has indeed happened.

To explain why the new approach was introduced during the late 1970s and officially recognized during the early 1980s, the changes in the demographic structure of the clientele of A-clinics were inspected. The figures given here are drawn from the 1985 annual report of the A-Clinic Foundation (A-klinikkasäätiön, 1985).[2] During the last fifteen years, the share of clients who are older than forty years has not changed markedly: in 1971 they formed 49 percent and fourteen years later 47.2 percent of all clients. In contrast, the proportions of those younger than thirty years on the one hand, and those in their 30s on the other, have changed remarkably. The years 1972-73 were the peak for the youngest client group: at that time 27 percent of all clients were younger than thirty years; ever since the figures have gone steadily downward. In 1985 their proportion was only 12.3 percent of all clients. This remarkable decrease was complemented by the rise in the proportion of those in their 30s. At their lowest the proportion was 27 percent in 1971, and ever since the figures have continued to rise. In 1985 the proportion of the clients in their 30s was 40.5 percent.

TABLE 1
Proportion of Age Groups of the
A-Clinic Foundation Clients in 1971 and 1985

	1971 %	1985 %
Under 30 years	24.0	12.3
30-39 years	27.0	40.5
40 or more	49.0	47.2

This remarkable change mainly reflects the differences in the sizes of different generations. By the beginning of the 1970s, those born during, or soon after, the war reached adulthood, and some of them entered the A-clinics at a relatively early age. This generation also differs from generations born before or after it—those born after 1955—regarding its drinking habits. As a distinct "wet generation" (Sulkunen 1979) they started the use of alcohol at an earlier age and also continued to use more alcohol than those born before or after them. By the mid-1980s, these people are in their 30s or early 40s.

Those recruited from the ranks of the baby boom generation who came to search for help with their drinking problems in their 30s were in a life situation that is quite different from those in their teens or 20s. The difference can also be seen by studying the statistics; as soon as the baby boomers grew older, the proportion of divorced clients rose, respectively, throughout the 1970s and 80s. The proportion of divorced clients has risen from 18 percent in 1971 to 26.5 percent in 1985, whereas the proportion of married clients has decreased from 50 percent in 1971 to 38.2 percent in 1985. The proportions of those never married and of those widowed have stayed practically the same.[3]

TABLE 2
Marital Statuses of the A-Clinic Foundation Clients in 1971 and 1985

	1971 %	1985 %
Never married	30.0	32.1
Married	50.0	38.9
Divorced	18.0	27.0
Widowed	2.0	1.9

It can be assumed that men who come to search for help with alcohol problems in their teens or 20s have developed their problematic relation to alcohol before any marriage. When treating them, a psychoanalytic framework, paying particular attention to early experiences and relations with parents, made sense from the standpoint of their therapists. But a great deal of those who have come to search for help in the A-clinics in their 30s probably developed their drinking problems only during or after marital life. In such a case a person is often preoccupied by marital crisis or depressed by a divorce. Since these clients were probably reluctant to dwell on childhood experiences, it was easier for the social workers to make them reflect on their adult life. The past fifteen years have seen a rise in this type of client and there was a social need for approaches such as family systems theory or some kind of brief therapy. The therapists have been willing to respond by seeking a therapeutic model more adapted to the clients' present situation.

In the interviews, the social workers themselves said that a change in the clients' attributions of causes of drinking has indeed taken place:

> *Interviewer:* Do the clients speak about their past?
> *Social worker:* It has diminished. Earlier there were probably more people who wanted to make up for themselves a difficult childhood. I guess the [social] worker's attitude has an influence in this respect. One can look backwards, if it is useful for the time being, but if it seems to be an excuse or a pastime; I won't buy it, I'll turn it back to today.

There are also other reasons that may have contributed to the increasing focus on the present. Because of changes in the job market and in the family life of the generations born during or after World War II, people seek help with alcohol problems at an earlier phase. Said one of the social workers:

> The clients come at an earlier phase; 15-20 years ago everybody had a very long drinking history at the arrival to the clinic, that is 10-15 years' drinking history behind them. Now one gets clients whose excessive drinking may be restricted to one to three years.

There are two main reasons for this development. First, the agreement settled between the employers' and employees' unions in 1972, by which a worker must be directed to treatment, instead of firing him

right away, has had an impact on treatment systems. The workers
directed to treatment by their employers have enlarged the proportion
of clients with a relatively short drinking career behind them. Secondly,
changes in the family life of the baby-boomers have also contributed to
the trend in the same direction. Divorce has become a more general
phenomenon,[4] so that facing a divorce is an ever-more realistic alternative in the case of family crises than for earlier generations. It may be
assumed that the fear of divorce makes the men seek help in an earlier
phase of alcoholism than previously.

To conclude, one can say that the introduction and adoption of
family systems theory and brief therapy has been understandable in
light of the changes that have taken place in therapists' practical working conditions during the past fifteen years. Due to the changed demographic structure of Finnish society, the typical life situations and concerns of the clientele have changed, and made the therapists seek or at
least be receptive to a treatment model that would be more in concert
with the situation. This makes understandable the fact that family systems theory made a breakthrough. Though it has not resolved all the
problems in the therapists' daily work, its widespread adoption among
therapists makes sense from their standpoint.

FEATURES OF CLIENTS' EXPLANATORY MODELS

To study how the clients' explanatory models and concomitant client
motivations are embedded in social conditions, the data will be now
approached from another vantage point: from the perspective of individuals trying to make sense of their life. Two overlapping dimensions could
be pointed out in this respect, the historical and the demographic. Changes
in Finnish society have had an overall impact on client motivation,
whereas the demographic dimension shows how one's conception of alcohol problems is dependent on one's socio-economic position.

On the basis of the investigation of the historical dimension, it
will be argued that many changes favoring the systems approach from
the therapists' viewpoint do not make sense when analyzed as factors of
client motivation. The changes in Finnish society discussed above have,
for example, had negative effects on client motivation in any kind of
therapeutic work. The worsening employment situation and the
increased divorce rate have, in some cases, given treatment provided by
the A-clinics a compulsory overtone.

As a consequence of the difficult employment situation, coupled with the new legislation discussed in the previous section, the assignment to treatment by employers often became interpreted as a punishment. These assignments are a new phenomenon, comprising a remarkable proportion of all new clients. In such cases, where the motivation does not come from the individual, it is natural that clients may not be particularly motivated to work on their problems in therapy.

It may be assumed that explanatory models and treatment motivations are dependent on the socio-economic positions of clients, and differ in terms of them. That can be studied by comparing the clientele in different kind of treatment. The Tampere A-clinic houses three separate facilities with differing services: the residential facility, the detoxification station, and the outpatient clinic. Therefore, factors of client motivation can be inferred by analyzing the client statistics drawn from the annual reports of the Tampere A-clinic from the years 1975-1984 (*Tampereen*, 1975-1984). Although it may well be that the assignment decisions made by counselors are dependent on their preconceptions of different types of clients, the demographic structure of the clientele of the three facilities also reflects the clients' own needs and preferences. First, although such preconceptions are based on prior practical experience, there is an interplay between the preconceptions and the social reality they maintain. Second, clients' stay in any of the facilities is based on their free will. Many clients make an appointment with the facilities themselves, without consulting anybody.

The clientele in the three departments mainly differs in terms of social class and marital status. These two factors were associated with a "mental-physical" continuum where the three facilities of the A-clinic could be put (see Wittman 1971).

The mental-physical continuum means that the three facilities vary in the extent to which they provide for the client's basic needs. The outpatient clinic offers the most in terms of therapy and the least in terms of physical or "bodily" relief. The only services that are not composed only of talking are the hangover medication provided by the nurse and the possibility of getting an appointment with the A-clinic's doctor. The detoxification station instead offers a shelter and full boarding from a few days to more than a week, in addition to medication. The possibilities for therapy are modest, mainly composed of optional discussions with the nurses. Finally, the residential facility provides shelter for several months. The only form of treatment provided is the prohibition on drinking. As a geographically isolated locale, the service is also a shelter from one's craving.

This continuum in the services corresponds with the demographic structure of the clientele; the more "mental" the means of cure of a department, the greater the number of married clients and the fewer the number of manual workers. The mean percentages of the yearly shares of married clients and manual workers in the three departments of the A-clinic of Tampere from the years 1975-1984 show that the share of married clients is highest in the outpatient clinic (39.6%) and lowest in the residential facility (7.3%), whereas the share of manual workers is lowest in the outpatient clinic (68.7%) and highest in the residential facility (87.2%).[5] The detoxification station is situated between the other two in both scores, the ten-year mean figures being 73.6 percent manual workers and 34.5 percent married clients.

It can be concluded that heavy-drinking single persons are most vulnerable, most often lacking a roof over their head, and single people in lower socio-economic positions most easily face the situation where they lose their job and home. In this kind of life situation, where a person does not have a job or a place to stay, there seems to be no sense in outpatient therapy, as one of the social workers says:

> Because it is a question of the basics of living for them, to get a roof over one's head. They are examples of their own subculture, and probably, from their point of view, this is a peculiar place for idle talk.

The statistical profile of clients in separate services and treatment facilities provided by the A-clinic institution reflects, I suggest, differences in the way people in diverse life situations perceive alcohol problems. In other words, the explanatory model of alcoholism that makes sense for a client is dependent on one's life situation, and professional and marital statuses are its essential determinants.

Middle-class people are especially apt to perceive alcohol problems in terms of a medical model. Manual workers, in contrast, tend to see alcohol problems more as reflections of social and moral conflicts, and tend to reject psychotherapy as "idle talk" because they eschew its middle-class biases and are more often in need of the basic inpatient services.

This class-based difference in the folk models of alcoholism is, I argue, also due to the differences in work conditions. In middle-class occupations, where one is expected to be responsible for one's work voluntarily, one has to internalize an especially strong sense of duty.[6] Because excessive drinking easily leads to failures in carrying out one's duties, and harms mainly oneself, it appears irrational from a middle-class viewpoint. A middle-class man is more apt to perceive his drinking problem as a symptom of a personality disorder or as a disease. Such an extreme sense of duty is for the most part lacking in the life situation of a manual worker, who is not expected to shoulder any responsibility of the work. Rather, he is expected to do no more and no less than what he is told.

The marital status of a client has a similar impact on one's explanatory model of alcohol problems. A married man has more responsibilities, and he is therefore more apt to think that uncontrolled drinking at the expense of his family is a symptom of a disorder that requires some kind of therapy.

These interpretations make understandable the pattern of assignment to the three departments of the A-clinic. The more "mental" the mode of treatment, the more the clients were married and the less they were manual workers. That distribution reflects, I suggest, a rule according to which the more internalized sense of duty a man has, the more apt he is to voluntarily seek help, and to perceive drinking as a form of irrational, involuntary behavior.

Though the middle-class may be a vanguard of a "civilizing process" (see Elias 1978; 1982), the Finnish history of treatment institutions (Bruun 1971) shows that there is an overall trend toward a more and more internalized sense of duty in the whole population. From the turn of the century onward, treatment models have laid more and more emphasis on the *involuntary* nature of the problem and the *voluntary* nature of the rehabilitative measures. The time span from the beginning of the twentieth century to the present day, which has meant the establishment of an industrial and an increasingly postindustrial society, has witnessed a continuation of the "civilizing process"; a further conversion of the constraints through others into self-restraints. Power and control have been buried in the self-discipline of the people, and the social meanings of drinking in the "nature" or the "unconscious" of the man, along with other desires. The developments could also be seen as a final elaboration of the process that according to Michel Foucault (1979) was pushed into motion by the birth of the prison.

The history of the treatment models illustrates the "carceral continuum," the replacement of the "offender" by the "delinquent," and further on, by the "deviant," and the simultaneous substitution of the prison by the inpatient facility and finally by the outpatient clinic. Also, as soon as the drinkers come to perceive themselves as "sick," confess it, and in this way express their willingness to be cured, coercion and imprisonment of "alcoholics" becomes irrational and dysfunctional. Instead of the prisons of the early 1800s, the problem drinkers are treated now preferably in voluntary treatment institutions.

THE FAMILY TREATMENT GROUP AND THERAPEUTIC DISCOURSE

There is, in other words, a social need for outpatient services in the population. But how is it with the explanatory model employed in therapy? Is it in accordance with the ways in which the A-clinic's clients make sense of alcohol problems? As far as the theorists and proponents of the family systems approach in psychotherapy are concerned, the new theory opposes a strictly medical view. As one of the theorists points out, the family systems theory does not regard illnesses as personal pathologies, but rather as workings of a system. A change is then brought about by making an intervention in the system.

Is that the way the family systems approach is applied at the A-clinic? In order to suggest an answer to this question, a family treatment group, one of the primary forms in which the new approach is utilized at the Tampere A-clinic, was studied. The object of analysis was the discourse, in terms of which drinking problems are discussed at the group level. This is how the individual differences are filtered away, and give way to the cultural structures, to the conceptual grid that articulates the perception of, and the measures taken by, the participants to deal with problems.

The group, which was the object of participant observation for nine months, consisted of four couples. Three of them were officially married, whereas one of them had cohabitated for five years. The marriages had lasted for ten, twenty, and thirty-one years. All the married couples had at least one child. In all the couples, it is the man who had an alcohol problem. The youngest of the men was thirty-four years, and the oldest fifty-four.[7]

The men's drinking careers that finally led them to the group were typical of the way the A-clinic institution works as a totality. All of them had first entered treatment by voluntarily going to detoxification;

one of them had made ten visits to the detoxification station. One of the men said that his employer had given him a couple of warnings about his drinking, and another one said that once he had stayed in a haven, an inpatient facility, for two weeks. In the station all clients are advised to make an appointment with a therapist in the outpatient clinic, which they had done. In the individual counseling they had been informed of the possibility of a family treatment group. One of the men said that his wife had suggested such a mode of treatment.

In the pages to follow, I will describe how the family treatment group worked during the nine months it held its monthly sessions (to be precise, the group gathered ten times). Along with description, I will then interpret and comment on the treatment discourse in terms of which the discussions were organized.

The family treatment sessions were started by the social workers, one man and one woman, who asked the couples to list the critical situations that may trigger the man's drinking. From the standpoint of family systems approach, it can be naturally reasoned that in order to manipulate the "alcoholic" family system, one first has to identify the problematic situations within the system. The listing of the risk situations and the discussion of them by each couple were video recorded and later viewed and discussed by the group. The next step was then to make each of the couples list the measures previously taken, or those that might be taken in the future, to reduce the risk and to prevent the relapse.

The lists of the risky situations, made by both the man and the woman of each couple, looked quite a lot alike. Being away from home because of work or because of an evening entertainment, being alone at home, a critical day like income tax refund, an impulse, stress at work, a hangover and the drinks to relieve it, going to work with a hangover when someone at work is on a binge, and the failure to take the anti-abuse pill, were the reasons that in some form or other filled up the lists of both men and women.

On a closer scrutiny, all the reasons mentioned have to do, one way or another, with the locus of control. The issue of motivation for drinking was scarcely touched on. And moreover, most of the reasons deal with the lack of outer control. It seems like the men drink whenever it is possible, every time the restrictions on drinking are missing or fail to be effective. It is taken for granted that a desire to drink is always there in the back of the man's mind. From this standpoint, the things to be classified into categories are the failures of different loci of outer control, whether it is the absence of the wife as the controller, extra money that enables one to drink, or the absence of anti-abuse drugs in the man's circulation. A hangover is discussed in the same vein: it is conceived as a pharmacological and biological state rather than a state of mind. Only "an impulse" and "stress" as reasons that trigger one's drinking may be thought to refer to *motivation*. But they may as well be interpreted to deal with the failure of one's self-control.

The locus of control and the agent of control also turned out to be the central theme in the discussions to follow. The concrete topics— confidence, the woman's revenge and nagging, explanations versus excuses, and control and manipulation—were articulations of, and artic- ulated by, this discourse of control. Let us now deal with the discussions in detail.

Confidence in the promises of the man is one of the issues that was frequently taken up by the women. Most of the time the men of the group were, after all, sober. But the woman's fear of the possibility of the next binge has an effect on the emotional climate of family life. In many cases, the man promises to abstain from drinking during a future risk situation but it often turns out that he does not keep his promise. For one of the couples, the husband does not like to go to her parents' home in the countryside, and so the wife goes alone. Despite plans of compensating activity for the man, and promises given by him, he always starts drinking during the time she is away from home. The same is true in all families of the man's business trips, or other inci- dents when the man is away from home. When the man, for example, has an entertainment evening, and he promises not to drink too much or stay very long, it turns out that "two beers and home at ten means ten beers and home at two" as the saying goes.

A lost confidence is difficult to regain. In the group discussions the men, who were primarily in the role of the defense, wanted to use examples of the more recent times when they had stayed sober, whereas the women drew on their experience of wet periods. The men com- plained that the wife does not appreciate a long dry period, that their scores are back to zero in the eyes of the wife once they have had only one beer. The women said that a drinking spree breaks down the con- fidence that has been built during a dry period. "First there is confi- dence, then disappointment, and after that there is suspicion," one of the women put it.

The discussions dealing with the woman's revenge illustrate the fact that the dispute over the proper locus of control in the families is not just a power play. The emotional bond between spouses makes the situation more complicated. Sadly enough, it seems to literally close the wife indoors. The woman's fear of her husband's counter-revenge, and of the final collapse of the whole relationship, often prevents her from leaving the home.

In one of the situations that was discussed in the group the man had secretly planned his weekend drinking well in advance. He had saved some extra money, changed his clothes, and left before she came back from work. She was naturally angry and would have wanted to leave for a dance restaurant as well, but because they have dogs that cannot be left alone for a long time, she stayed at home because, as she says, she is such a responsible person.

In the individual interviews the women told about situations in which their absence from home had made their spouse drink in response:

> *Interviewer:* How do you think your husband would respond if you'd go out now with some of your girl friends, say?
> *Wife:* He has almost always started drinking when I have left somewhere.

> *Interviewer:* Imagine you would go to a dance restaurant. What would your husband do?
> *Wife:* I don't know. He always says that he would not drink because of such a thing. During the one and a half years we have gone to the clinic, I have been very much at home. I have gone practically nowhere. Twice it has happened that when I have left, he has started to drink. I went to Sweden the summer before the last one with a female friend of mine. He started to drink the very evening we left. We had talked about it and he promised that I don't have to fear. I called from the other side of the sea and asked him. I noticed it already in the phone that he had been drinking.

Because of the women's fear of a cumulative effect of strong measures, they most often express their hurt feelings in a more subtle form. If the man drinks at home, the women said they don't want to talk to him at all. One leaves to meet other people and speaks about everything else but alcohol. "A drunkard terrorizes the whole family," one of the women said. During this discussion, the women suspected that according to the men they do not have the right to get mad or leave. The men asserted that it is irritating if the wife is speechless.

During the husband's binge, the women also usually abstain from sexual intercourse. It is another reflection and expression of the wife's hurt feelings. On the other hand, the man might be in such a condition that he does not even suggest any sexual activity. But the refusal of sex may be used also as revenge after a binge. One of the couples touched on this sensitive topic in the group discussion: "When I'm sober the practical business is okay, but at the emotional level we don't meet at all," said the husband. "Liquor always makes a backlash in the search-ing for the 'common tune', and every relapse hurts," was the wife's response.

Another form of revenge often used by the women is so-called nagging. According to the women, nagging is not something that has been planned; it is a result of losing one's head. Nagging serves the function of a safety valve. But it also seems to have its dysfunctions. Nagging is an expression of the wife's helplessness in the face of her husband's drinking, but according to the men it may nevertheless make the tension between the spouses ever more critical. One of the men said that when she loses her head, it causes a quarrel during which he already thinks that he will go out, drink more, and return home smashed.

But as a consequence of the lack of confidence, the women might not necessarily trust in such statements of the consequences of the woman's behavior. It was often discussed whether the accounts men gave of their behavior were honest; were they explanations or excuses? When discussing the couple, Matti and Maija, where the husband does not want to go with his wife to her parents' home, one of the women in the group suspected that his unwillingness to join her was just an excuse. One of the men doubted that it has become a habit for Matti to drink every time she is seeing her parents, to look forward to her trip. Similarly, one of the women suspected that her husband arranges him-self business trips in order to be able to drink. Her husband admitted that sometimes it is true, not always.

The men were almost as eager as the women to doubt that the accounts given are only excuses, or that an argument with the wife before a spree is an excuse rather than the reason for drinking. More-over, some men were suspicious of their own behavior. One of the men said that the decision to take a drink may be made in just ten minutes, but unconsciously it might have ripened for months. An instant situa-tion may in fact be planned.

In such a state of uncertainty of the "real" reasons, it becomes tricky to speak about motivations for drinking. As far as drinking is concerned, all reasons may be interpreted to be at least unconscious excuses. All that is left are the means of somehow blocking the ever-existing desire to drink. That was the task given by the therapists to the couples after discussing the risky situations; they had to figure out what means they could use in preventing relapses.

For women, there seemed to be mainly two alternative means available for reducing the husband's drinking or stopping him from drinking: control and manipulation. In the discussions of this issue, the men and the women tended to be divided into two camps. The men emphasized that open or covert control does not prevent them from drinking, that it rather irritates and causes further drinking, whereas women suspected that they are simply forced to take care of the family and economy.

The women told of using open control, especially during a drinking spree. They might hide the money or the clothes of their husband, or even sit in front of the door, to prevent him from going drinking. They remarked that they had not been very successful with these measures. Some way or another, the man gets the money to drink.

In some cases both drinking and controlling take on a more covert form. Some of the men who drink at home are in the habit of hiding their liquor. One of the men, for example, used to save liquor at home before he went to a restaurant with his wife, so that he would not run out of it. In these cases the wife tries to find the hidden liquor, pour it down the sink, or dilute it with water. Whether the control of the wife is open or covert, the men emphasized that it does not prevent or even restrict their drinking. The man whose wife used to dilute the liquor, for example, said that he had noticed it. It had irritated him, and as a consequence he had purchased more alcohol.

"Manipulation" is another way of trying to take care of the husband's drinking problem. This method means that the spouses, either alone or in cooperation, try to avoid or change the situations that easily lead to a spree. One of the forms of manipulation could be called "nursing." In this case, the form of control employed by the woman is clothed in the uniform of an emphatic nurse. The wife treats her husband as a patient. One of the women, for example, told of nursing her husband's hangover by serving him soft drinks and food in bed, and by using baby talk. The men were, in general, in favor of this kind of approach.

But the method has its limits, which the women are sensitive to recognize; "nursing" may be easily transformed into "mothering," a situation where all the responsibility of the husband's abstinence is put on the shoulders of his spouse. One of the men suggested that his wife, while out of the home, should give him a call every now and then. He also suggested that they should make a deal with his wife about the evenings he goes out; how much he drinks, where he drinks, and what he drinks. The wife was not eager to make the deal. "It is not my duty to set limits," she answered. According to her, it should be enough that he knows that she does not like his drinking.

On the other hand, the men often tried to prove to their spouses that they can handle themselves. One of the men wanted to convince his wife that soon he will learn to drink in a controlled way again. But mainly the men were trying to find ways to convince their spouse and themselves that they are perfectly able and willing to take care of their continued abstinence themselves.

For this purpose, antabuse, which seems to be a good solution, was tested by two men of the group. First, it is an obstacle for drinking because once you have taken the pill, you just cannot drink. But second, it was one's own decision in the first place. This is why it is not a form of outer control and surveillance, it is just a "mental crutch," a form of manipulation of risky situations by the alcoholic himself. One of the men thought it is a good means of controlling one's behavior. "When you take Antabuse, situations have to be built in a new manner in advance." But the other man was not that content with antabuse and the reason why illuminates the dispute over the locus of control. His spouse said that if she does not put it into his mouth, he tends to forget about it little by little. He emphasized that when he is compelled to take it, it, it is like being in prison. He does not want to depend on antabuse all his life, his spouse has made it such an unpleasant activity. In this way, antabuse had become just another form of control employed by the wife. As the man's response, it had lead to secretly planned binges.

To conclude on the discourse of the family treatment group, it seemed to the discussants that the universe of thinkable solutions to the alcohol-related family crisis is a closed system, a vicious circle. Suppose a man wants to prove to himself and to his wife that he handles his desire, that he can stay sober or drink moderately. Because he has failed before, she cannot trust him, and cannot help trying to prevent or control his drinking. But because a dry period achieved in this way is not actually of his own making, the man feels that he is in a kind of prison. So he starts to behave accordingly; he deceives his wife and uses every chance for drinking. But it only proves that control is needed. In this way, all the methods used by the spouses in coping with the problematic of control, self-esteem, and drinking, seem to get the spouses back to the starting point.

FAMILY TREATMENT AS A MEETING POINT

It would be tempting to regard the description of the therapeutic discourse presented above as the one dealing with "real life," as a description of the clients' marital life and the role of drinking in it. This is particularly tempting since the participants' accounts appear to be honest and sincere. However, one must bear in mind that the whole picture is based on a therapeutically guided treatment session. The discussions are approached from the viewpoint of a therapeutic discourse; a discourse which is formed at the meeting point of the participants' EMs, and which then gives a point of reference for individual participants' contributions to the discussions and debates.

What is the therapeutic discourse of the family treatment group like? In other words, in what form was the family systems approach applied in the group?

In order to answer this question we have to recall the specific form in which the explanatory model of alcoholism, inspired by family systems theory, was introduced in the group. First, it was made clear that there are changeable factors that cause, or at least contribute to, the relapse of the husband. Second, the spouses were asked to figure out new, better, or more effective ways to prevent relapses. Help was then supposed to be brought to the couples in the form of a better awareness of the most common pitfalls and dead ends of the Finnish marriage.

On a microlevel, the discussions were guided by a search for interactional factors of drinking, but these discussions were structured with the preexisting alcoholism framework. The family life was divided into normal and pathological, in this case to "dry" and "wet," periods. While the empirical reality of binge drinking was the starting point for changes hoped for by the group members, the dry/wet dichotomy was also accepted as a taken for granted frame of reference in the discussions dealing with alternative behavioral patterns.

Though controlled drinking was accepted as an alternative goal, and though the behavior of the spouses during the man's drinking spree were touched on in passing, the macrostructure of the group treatment was directly adopted from a cyclic behavioral pattern. First the spouses were asked to list the risky situations easily leading to the man's relapse, then they had to invent and discuss the tricks to be used to lessen such risks.

From the frame of reference formed in the family treatment group, the spouse's means in handling risky situations seemed to be quite ineffective. From the wife's viewpoint, it seemed to be all the same whether she tried to guard and control her husband in order to prevent relapses, or whether she showed her confidence, tried not to carry the responsibility, and in this way irritate him with open surveillance. In both cases, it seemed, the man sooner or later started drinking again. The women did acknowledge that the atmosphere at home was often tense before the man's relapse, and that it often culminated in a quarrel, followed by his drinking. However, even the men admitted that the fight was an excuse and that the drinking was often planned. From this standpoint it made more sense, at least to the women of the group, to think that the beginning of a spree is caused by the natural craving for alcohol that grows stronger and stronger during the dry period. The whole alternation of dry and wet periods seemed to be independent of marital relations. It seemed to be like a pressure chamber of craving with the safety valve of drinking. As the women put it in one discussion:

> Tarja: A drunk is always a drunk.
> Maija: One out of a thousand recovers.
> Aino: The man needs a backbone, needs to straighten up. The liquor destroys the head, the intestines, and the liver. It changes the personality. The brain grows smaller. . . .
> Tarja: Alcoholism is a disease of the metabolism. The craving for alcohol is caused by a change in the organism.

THE DOUBLE EPISTEMOLOGICAL STATUS OF EXPLANATORY MODELS

In conclusion, the form in which family systems approach was applied in the family treatment group did not radically challenge the alcoholism frame. Rather, it turned out to host many elements of it, and in that sense allowed the participants to make sense of their marital problems related to alcohol use in terms of it. It was possible for them to conceive of a family system as an external factor in either worsening or improving the identified patient's condition.

The form that the therapeutic discourse took was influenced both by the clients and the therapists. One can say that the therapists would not accept a biomedical model suggested by the women of the group. However, as easy as it would seem to deduce that the ingredients of a medical model were added by the clients, one must remember that elements of the alcoholism frame were already embedded in the macrostructure of the series of sessions introduced by the therapists. It, in turn, had been worked out on the basis of the therapists' prior experience of family treatment groups.

Therefore, one may conclude that the family systems approach adopted by the A-clinic institution has taken its shape as a response to the social need for a medical view of alcoholism. In that form, the new family systems approach reflects changes in Finnish society. Founded in the early 1950s, the A-clinic institution reflected the process of modernization in Finnish society by being ideologically based on voluntary treatment. On the other hand, it took a middle ground by subscribing to a social-psychological theory of alcoholism. In terms of that theory, alcoholism is accepted as a form of involuntary condition, not just a choice of an individual. But the social and cultural aspects of alcohol problems are acknowledged as well. The proportion of people with middle-class occupations—that is, those doing "mental" work—is increasing in the population,[8] which enhances the motivation for psychotherapy. But middle-class people are especially apt to perceive alcohol problems in terms of a medical model. Manual workers, in contrast, tend to see alcohol problems more as reflections of social and moral conflicts, and tend to reject psychotherapy as "idle talk" because they eschew its middle-class biases and are more often in need of the basic inpatient services.

Consequently, social reality is beginning to resemble the conceptual grid of the folk model within which alcohol problems are approached. In this sense the disease model—like any folk model employed by all the parties involved in coping with a problem—acquires a *double epistemological status*—that is, it becomes a part of social reality. The very model structures the empirical phenomenon itself because it is used by the people in their effort to make sense of their or the clients' situation. Kettil Bruun's assertion, made in 1971, that intoxication, not alcoholism, is the major alcohol problem in Finland is probably historical. Drinking problems are more and more unanimously conceived in terms of the disease concept of alcoholism.

Chapter 6

A Technique of Desire:
The A-Guild

Folk Models and the View of Life

The following case study of the Tampere A-guild is an analysis of the way the guild treatment modality works. However, the study is not representative of what is known as evelution research, since the idea is not to measure how effective the treatment program is. The point is, instead, to study how the guild philosophy fits in with the worldview or Weltanschauung of the social strata from which its members come and to which it appeals.

The study was guided by my conviction that an alcoholism explanatory model peculiar to the group being studied cannot be recognized and separated from other group activities, and neither can the latter be regarded as a way of life in which the explanatory model could be rooted. The group activities, views of alcoholism, and practical methods of recovery all form a totality. The interest is focused on factors that render the views of alcoholism, intertwined with all the features of the group life, like the normative rules or pieces of advice, intelligible for the individual members. The guild is, in other words, treated as a cultural group that shares a particular view of life. Though there is always some normative pressure in a social group, especially in one that has a preset goal and that has been institutionalized to a certain extent, it is argued that social norms are only of secondary importance in the guild. The function of the group is not to guide and support its members in internalizing certain social norms into a self-discipline that prevents them from drinking; the idea is rather to remove the desire for alcohol by a means of transforming and modifying their overall view of life. The guild philosophy is, it is argued, a technique of desire.

PARTICIPANT OBSERVATION OF THE TAMPERE A-GUILD

The Tampere A-guild is a local member of a Finnish self-help organization, the Union of A-guilds (*A-kiltojen liitto ry*). The first A-guilds were established in the early 1960s by the clients and personnel of local A-clinics to offer help, support, and information to anybody who came to ask for it. A-guilds operate in all towns where there is an A-clinic; in 1986 there were fifty-five A-guilds in the country. In 1984, approximately seven thousand persons took part in the guild activities.[1]

The guilds are institutionally affiliated with the A-clinics where they were initially born. Most guilds are physically located in the same residence with the A-clinic, and most of the guild members are present or former clients of the clinic. The institutional connection has certainly had an impact on the view the organization has taken toward treatment by the guilds, but the A-Guild Association nevertheless has its unique philosophy. In many respects it can be compared with AA, who also operate in Finland, but in some points it is in opposition to the AA ideology.

Like any indigenous treatment models, the A-guilds are spontaneous products of the group members' parent culture, informal and autonomous groups that themselves plan their shared view of life. According to the members of the studied group, the A-guilds are even more informal than the other major self-help organization, AA.

The Tampere A-guild has approximately two hundred members, though only a minority of them go to the meetings on a regular basis. About 70 percent of the members are divorced or otherwise single, and a great majority of them are men; of the few women active in the guild, most are nonalcoholic wives or cohabiting spouses of male members. The guild is therefore a male-dominated community, which is reflected in its philosophy as well.

The activities of the guild consisted mainly of daily morning sessions from 10 to 12 A.M. and of evening sessions from five P.M. onward on Tuesdays, Thursdays, and weekends. The sessions did not have any program whatsoever; people just gathered around the table in their relatively small room and chatted with each other in an informal fashion. In addition to these sessions, the guild organized flea markets, sauna evenings, and volunteer work sessions—for example, to cut and axe the firewood for the fireplaces in a summer place made available for their use by the city of Tampere.

The daily meetings formed a natural setting for participant observation, which was the primary research method. With the help of one research assistant, I went to the morning sessions two or three times a week for three months. The evening sessions were visited by us on a less regular basis. Once we also visited the guild's summer place. Furthermore, I reviewed the newsletter of the A-Guild Association, *Vesiposti*.

The material gathered during the fieldwork consists of field notes, recordings of group discussions, as well as six interviews of individual guild members. It gives a fairly reliable picture of the activities and attitudes of the local guild. However, the relation the Tampere case to the other guilds can only be indirectly concluded; the attitudes and lines of reasoning of the local guild are largely in concert with the general or "official" views presented in the association's newsletter. Analysis of the local case shows how these separate attitudes and opinions more or less form an internally logical whole. It is reasonable to assume that the way the other local guilds make sense of the guild ideology is comparable to the Tampere case. Or one might at least reason that there are limited ways of making sense of the guild ideology as an integral part of the members' everyday life.

The idea of the study was indeed to make a "thick description" (Geertz 1973) of the guild: to give as thorough a picture of a culture as is needed in order to grasp "the informal logic" of actual life. Such an orientation does not mean, though, that all theories or theoretical concepts should be put aside. If one thinks about the vastness of the undertaking, it becomes obvious that a student of culture cannot start intellectually empty-handed. Particularly when one studies a subculture of one's own society, as is the case here, one needs theoretical ideas and concepts in order to break through the natural attitude, the horizon of taken for grantedness, that prevents one from paying attention to any other aspects of the cultural group except the ones that deviate from those of researchers themselves. A mere list of the deviating features of a group does not pass for thick description; it would not account for the systematic rules or conceptual structures that inform the acts of the members of the culture being studied.

The guiding principle of thick description, and of cultural studies in general, is simply the enlargement of the human mind. It is achieved with an open mind and with the help of conceptual frameworks, whose function is not to restrict one's scope but rather to open up new ways of making sense of social and cultural phenomena. Theories are not used as conceptual grids that are forced on empirical observations; rather, explanatory frameworks are developed in the cross-fertilizing process of ethnographic fieldwork and constructive attempts (Malinowski 1961, 13), informed by previous knowledge and understanding of the nature of the phenomena being studied.

CHARACTERISTICS OF THE GUILD

The Coffee Ritual

The first thing that attracts the attention of a newcomer in the guild meetings is the importance of coffee drinking as a ritual. When the first participants of the morning meeting show up around ten o'clock, making coffee is the very first thing they pay attention to. If the chairman has not arrived yet and put the coffee pot on the electric plate in the kitchen, which is often the case, a friendly argument will start: Who will be the one who makes coffee this morning? When the humorous argument is finally settled, the key to the coffee closet is fetched from its hiding place and someone will go out to the kitchen. Meanwhile, other guild members will show up one after another, and the first comment they often utter is whether coffee is available or whether it is being made. Men may also converse about the amount of coffee they have already drunk during the morning, and compare the numbers of cups each one has consumed.

When the first pot of coffee finally arrives from the kitchen, it is the high point of the morning, so it seems. The whole atmosphere around the only table in the tiny meeting room, where all are gathered, immediately becomes more lively. The discussion, which this far has consisted of a quiet, infrequent murmur, involving only some of the people present, gains more speed, the voices rise, and the first loud bursts of laughter can be heard.

As in any ritual, there are rules which the participants follow in this one, too. The guild uses plastic coffee cups, with detachable handles. The person with the coffee pot pours coffee into as many cups as there are members in the room, another attaches handles to each cup, and then the cups are passed on from one end of the table to everyone. Simultaneously a tin box for coins is also passed. Though there is no fixed price and someone who is totally broke can have coffee for free, everyone usually puts some change into the box.

One is not supposed to take the first cup handed over, as my research assistant did the first time, but rather to pass it on until the person at the end of the table has been passed a cup, so that the last one who gets coffee is the one pouring the coffee:

> The vice-president brought the pot, poured into a disposable cup, and handed it over to me. Because I did not master the strict rules of coffee drinking, I immediately started to drink it myself. The man sitting at the other side of the table said to the vice-president to pass the next one this way. So he did, and the cup traveled from hand to hand to the furthest man. With this system everyone got his cup of coffee. [A-guild September 11, 1985]

The second cup of coffee is served by using a different system. This time the pot itself is passed on from hand to hand around the table, and each one wanting to have more coffee pours a second cup. This variation of the coffee ritual is then played out repeatedly throughout the daily session; new pots of coffee are continuously being made, and every now and then the pot is passed around to those wanting to have still another helping.

Most of the participants want to, and it is extremely difficult to abstain from drinking coffee in the meetings. It is a social norm that one is expected to take part in the ritual. After one has already had the first cup of coffee, one is supposed to have another and another. Not to pour oneself a cup needs an explanation:

> A man sitting beside the vice-president astonished the company by refraining from coffee. When he was eagerly asked why, he based his abstinence on the fact that he had had three cups of coffee in the morning, just before leaving for the meeting That is why he did not have a taste for coffee. When pouring the second round the vice-president asked whether he now wanted a cup. He did

not have one that time either. As there were people coming and going, in the third round the vice-president made a miscalculation, pouring one cup too many. That cup he gave to the abstaining man, saying that now you have to drink since it's already been poured. The man did take that cup in his hand and said that okay, I guess I have to drink it then. This time the pot was not passed around; the vice-president conducted the ceremony one cup at a time. [A-guild September 11, 1985]

The consumption of coffee is enormously high in the guild. And the members are well aware of the exact amount of coffee consumed annually; it is in fact one of the permanent topics in the guild:

I asked how much coffee they consume. A young man replied that more than a hundred kilos (well over two hundred pounds) might be consumed in a year. Last year the consumption was 90 kilos. The vice-president confirmed the information, that it is correct, that a lot is consumed. [A-guild September 11, 1985]

The reason why they know the amounts so accurately is that they purchase a small stock of articles—cigarettes, bottles of soft drink, and coffee—with the money they give to the tin box being passed around in the meetings, and they keep a record of the amounts. It is, however, significant that the exact figure of coffee consumption produced by bookkeeping is passed on as general knowledge among the guild members, and that it is publicly discussed and commented on in the meetings. It reflects and underlines the fact that coffee drinking carries a particular cultural meaning in the guild. Its cultural significance as a ritual and as a reflection of the A-guild ideology is obvious and transparent. Not much of its symbolic content seems to belong to the sphere of *doxa* (Bourdieu 1977), the universe of unconscious, undiscussed, and undisputed structures of meaning underlying any shared view of life with its explicitly expressed attitudes.

For the A-guild members coffee is a substitute for alcohol. It can be both a way of sobering up after a binge, when returning to the guild, and a way of staying sober and keeping one's head clear, so to speak. Smoking cigarettes and drinking coffee are activities that fill the idle hands of the company of men and women used to holding glasses and drinking alcoholic drinks. Its function as a substitute is so well known and acknowledged that the issue was even discussed in *Vesiposti*, the newspaper of the association of local A-guilds in 1985, the year when most of the fieldwork of this study was done. The article "Kahviko korviketta—ei kai" (Anonymous 1985, 30-31) reviewed a social survey, mainly conducted in the social hospital of Järvenpää, where the patients or clients, who were having treatment of their alcohol problems, were reported to drink up to twenty-one cups of coffee daily. Those drinking ten to fourteen cups of coffee formed 23 percent of the clientele. To the question whether coffee was a substitute for alcohol for them, 44 percent responded that it was.

It is no wonder that coffee is used as a substitute for alcohol. Its property as a stimulant and therefore as an opposite of alcohol, which pharmacologically is a depressant, is well known; unlike alcoholic drinks, coffee does not cause intoxication. It only refreshes, and it is therefore widely believed that coffee is effective in sobering up a drunken person. A good deal of these beliefs are probably due to the social history of coffee, which from the fifteenth century onward, increasingly replaced wine and other alcoholic drinks as a substance used in social life.[2] Coffee drinking has an especially important role in Finnish culture, at least if the consumption figures are accepted as proof. The Finns are among the heaviest coffee drinkers in the world. All in all, it is quite natural that coffee has gained such an important position in the social life of the A-guild, a company of people trying to stay abstinent.

However, there are many lessons to be learned from a more detailed analysis of the various aspects of the A-guild coffee ritual and of the social meanings attached to coffee. The coffee drinking habits differ from the ordinary Finnish coffee ritual and reveal that the guild coffee ritual parallels and reflects "the structure, style, typical concerns, attitudes, and feelings" (Willis 1978, 191) of the guild. There is, in other words, a homologous relationship between the coffee ritual and the particular cultural forms of the guild. The structure of meanings related to coffee drinking provides us with a partial, microcosmic picture of the shared view of life of the guild members. One could alternatively say that it both reflects and modifies or strengthens, consciously and unconsciously, the particular form of consciousness and social identity developed and sought for in the guild.

Consider, say, the way coffee is served in the meetings, or rather the fact that it is not *served* in the usual meaning of the word. That is, I suggest, due to the way coffee drinking habits are already culturally "marked" by their previous uses in Finnish culture. The central role that coffee traditionally plays in everyday life has made it especially fit for the use of the guild. On the other hand the group has to take into account shades of social meaning of coffee drinking that are in contradiction with the attitudes and feelings that the guild seeks to express and strengthen. Coffee is, indeed, perceived as an opposite and alternative to alcohol, which well suits the purpose of the guild. As such, though, there are certain feminine shades to it. The victory of coffee over beer and spirits as the sole drink of "decent" social gatherings certainly also was a victory of women as strong supporters of temperance, even though Finnish temperance was far from an entirely female social movement. As was discussed in chapter 2, in Finland the workers' movement came to support prohibition at the turn of the century. However, Finnish coffee drinking is also a very female ritual. It is conducted solely by women, and in many respects it is also an expression and celebration of female values, even of matriarchal features in Finnish culture. As a counterpart to it, the making and especially serving of coffee is traditionally left entirely to women. A man serving coffee would easily be deemed as feminine. Therefore, coffee is not properly *served* at the guild table, but the coffee ritual is carried out by means of the self-service described above.

One should not, however, overemphasize the feminine tone of Finnish coffee tradition. There have been many all-male groups—like the lumberjacks in their cabins in the forests—who are used to having coffee among themselves. Such male groups with their peculiar coffee drinking habits have certainly provided the guild with sources from which to draw models for a male coffee ritual without any feminine tones. Nevertheless, the fact that the guild has adopted a particular modification of the standard Finnish coffee ritual shows how important a role masculinity plays in the cultural production of identity taking place in the male-dominated guild. All threats to masculinity are taken care of in one way or another.

The normative pressure used against those trying to abstain from drinking coffee also deserves attention. With a functionalist frame of mind one could conclude that the coffee ritual functions to reinforce the community of the guild members. Furthermore, as the main purpose of the guild is to provide the individual members with a supportive group that helps them in their effort to abstain from drinking, the unity of the guild is protected by not easily letting anyone refrain from rituals serving as symbols of the community.

However, that does not explain why a particular ritual is needed;

Why is it not simply enough to attend the meetings and stay a teetotaler? As useful as it is to pay attention to the manifest and latent functions of an activity, one must bear in mind the fallacy of functionalist explanations, a "cannibalism of form by function," as Sahlins (1976, 77-78, 83) puts it: "the more distant and distinct the cultural practice from the register of its purported function, the less this function will specify the phenomenon." Instead of such a functionalist reduction, let us consider the coffee ritual as a whole, with the forms of interaction particular to it. It greatly resembles that of another scene: a Finnish drinking group. When the coffee pot is replaced with a bottle of booze, the resemblance is astonishing. In a traditional Finnish male drinking circle, drinks are seldom served, but among real friends or in a hospitable house the bottle is passed on from hand to hand. One might compare the guild meetings to a group of men at a bar table, with the cups in front of everybody, cigarette smoke hanging thick in the air, and the loud, freely flying conversation going on, interrupted only by bursts of laughter from time to time. This is the scene one of the men described when I suggested I would like to make a recording of a meeting the first time:

> One guy a long time ago, when we had an open group at the end of the 1950s, suggested that we might record a meeting on tape. But we did not know when it would take place. It was a round table with the microphone on it and the tape recorder under the table. He had made a pirate recording, goddamit. The next time we had the meeting he said first let's listen to the previous assembly. Goddamit, there was a lot of noise, it was just like being in a bar and we were only seven men!

A socio-symbolic homology between a circle of men having a drinking bout and the guild meeting becomes even more obvious when the discussions going on are considered, which is considered in the next section. However, the similarities as well as differences between the members' previous life events and the activities of the guild must be discussed in more detail before one is in a position to estimate the significance of these observations as a whole.

Memoirs of Past Drinking

One of the permanent topics in the guild meetings are stories and anecdotes told of the members' previous lives as drunkards or alcoholics.

Since the group of regular visitors to the meetings is quite restricted, there is in fact a limited repertoire of individuals' memoirs, transformed into a local form of oral tradition recited over and over again. Though all areas of life are covered in these stories or anecdotes to some extent, stories of past drinking are dominant.

In that respect the meetings resemble a group of heavy drinking men on a Monday morning, recalling and telling each other the incidents that have taken place during the weekend's drinking spree. The only difference is that in the guild some incidents being recited may date back even thirty years. Nevertheless, they are made afresh in the stories over and over again.

There is, in fact, a funny paradox in their stories when compared with those of a group of men in a bar; while the guild members talk mostly about drinking when sober, those actively drinking often talk about work. The men in a guild meeting shared this observation, when I presented it:

> On the job I once discussed the guild with a buddy, and told him that we don't talk about work that much. He said that that is because one does not drink there. He regarded it as natural that when one does not drink, one does not have to work either. And I guess that one's occupation is revealed in a boozer. I have noticed it myself when hanging around in pubs that every second guy claims to be at least a psychologist or a civil engineer; one hardly finds a guy with a lower status. Back in the 1960s, when I practically lived in a bar for six or seven years, the porter used to come to us and say that okay you masons, go home to sleep for a while so that we can clean up this hole. You splash too damn much cement around.

One of the themes in these guild members' stories of drinking deals with conflicts with employers, and with the numerous times the men have "drunk their job." Sometimes one might be lucky enough only to get a warning:

> I got one warning during the time (he worked at a military depot as a civilian worker) but that was partly because of reckless fooling around. It was my name day which we were celebrating (on the job). All the officers were at an auction, and therefore we went several times to Nokia (the town nearest to the work place) to get wine,

several big bottles. Can you imagine, my work mate rode a bike and I on the back of it. He lived at the auction place in one of the barracks. So we swooped down there. . . . The maintenance officer saw us . . . my buddy was riding the bike, barely keeping it upright, almost falling into the ditch. So we stopped there. He was looking at us, said where are you brothers coming from. My mate said that from work of course . . . it was half past three . . . one comes from work at half past three, where else. . . . Dammit, he said, we're gonna talk this over later on, now go to your hole. Three or four days later we got an invitation saying that the boss wanted to see us. I got a warning but for my work mate it was the final one. The miniature statue of Mannerheim (a general and president in Finland's history) on the boss's desk jumped whenever he pounded his fist on it. Mannerheim was changing his position over and over.

The guild members' inclination for telling biographical stories resembles the AA program, where telling one's story after one has "got it straight" is an inherent part of the whole program. In the case of AA, the important details and events of one's life story have to be told in terms of a strict format required of an AA story; a format that is nevertheless the AA ideology in a condensed form: "Through the stories he (an AA member) comes to understand his life as more intelligible; he views it with a different structure and logic than he had previously" (Thune 1977, 80).

It is obvious that in the guild storytelling has a similar function as a way of reconstructing one's past and therefore one's identity as well. However, the guild storytelling is much more informal than it is in AA speaker meetings. The AA stories typically consist of two parts. The first part describes the horrors and human degradation caused by one's drinking. The second part tells of the joy and peace achieved after finally coming to the program. The guild stories mainly concentrate on the incidents experienced during drinking and the mess a man makes of his life by it. Still, the stories are not that sad. Rather, they are told with a humorous tone; the hero of the stories is a crazy and clever guy who does not care about anything, even though he is often faced with serious trouble and repeatedly ends up in a ditch. One could say they represent the genre of heroic stories; there appear many classic themes in them, like that of a totally free tramp. Consider one of the men who told about his time working in another town, Nurmes, which is situated some two hundred miles from Tampere in eastern Finland:

It took me eleven or twelve days to get back from there. I took a train that goes through Kajaani (another town). The first thing I did when I got there, I made a call to say send me money, for Christ's sake. I only got a per diem back there. I was calling my firm to ask them to send me money so that I could go on with my trip. And they did. Next I got to Varkaus, and called them from there: send me money. They said that, damn, Varkaus is not even along your way. I said dammit, this is Varkaus all right, at least that's what the sign says. Somewhere along the line, it must have been in Pieksämäki, I must have stepped on the wrong train, and swooped down to Varkaus. When I finally managed to get out of there, I found myself in Mikkeli. One more time I called to ask them to send me more money, even just the price of the ticket. They said fuck you, this is the last time we send you any money. We're gonna fetch you from there if you are not here in three days. They sent me money all right and I got out of Mikkeli. When I bought the ticket and cigarettes, I had no money to go to have a drink. I just had to come to Tampere nonstop.

The men's encounters with their wives, during the time they still were married (most of them are divorced), are told in the same vein. The men use every possible means to get more alcohol, with no regard for any moral behavior. One of the several stories is reported in the field notes:

> The chairman of the guild told of a phase (in becoming an alcoholic) when he tried to agree with his wife that he would only drink at home. So he kept a bottle in the fridge, but his wife would remark every now and then about why it was necessary to drink the whole bottle at once. So he put one bottle in the fridge and another one in his boot-leg. As a consequence, the level in the bottle in the fridge naturally sank more slowly.
>
> Another man reported a similar experience. He said that he had one bottle in the house and another one in the garage. His wife of course found out about it, since when only half a bottle was gone, the man was nevertheless all boozed up.

Some of these stories do state in a plain and revelatory form the utmost degradation of the drunkard, who cheats, uses and harms anyone and anything in order to gratify his bottomless craving for booze.

Since most of the stories are biographical, the ease with which they are told is amazing. In fact it is only the ease and the ability to laugh at one's own past encounters that enables the storyteller to distance himself from the person he used to be when drinking. What is interesting, though, is that such distancing is far from complete. The story ends in a comment on the practical impossibility of repeating a dirty trick, not in any kind of moral disapproval of it:

> I had beaten it out of home already. I used to go back there with my own keys when my ex-wife was not home to find something with which to finance my drinking. Once I took a painting, and damn if I didn't swap it into two big bottles of Gambina (a strong wine). T'was a real painting affair. And my old woman changed the locks to the door. No way to get in there any more to do business.

There are also stories told about other people, met somewhere along the line, or guys who once used to come to the meetings. Such stories are used, for example, to describe different types of drunkards. The guild members stress that there are numerous ways of drinking, and consequently there should be nearly as many treatment programs as there are problem drinkers. The similarities among individual alcohol problems are, according to them, only limited:

> There was an electronic mechanic working for Rauma-Repola. He used to stay sober for four or five months and then drink for a month. The first month after his binge he used to behave damn well. But then he would start buying an afternoon bottle to stash. Only when he had fifty or sixty bottles put aside did it pay to start drinking. He did not go to work. He arranged some food and the bottles beside his bed, and a small table beside the bed with an ashtray and cigarettes on it. He would only get out from under the blanket to go to the bathroom. Dammit, that's a way of drinking all right. Took a drink and rolled back over again.

Even though the members emphasize that there are numerous drinking habits and, consequently, various ways in which alcohol can be a personal problem, the most popular encounters of previous life as a drunkard deal with heavy drinking. One could argue that to tell how hard one used to drink, without any built-in restraints, is a form of boasting. That is reflected in the way stories about a more "civilized" drinking, which nevertheless cause problems to an individual, are responded to. The field notes report of such an incident:

> A man told about his effort at moderate drinking after eight months of abstinence. He would drink only a small bottle of cognac each day plus a couple of shots in a bar. At that time he thought that that was moderacy, but he had to have that amount every day. Another man responded that this was normal drinking all right. There should be no problems because of it. The president said that maybe it would be normal for you, but if someone else felt it was a problem, then it was problematic drinking for him.

The president defended the spirit of tolerance toward everybody coming to the guild; there is the principle that everyone has the right to define what is a problematic for him. Nonetheless, the guild members tend to make mitigating remarks about the member whose alcohol problems used to be less severe, and typical of those often observed among the middle class. The fact that the president reacted to the incident shows that an idealizing attitude toward "real" problem drinking does prevail, and secondly it shows that such an attitude is perceived as a problem. In the group discussions the men first tended to deny the very existence of this attitude, but it was admitted, though, that there is a tone of boasting in the stories told about previous drinking:

> Sure, sometimes it leads to the fact that you remember the good sides and the bad ones are left out.
> PA: You boast how damn much you have drunk?
> You know, nobody remembers a bad hangover.
> PA: But one may boast with that, too. Where does this come from, it appears strange to me. When you talk about past drinking, there's always a taste of boasting?
> You color the story for your own good. In a large crowd you color the whole story one way or the other, no matter what it actually was.

The Guild Activities

The members are proud of the additional activities the guild arranges; it is more than just a group of passive ex-drunkards sitting in their quarters and endlessly dwelling in their problems. In that respect they think they differ from AA:

> PA: What do you think, what kind of a person fits in here and which kind to the AA group?
> For example a person who is interested in activities comes here. We have more leisure activities. AA is nothing but a sheer therapeutic convent. If they have any hobbies or other activities, then they are private. We have the summer place and other things as well;we go to pick mushrooms and berries. And we make trips. We make trips now and again to meet with other guilds. We have these trips more than the AA. Those who are interested in such things remain here.

Contrasted with the weight the members give to various guild activities, it is somewhat confusing that they nevertheless perceive the laziness of the members as a problem. The laziness of the members is in fact one of the favorite topics in the conversations. "How lazy this bunch can be," is an expression that is often heard. The problem is especially acute as regards the various activities and duties in the summer place, an old farmhouse and a sauna with a wooden stove. There are always things to be done together, but the problem is that the members seem to have developed an avoidance of all work into an art form. Here is one of the discussions dealing with this subject, reported in the field notes of a sauna evening at the summer place:

> The central topic of the discussions was the laziness of the guild members. "How lazy this bunch can be. If you announce beforehand at the guild in the morning that there's gonna be a work party, nobody shows up." That is what happened when they needed firewood. It is of no use to expect anyone to come in the evening, if the people know that there is firewood to be cut. It should not be mentioned beforehand at the guild at all, but only after everyone has arrived. But then people invent excuses in order to get out of preparing firewood for sauna. One guy had once used the excuse that he had new pants. The men made jokes about the members' laziness and repeated many times that dammit if this is not a lazy bunch. People don't even care about making coffee. They would rather ask someone else to pour rather than to pour for themselves, not to mention actually making the

coffee. Even now people had to ask first if there is coffee made; everything is expected to be received ready-made.

When asked about it, people interpret the guild members' laziness in various ways. Said one man: "Once you have given up drinking, you feel you deserve to get everything ready-made, you think that you don't have to trouble your head with anything. Since one has given up drinking, one is entitled to services, that's enough." Other interpretations stress the envy of the alcoholics:

> PA: In the summer you complained several times that when there's something to be done by a work party at the summer place, there are no volunteers. Have you thought, why is that?
> Laziness.
> PA: But what is the reason for laziness?
> There is the attitude you see, that someone else will take advantage of my work. That is the biggest factor: envy and bitterness. There is the feeling that, for Christ's sake, the others don't come to do shared work either. Why don't the two hundred other members come to help out, since there are that many members? If I go to cut firewood, I'll be damned if someone else will be bathing in the sauna heated by my wood, without having done a damn thing. That's the worst problem. Alcoholics are damn bitter and envious toward another one. There's no solidarity.

Such psychological interpretations, drawing on the notion of a personality type peculiar to an alcoholic, are interesting for the simple reason that they prevail in the group. However, the enterprise of grasping the inner logic of the people themselves by analyzing their actions and accounts in terms of the native concepts that I am engaged in here does not mean that one could or should take accounts at their face value. One must bear in mind that these accounts are but one aspect of thought, speech, and behavior; accounts often contradict actions and each other. In fact, when studying the cultural forms of a community one often comes across explanations of a second order, so to speak. Since many aspects of a cultural system are below the "horizon of the taken for granted," unarticulated and only partially conscious for the actors engaged in the practical activity of everyday life, questions concerning such cultural features are responded to by giving an ad hoc interpretation. In this particular case, the interpretations of a persistent feature of laziness were drawn from the framework of the folk models of psychology.

What, then, is the reason for the attention paid to the members' laziness? To approach an understanding of this cultural feature, let us place it in the larger framework of the guild members' view of life.

The problems connected to the members' laziness are not, it seems, caused by a discreet attitude, a general reluctance to carry out tasks and duties in the guild only. On the contrary, it seems that they are a reflection and a symbolic expression of a critical stance toward the prevailing "Protestant" work ethic taken in the guild philosophy. A certain carefulness and suspicion toward all toil is part of the social identity that is being developed and strengthened in the guild. That, in fact, explains the contradiction that prevails between the actual active- ness of the guild on the one hand, and the continuous complaint about the reluctance of the members to carry out the activities on the other. To complain about the laziness of the guild members is an acknowledge- ment that they are conforming to the social identity that is striven for and respected by the members socialized to the profane philosophy of the guild. Remarks about laziness are expressed in the form of a com- plaint only because of the practical problems it causes and because it is a deviant attitude toward work; the tone of boasting in such complaints is barely concealed. In many of the stories expressly dealing with work life, the men, indeed, boast about and laugh at the cleverness with which they have avoided hard work and cheated their employer. Let us take one story reported in the field notes, as an example:

> A man told a story about how he and his buddy painted a house for a farmer in the countryside. They were supposed to under- take the painting on a week's contract, according to which the house was supposed to get two coats of paint. The farmer was not home during the time, so there was no supervision. They painted only one coat, dug a hole in the field, and dumped the rest of the paint, thirty liters, into the hole. They had the empty cans as proof that they had actually used all the paint, so they got a week's wages. The farmer was half blind, so he noticed nothing at that time, at least. The storyteller repeated the main points of the story several times while others were laughing.

Reminiscences of the social relations between the fellow workers, or rather those between older skilled workers and novices, are also told in the same light. Instead of glorifying solidarity and friendship among the workers, or celebrating the masculine tone of strength and skill required in manual work, these stories shed light on the hierarchical nature of work groups. The field notes report of a man recalling the 1950s:

> He thought back to the time when he got to be an apprentice to a skilled worker who installed the insulation on hot water pipes. He promised his two assistants that if they were able to put cloth tape around the pipe as fast as he went in installing the insulation material, they would be allowed to share the work contract with him. The first two days were pretty tough for the assistants, but then they learned the job so well that they were breathing down his neck. It was then that this guy stopped to see: "Well, how have you placed the cloth tape, after all.?" He went to see, and said that it was all upside down. In fact it made no real difference how it was installed, but they had no choice but to tear it all down, wash the cloth, and put it all back again. It was around three hundred meters of pipe that they had done with the cloth tape by that time. Therefore they did not catch up with the work contract and were not paid according to it.

VIEWS OF ALCOHOLISM TREATMENT

The Relation to Professional Treatment

It is not an easy matter to pin down an explicit theory of alcoholism and the concurrent, detailed method of recovery that is an explanatory model of alcoholism shared by guild members. They are quite reluctant to express their individual views, and there is not an official one. The individuals do have their private thoughts about it, which are often in accordance with the usual, public ideas about alcoholism. One of the members, for example, said he had concluded, based on his experience, that there were two types of alcoholics, habitual alcoholics and those with a reason. For the habitual alcoholics it was easier to give up drinking, he figured. He himself was one of them. He had been drinking for twenty-five years, first moderately on a regular basis, then the rest of the time constantly. "One becomes an alcoholic by drinking." Another man also stated that for him drinking was just a habit; he did not need to have any reason for it. He had an apartment of his own, a wife, and a child, but despite all that, he just had to buy a weekend bottle every Friday, without any reason. It was just a habit.

The alcoholics with a reason, the man went on, were those who had a nervous problem of some kind in their head. "Not all of those drink who would really have a reason to do so. No matter how hard it may be, some people do not drink." An older man added that the drinking of poor people is immediately visible; the rich can drink as much as they please, but it will be kept secret.

The bipartite typology outlined above is not much more than a way of refusing to give any definition of alcoholism; it simultaneously succumbs to any views and theories of alcoholism, whether they be moral, sociological, psychological, or medical. That is the whole point in the guild views on theories of alcoholism. "The alcoholics have been studied for forty years," the men remarked when discussing the issue, "but the situation has not changed a bit." For them, alcoholism treatment is a very practical matter. It is a practical, not a theoretical, matter, not to drink, at least in a way that causes problems, they figure. No matter what the reasons *behind* one's drinking or even if there are any, one has the same goal *in front* of him: to stay sober. Therefore the men are often skeptical about the usefulness of digging into the past, to the original reason behind one's drinking. This is also their view of the similar habit in psychotherapy in the A-clinic or in other treatment institutions. The only advantage in individual therapy, according to many of the members, is a better opportunity for privacy, a chance to tell about issues that are too sensitive to be told publicly in the guild:

Chairman: And often it is of no use to start recalling old things. When you shake up shit, it stinks.

A man: It stinks no matter how long you shake it up.

Reino: But when I had the same therapist for a half year, we went through it all. And when I was leaving she asked if I had let it all out. I did talk it all over in the sense that I did not have any big secrets in the first place. Somehow I got a lighter feeling after telling all I remembered from as far as my childhood onwards. You don't have to discuss it another time once you're through with it.

Chairman: You cannot talk about childhood the way you talk about the present.

> *Reino:* We went all the way down from childhood to the present all right.
> *Chairman:* So, figure it out now, what was the use of it all.
> *Reino:* I was pleased. . . .
> *Chairman:* Yeah, but you wound up in the slammer after that, anyhow.

The disputes in the views toward professional therapy on the one hand, and the official tolerance often expressed toward differing views on the other, and finally the refusal to make official statements about the theory of alcoholism supported by the guild, all derive from the fact that most of the members initially came to the guild through the A-clinic. Moreover, many of the newcomers are still in the intermediate stage; they go to see their therapist on a regular basis while simultaneously taking part in the guild meetings. As an association, the guild cannot therefore take a totally opposing stand toward the mode of treatment practiced in the A-clinic. The guild has, however, its own views and a critical distance toward professional treatment:

> PA: Isn't it quite strange that you've all come here through the clinic to some extent, and this is nevertheless a bit in opposition to it?
> In opposition to a healthy extent. We do say that if a guy is having a hard time, we give him advice to go there to see the therapists, nurses, and doctors. In that respect we are in cooperation. But then again we don't place them in the position of God, that they would be almighty or know everything, that they would help you out of a crisis. A guy makes it here as well as there. Better here.

The main distinction they make between the clinic and the guild, for the advantage of the guild of course, is the weight they give to the personal experience of alcoholism as possessed by guild members. According to the men, the therapy is often quite shallow in many respects, since they do not have "field experience":

> Quite many of them, since they don't have the same kind of problems themselves, just study the symptoms in the books they read. A guy who has gone through it all, has drunk and then started another life, the sober life, the way of life free from alcohol, a guy like that is easier to talk with, since he's had the experience of the same symptoms.

During the time the fieldwork for this study was done, a greater independence from the A-clinic was a hot topic. The guild had been looking for a location of its own, to get more space and an image of its own. Quite shortly after the study was completed, they indeed managed to find a house of their own:

> PA: You are looking for a place of your own. Does it somehow disturb you that you are located in the same building with the clinic? What is the guild's relation to the clinic? You are a registered association, aren't you?
> There are some disadvantages in the sense that we don't get a sufficient amount of keys. . . . Nobody can use this space for any hobbies during the times when the group is not holding its meeting here. But when we get a place of our own we can have more spare keys. Then the number of the guys who can go in is bigger. We can switch the guys every now and then, instead of fetching the key every time. And since you talked about the disadvantages, it has happened a couple of times, that when a newcomer first comes, and there's a guy in the corridor staggering on his feet, they connect it with the guild, like there they are already drunk. It cannot be prevented in this location, that such people are mixed with the guild people.

The men also pointed out that nonsmokers and especially allergic people cannot come in the guild since there is only one small room full of smoke. Neither is it easy for a newcomer to approach a loud group packed in one, small room. More private or confidential discussions with newcomers or others having hard times, as well as a separate group for women, are impossible.

On the other hand, the guild seem to have made the outer constraints into virtues by undermining the relevance of therapeutic discussions. Seemingly in contradiction with the fact that past drinking is evidently an important topic, they also claim that psychotherapy centers too much on drinking, at the expense of other aspects of life:

> *A woman:* One doctor once said to me, that in the A-clinic, the therapist talks about alcohol, so alcohol is talked about all the time and it is always on your mind. But when one hangs around in the guild, there people do not talk about alcohol all the time during the two hours; they

> talk about other things as well, so you forget about it
> little by little. But when the therapist talks about alco-
> hol, it is all the time on your brain. It doesn't go
> nowhere, said the doctor, a specialist.

By listening to the talk in the guild it is hard to believe there is any
truth in the above statement at all. However, there is the difference that
the guild activity is not based on any kind of therapy at all. Whatever
one talks about, it is not done in the spirit of a confession of any kind,
which is, I suggest, typical of a therapeutic or a spiritual discourse:

> This is all based on togetherness and on staying together. And
> since this is the foundation, it includes all other things. One has
> certainly talked about alcohol enough and without any result.
> What I mean is, it is of no use to dwell on the issues of alcohol.
> With that talk, one only ends up drinking.

So one can conclude that the process of recovery in the guild is not
based on psychotherapy in any official sense of the word. The informal discussions, and the numerous stories told about past drinking and
of other subjects, however, have their function and meaning. It is
through these stories of personal experience that the guild conveys its
practical knowledge and beliefs about working methods of recovery, to
be flexibly applied by individuals:

> Here, when you listen to someone else's story and know your
> own, you can take a bit from here and a piece from there, and
> apply a lot of it to yourself and see what fits you. You'll learn
> something from it. You really don't have to learn quite all of it
> the hard way. Some things can be learned without one's own
> experience.

Claude Levi-Strauss's (1966) concept of *bricoleur* fits the guild
members perfectly. According to him, a bricoleur is someone who "uses
the means at hand" to produce something, to work out a solution. The
same goes for the idea of the guild meetings. It is not to transmit a fixed
ideology backed up and defended by a strict normative structure prevailing in the group, but rather to provide the participants with a wealth
of material out of which to make up a totality that makes sense for the
individual in question.

That is not to say that anything goes, that the materials at hand in the group fit any production of an individual identity enabling one to abstain from drinking. It is only that the bits and pieces attitudes expressed or pieces of advice given by the members are not offered in a ready-made, neat package. They make sense only in terms of a particular frame of reference provided by one's previous life and position in society, which are largely shared by the members. Informed by this frame of reference—that is, the cultural forms of manual workers—the individual members are able to make sense of the bits and pieces, to arrange them into a whole, the internal logic of which will be outlined in the last section of this chapter.

It is precisely because those who fit into the group already share a point of departure about life and the issue of drinking problems that the "treatment ideology" of the guild does not need to be spelled out explicitly. It has been largely taken for granted; the interest has been, instead, directed to specific issues deemed important in the mutual enterprise of working out a philosophy of sober life that makes sense in terms of the shared frame of reference. Nor would it have been an easy task to make it explicit, since the whole profane philosophy has been worked out according to the principles of *bricoleur*. Particular pieces, borrowed from different sources known to the members, have not been selected according to formal, explicit criteria, but according to the feelings of the group, initially constituted by the cultural forms of manual workers, and later on increasingly by the inherent logic of the totality being shaped in the process of identity formation and transformation.

The Relation to AA

In a "treatment ideology" worked out this way, the views of alcoholism and its cure are typically expressed in relation to other programs and institutions known to the members. The deviations from, on the one hand, and the views shared by the A-clinic, on the other, have been discussed already. Another institution that is important for the guild as a means of articulating its philosophy is Alcoholics Anonymous.

Some of the modes of discourse used in the guild are clearly loans from the AA ideology. One of them is a more or less explicitly expressed belief in a drinking career that one has to go through before one is ready, prepared, and adaptive to abstinence and the guild. In other words, just like the AA, the guild members sometimes say that one has to hit the bottom first, though they are quick to add that the bottom is individual; some reach it and come to their senses at an earlier stage. The theme of one's hitting bottom was, for example, touched on in a discussion of the basic rules of the guild, recorded in the field notes. The first rule says that anyone who is sober and willing, can enter the guild:

> I made a comment, as a joke, that "don't you have any per mill limit?" The guys responded that you cannot set any limits; they wouldn't hold in any case. One guy said that it wouldn't make any sense. "If a guy drinks, he goes by a place like this at a safe distance. A guy who comes here drunk has a huge vat of booze left undrunk somewhere in the world. It's needless to come here. He better drink his vat first, and if he manages to do it before he's in his grave, it's only then he'll come here."

The habit of telling life stories has probably also been influenced by AA. The differences between the guild and AA are however significant and important for the members as well. One of the differences is in their relation to teetotalism.

> We're all allowed to deal with the issue of drinking the way each of us wants to. If a guy wants to reduce his drinking, so let him try. AA stands for unconditional abstinence only, but with us everyone makes his own program. I do recommend abstinence for all of those who have already reached an advanced stage of alcoholism. That way you certainly get away with less distress and damage. What I mean is, it is easier to reject the first drink instead of third or forth. It is impossible for God's sake to reject anything after two or three drinks. The first drink you might be able to reject by using some damn trick. But after you've had one, you have kind of sold your principle, and so you say okay, today may go down the drain alright, but tomorrow we're gonna start a new life. And then the new life starts to be pushed further and further ahead, until your next trip to the detox.

In practice the guild members are for total abstinence as the best way out of alcohol problems. The members said they knew only one man who had probably succeeded in controlled drinking. That they do not make total abstinence part of an ideology and policy is, however, more in accordance with the more informal nature of the guild philosophy. The final solution is in that way left up to the individual member;

it is the individual who has to figure out that teetotalism is more in concert with the guild philosophy.

The differences between the two self-help groups are, however, not restricted to nuances in emphasis due to a more informal nature of the guild when compared to AA. There are real differences, totally opposing views between the groups, which appear to stem from a difference between the average social background of the members of the two groups. The AA ideology is, to a greater extent, a continuation and modification of the middle-class worldview:

> PA: Do you think it matters which occupational or social group you come from? Those in AA are probably coming from somewhat higher social groups. There are more directors and such, and all of those entrepreneurs. We have got only a few of them. Usually we have, let's say, one entrepreneur. We have a lot lower level than at AA; there they appear anonymous.

The guild members associate the social position of the AA members with the social norm of anonymity of AA members. The guild, instead, takes the stand that it is fair play to use one's real name:

> We, instead, think that we go by our own names here because one drinks by one's own name as well. We would rather like to drink using a fake name, but the problem is that it doesn't work. I once tried to use a fake name when I had wound up in the slammer. Dammit if it wasn't a police officer that knew me. He asked my name and I said Virtanen. (In the morning) there was no Virtanen in the jail, so Virtanen couldn't get out either. The police officer then came to ask, Do you remember your name by now? I said I have remembered it all the time; Why in the hell would a police officer who already knows me ask my name? He said that at that place everyone goes by his own name, and here we've been calling Virtanen, but there is no Virtanen. . . . And what is there to be ashamed of to appear by one's own name. At AA they try to be anonymous. In such a small town as Tampere, you cannot do it more than a couple of weeks. Your name will come out; you just can't prevent it.

Another grave difference that the guild members feel exists between the guild and the AA is the two institutions' relation to religion. While the AA ideology has a strong religious, or, to be precise, "spiritual" foundation (see Kurtz 1979), the guild does not accept religion as a topic. It is their feeling, as all informal male groups seem to point out—in taverns, for instance (Sulkunen, Alasuutari, Nätkin, and Kinnunen 1985)—that there are two topics that cause quarrels and are therefore forbidden: religion and politics. Though it is true indeed that AA does not officially subscribe to any particular Christian or other religious sect to prevent the ideology from being restricted to a small section of people, sobriety is in AA nonetheless achieved by a strong "spiritual" experience. AA members are encouraged to believe in "Not-God" (Kurtz 1979), in "God, as we understand him." The guild members do not accept such a backing of one's sobriety:

> It is difficult for many of us to accept that a God of some kind directs us somewhere. What in the hell have we done so that we've been directed to drinking? He could have prevented us from drinking as well, and made us sober also. I don't believe in such things for no reason. It is me that has to do what I do.
> There's a bit of fanaticism in it, you know. One stays sober as long as the ecstacy prevails, all right. It is the same as in faith, in a religious sect. It is all the same.
> Have you tried to become a believer, to join the sect? Well I haven't succeeded. I have tried it at AA several times, and hell, I never learned to believe in a Higher Power. I am myself the Higher Power.

One might get the impression that the guild is more individualistic when compared to AA. They do not have any formal program or shared view of alcoholism; do they not succumb to any power higher than themselves as a key to the hall of sobriety; and finally, they appear by their real names, as self-sufficient individuals who have to set their goals and make up their minds on their own. This is not quite the case, though. They do emphasize the importance of group support; it is only that they do not think that any ideology or authority backed up by a Higher Power of any kind does it. If there is an official belief system of any kind, there is always the chance that some day one loses one's faith or that one is not honest, that one has to pretend, the guild members seem to think. The solidarity and sense of community of the group must be based on total honesty, not on a model of conformity dictated from above by an ideology: "I have observed in AA when they try to preserve their faith half by force. That it does not work at all.

In fact the guild members criticize AA for an attitude of total individualistic laissez faire among their membership. In their view, AA has a weaker sense of solidarity than they do:

> What I hated more than anything else during the time I tried to go to AA were the guys who, for God's sake, became bootleggers when they had gained sobriety. Damned if they didn't sell to the AA members as well, and what's more, they gave them booze on credit. I was really pissed off by that. When some of those I knew came to the guild, I drove them away, get the fuck out! Don't you come here for anything.
> PA: Do they accept that in AA?
> Anything goes there, you see.
> Everything's permitted; everyone is looking after their own interest. All activity is accepted.

On the basis of the guild members' opinions about the local AA group, one is in no position to judge the real differences between the two rival self-help groups, let alone the characteristics of the local AA. The distinctions drawn between the guild and AA by the guild members only serve the purpose of articulating the peculiarities and the inner logic of guild philosophy. Moral judgments notwithstanding, one can say that both groups share the view that group support and solidarity are of great importance in an individual's effort at sobriety. Moreover, both groups leave the final decision up to the individual; it is he who has to get it straight in the final analysis. The differences between the two groups' differences stem from the average socio-economic position of the memberships; can be understood only in terms of the total composition of particular traits.

When looked at within the framework of the AA ideology as a totality, the peculiar traits of the AA program do make sense. It is the inability or unwillingness of the guild members to grasp the inner logic of the AA ideology that explains their skepticism toward its characteristics.

The fact that individual members appear anonymous, for example, serves several purposes. First, this rule stresses the idea that all men should be equal. Despite a possibly high position in society, any member in AA is just a recovering alcoholic, no more and no less. Second, the anonymity rule protects members from becoming renowned as AA members and former alcoholics in life outside the meetings. Therefore it lowers the threshold to AA, and makes personal confessions in the meetings easier. What the guild members seemed to criticize, however, was the implication of a two-faced life: one has an official front and the secret "disguise" as a former alcoholic on the other. For ordinary people, manual workers, such a double life is seldom possible. A worker just cannot carry on with an official on the one hand, and drink secretly on the side. Since the guild members' drinking problems were made public and caused serious problems in their work and marital life from the very beginning, why should they keep their sobriety secret?

The meaning of religious experience in the case of AA cannot be spelled out as easily as that of anonymity. However, one must bear in mind that AA is not officially a religious organization of any kind. As an organization that provides its members with a total worldview and code of conduct it can quite well be likened to other Protestant revivalist movements, as Kurtz (1979) has shown, without doing too much injustice to it. But in that sense, any living form of revivalism cannot be treated en bloc as a dogmatic system. True religious experience is based on its ability to play the strings of one's soul; it stems from a shared cultural background of its members, and can be only poorly understood by listing its outer characteristics. As such, it did not seem to succeed in finding resonance in the souls of the guild members who had tried it. Therefore, for them the religious sentiments expressed by AA members appeared as acting. Similarly, since they did not "get it," the inner logic of the AA program did not make sense, the rules that were followed by AA had no authority in their own minds and as a consequence they appeared to be only ridiculous social *norms* supervised by a patriarchally ruled formal organization:

> I have been told that you may believe in an ashtray or anything. But I know that an ashtray does not make me temperate, so why on earth should I believe in a backwoods fur or anything, 'cause it doesn't keep me abstinent? There must be some other damn system which would help me achieve a mental awakening. To become abstinent, one doesn't necessarily need a spiritual revival. You need other things except your own will; you cannot do it alone.

Instead of trying to find a belief system that makes sense, the guild members have created a skepticism toward any explanations for an alcoholics' drinking. They reject any theories of alcoholism because any theory is, in their view, used as an excuse by an alcoholic:

> It's me myself who decides. God cannot make me drink. Of course it did make me drink when I sometimes got angry and left AA for a saloon.
> We find an excuse all right.
> We are specialists in looking for an excuse and finding one, too . . . using any opportunity. If you hear only one cross word, you immediately pull your hat over your eyes and swoop to a joint before your buddy finds the time to take back his cross word.

One should not, however, be fooled into thinking that anyone can do without any belief system at all. The guild has got its own creed as well; the conviction that all explanations for drinking are but excuses is a good example.

However, the guild is capable of reducing the role of theorizing to a minimum by sticking to pieces of practical advise given to new-comers wanting to achieve temperance. Such pieces of advice are also given by AA, but those of the guild differ from them. Those of AA can be said to consist of two basic rules, the first of which is that the task is simple: to take one sober day at a time. In other words, one must not set grand goals for far into the future. One only has to make the decision every morning that today I am not going to take a drink. One can assure oneself of the advantages of such a view of life by looking back, by looking at how much damage one has caused by drinking, and how much one has achieved since making that deci-sion. According to the guild philosophy, however, those at AA have no future at all:

> We've had this line as a kind of a guiding star: yesterday is yes-terday, and it's of no use to delve into it. We live in this day and from now on. There's nothing we can do about yesterday, it doesn't pay to pick on it. Of course it's good to have it stored back there, so that you can look at your situation from that perspec-tive. When I face a crisis of some kind, I can recall how I've behaved in a similar situation. But no . . . In the parallel organiza-tion [AA], you know, they pick on it from day to day, year to year.

They live entirely in the past, goddammit; there's no tomorrow at all, only yesterday and today. We, instead, try to forget about yesterday and live for tomorrow.

Guild members note, paradoxically, that the nonexistence of the future in the philosophy of AA leads to a lifelong affiliation and membership in AA. The second basic rule of AA encourages its members to permanently take part in the group activities, initially to support oneself in abstinence, and in the final stage to act as a member available for others in distress. That is, to "work the twelfth step." The guild, instead, does not expect its members to retain their active membership eternally. They regard their involvement as first aid whose purpose is to make itself useless:

> We have a lot of guys who have come here for a year or two and disappeared back into the world. They lead their life, and they are sober and doing all right. At AA I noticed that they set the goal that one should stay for as long as possible, for ten years or twenty years. We haven't advised anyone to set that kind of goal, which would force you to come here all the time.
> PA: But this becomes a habit as well.
> Yeah it does, but only for some. Some are in the habit of at least coming and writing down their name in the book, to sign in and out, so to speak. But it's not like that crap in AA. Some drop by once, after a year or two, to look around and see if any of their old buddies are here still. And many times when someone has achieved abstinence for a long time through the guild, they will come back to see how they gained their temperance.

The AA members do not, however, give up their "worldliness" by concentrating on the group and on today. It is of crucial importance for them "to make it" in everyday life and in one's career after joining AA, because it proves that it has been useful or, more strongly, a blessing for the individual to join AA. One must bear in mind that the description of success after joining AA is the latter part of any life story told in the AA speaker meetings.

In this respect the guild is again in total opposition to the AA program, as has already been implied by the fact that the life stories told in the guild do not have the latter part, the success story. The guild members say that nobody can live up to the program of AA; they totally reject the idea that one should go on or even enhance one's speed in the rat race: "It does not work out in practice that you give up drinking, and in a year you have a new Mercedes."

Instead, the guild advises newcomers to take it easy after sobering up with the support of the guild. Usually it is stressed that it is of crucial importance for a guy who has recently given up drinking to get back on his feet economically, to get a job. Contrary to the typical advice of a social worker, the guild members hold the view that one should first clear one's head:

> But these guys who, after a visit to the detox, stuck on the idea that they have to get a job, go to the detox two or three times a year. But they still cannot hold their jobs. I've tried to explain to many of them that for God's sake don't get caught in a hustle by taking a job, because you cannot keep it anyhow. Clear your head first.
> PA: Working disturbs sobriety just like it disturbs drinking?
> After a year one thinks in another way than one does after a week or a couple of months. One's views have been changed. One thinks that I am a good guy after all, because I got a job right away. But fucking goodness ain't nothing if nothing has happened in your head. The old drunkard's way of life is still there: I get a job all right, there are plenty of these. There has to be a change in that way of life if one is going to keep his job and manage in life. It pays to make a sacrifice and stay unemployed for a half year or one year . . . and to fix one's head.

By fixing one's head the men mean that one should get out of the rat race for good. The literal translation of the term, which comes up in the discussions repeatedly, is in fact the "squirrel wheel," by which the men mean that one goes to work and drinks the wages, over and over again. The men stress that one should free oneself from that frame of mind before getting a job. By that term the members direct criticism against a "bourgeois" way of life. The only man in the guild who has held on to his job throughout his drinking career and recovery is suspected of never really changing his views, of never stepping out of the squirrel wheel, as the field notes tell:

> The only man of those present who goes to work told that when he still drank, all of his extra money went to drinking. A man in his forties said to him that you are still in the squirrel wheel. You

have always been and you still are. The first man responded that it is no squirrel wheel for him, but you can think like that if you want to. The other man answered that you have stereos and videos and other appliances. The first man snapped that he hasn't got them yet. The vice-president interrupted by saying that it is only good if one has taken care of his money in such a way that one has paid his bills. There are also those who have left everything unpaid. It's only good if only the extra money goes to drinking.

The discussants referred to the fact, well known by the guild members, that the man in question had indeed made a whole purchase program for the future. In an individual interview he told about his private economy:

> My therapist asked me last fall, how has it been going. I said that for two or three months it has been pretty balanced. She said that it's abnormal for it to go so smoothly for such a long time. So I booked a trip to the Canary Islands for a winter holiday. I got so excited; it was such a wonderful trip, that last summer I decided to go there again. So I will spend two weeks there next winter. I will be leaving in less than five months. In the summer I went to the USSR, to Rica and Tallinn. It has been pretty good for me economically; I've got an apartment of my own and a steady job. I've put aside money for next fall and I'm going to buy a new color TV, stereo and video. This whole program will cost me 12,000 marks.

Most of the guild members do not seem to approve of such bourgeois plans, which is contradictory, because neither do they accept that one drinks away the money instead. Being on the dole or otherwise short of money appears to be practically the only way that suits their view of life. This issue will, however, be discussed at greater length later on in this chapter.

WORKING-CLASS CULTURE AND GUILD PHILOSOPHY

It would be tempting to grasp the inner logic of the guild program by rooting connecting its notions of alcoholism treatment to the wider life they live; that is, to separate their explicit notions of alcoholism treatment discussed in the section "Views of Alcoholism" from other discourse and activities described in the section "Characteristics of the Guild." An explanatory model of alcoholism, made up of the views held by the guild, could then be made intelligible by relating it to their way of life. However, such a notion of an explanatory model is too restricted; it tends to isolate ideas, opinions, and behavior particularly related to drinking from other aspects of a whole way of life. Although the central idea of such a research setting might be precisely to explain the explanatory model used in the group by relating it to the wider life they live, there is still a case for criticism. There is a danger that the notion of an explanatory model is nothing but a theoretical construct in the first place, an empty abstraction that does not serve to illuminate either drinking or efforts at abstinence as an integral part of everyday life.

The truth is that the guild could be likened to a subcultural informal group. The guild program is an attempt "to develop some meaningful account and representation of the world, of cultural members' place within it and to experiment with possibilities for gaining some excitement and diversions from it," as Willis (1978, 173) puts it when dealing with subcultural groups. The task of the guild is, likewise, to provide its members with a view of life that is enjoyable and makes sense for them. The only difference is that the hedonism of an informal subculture would not do, because it has led the group members into distress and misery in their previous life. In the course of a cultural production of identity, the guild has had to come up with diversions and pleasures other than drinking. The guild program is *a technique of desire* in the sense that it aims at changing and modifying a view of life in which drinking has appeared excessively desirable to the extent of becoming a craving.

The transformation of identity fought for in the guild philosophy is in part nothing but the replacement of alcohol with other substances, in a social setting and a way of life that otherwise remains as unchanged as possible. The particular importance of the coffee ritual, for example, stems from this replacement logic. The social setting of the meetings has a remarkable resemblance to that of a male drinking group. In that way, those coming to the guild from such groups do not have to give up the spirit of male camaraderie found in the drinking group, which, it appears, is part and parcel of the desire for alcohol.

The same can be said of the guild's advice to stay unemployed for a half-year or a year after one has gained sobriety. In that way, the *logic of freedom*, characteristic of Finnish alcoholic thinking, as I argued in chapter 4, is employed also when one is taking the first steps of sobriety. Instead of using self-control, one delegates every kind of self-restraint to other people or externalizes it to outer constraints. When one is short of money, there is less danger of a binge. One feels free and safe when one can do almost whatever one wishes to, because the space available for realizing one's desires does not allow one to seriously hurt oneself.

The guild's recommendation to stay on the dole for some time after gaining sobriety stems partly from this. The old-timers have a vivid recollection of the difficulty of walking around with some money in their pockets for the first time after having recently achieved abstinence. The money "burned" their pockets, they said:

> One thing that was difficult was handling money. You had to relearn it right from the beginning like a little boy. It was difficult, the money. . . .
> It was almost always when you got money in the beginning that you had to fast spend it on some stuff, so that there's not much left of pocket money.
> It doesn't affect or bother me any more. In the beginning it did.
> When you watch these guys you see around here, you see that they have exactly the same phases. It takes a long time for them to get over the habit of each time drinking their two week's wages. That's what I did, too. I lost many a job in that way. You couldn't stand the flow of money. You went to the bank and you'd get the money, and you thought that dammit now this time I'm gonna buy some clothes for myself. It was an achievement if you could just buy a pair of socks.

The "squirrel wheel" of hard work and heavy drinking can be broken in the easiest possible way by staying out of work. However, the central concept of the squirrel wheel refers to other things than just the manual workers' inclination to think that a hard worker deserves the right to diversion, usually in the form of drinking. In the guild usage, it denotes their previous way of life as a whole; it is the name for the guild's form of cultural critique directed at the view of life of manual workers, the one their alcohol problems stemmed from. As a modification of the members' previous mode of life, the guild philosophy is, naturally, a *reflection* of working-class cultural forms, but it would not be effective in the long run if it just mechanically reproduced its features on another symbolic level by simply replacing alcohol with coffee and preventing the members from drinking by recommending that they not go to work. The guild philosophy also *reflects on* some taken for granted features of the workers' way of life. It would be an error to claim that the creed of the guild is a well-founded cultural critique or the truth about alcoholism, as tempting as such a romanticizing of an indigenous treatment ideology would be. It is nonetheless true that the structural position of alcoholics trying to figure out a remedy to their problems compels them to both consciously and unconsciously probe their world and its fundamental organizational categories.

The profane cultural critique of the guild centers on one particular aspect of the workers' way of life: the work ethic. In various ways, the members undermine and ridicule the sense of hard work, because it cannot give one anything but money, and money leads to a binge:

> Most alcoholics are of the type that when they quit drinking, they are thrown in a terrible hustle to get a job. They imagine that it'll be all right when I get work, get wages, and pay my debts. They are unconsciously preparing for their next binge. For years I did this. I often felt I had accumulated enough points that I felt I owed myself a drunk. I thought that was a good situation to drink, to sweat it out for two or three months. Then I finally realized that I always start from the wrong end and I began another practice. I stayed out of work for a half year and didn't even apply for a job. I just cleared my head and thought about how this thing should be handled. When I'd finally got it all straightened out as regards my thoughts about alcoholism, I was ready to go to work. In other words, I was no longer going back to work in order to get money for drinking.

Though the line of thought presented above seems to be a simple revelation of false "alcoholic thinking," it in fact criticizes the "bourgeois" elements in the blue-collar way of life. Guild members do not approve of saving one's money to purchase fancy commodities like videos or stereos, as it appeared in the previous section. But for guild members, working in order to get the money for drinking is just another form of conspicuous consumption. They argue that the whole (Protestant) work ethic has to be changed:

> But now as a consequence I've got to the point where I don't go to work for the money. I got out of the squirrel wheel simultane-

ously. What I mean is, with the work I do now, I make thirty percent of what I made previously. I'm doing all right with that and I have quite a gratifying life. Certain values change when you get it straight for yourself. One realizes: What do I need the money for? What do I stash it away for? Previously it was, after all, gathered for drinking.

The guild line of thought is in this respect an interesting partial extension and inversion of the one I came across in my previous studies dealing with local taverns, discussed in chapter 3. For the regulars of the taverns, playing darts and having a beer with the friends were an alternative to the bourgeois way of life, to the meaningless pursuit of collecting the pennies. As the members of the darts club put it:

Pekka: I mean what's the point with stacking your money up under your bed?
Ale: It's stupid (laughter). Then you have to buy a new house so that there's more room for the money.
Aki: And you're in debt again.
Pekka: Life is not meant for being stingy.
Aki: No it ain't. You should live like it was your last day.
Ale: It'd be stupid for me to save up a million and then . . .
Pekka: And then kick the bucket. Shit, think of the waste.
Aki: Shit, yeah.

The guild members could not agree more on the disapproval of a "bourgeois" way of life, an attitude that appears to be one of the central features of blue-collar workers' view of life. However, drinking as a form of cultural protest toward a bourgeois way of life has led them into a dead end, and therefore they have been obliged to give it another thought. The result is a reworked version of the rejection of the bourgeois way of life, an enlargement of it. For the guild members, drinking is just another form of conspicuous consumption. It is all the same whether a man works hard in order to finance his drinking or to buy fancy goods; in both cases one is in the same rat race. The guild members argue that the whole (Protestant) work ethic has to be changed.

It is not that enjoyable, the members reason, to work like hell in order to drink like hell. Instead, to really enjoy life, one has to take it easy and relax. That is why, when the members make remarks about the laziness of the group, it is to give credit to their healthy attitude toward life.

The attitude toward work held by the guild members is, indeed, in partial opposition to that of "normal" blue-collar drinkers or active alcoholics. However, it is just their solution to the quest for a sensible and enjoyable way of life in a wage-labor society, so central to the cultural forms of manual workers. It is an argument that belongs to the same discourse, so to speak. In many other respects, the characteristics of the guild also stem from the workers' cultural forms.

One of these features is the rejection of theoretical knowledge detached from concrete practice, which is, according to Corrigan and Willis (1980), the central feature of working class cultural forms. That is reflected, for example, in the guild's refusal to make any official statements about the nature of alcoholism. Likewise, they have suspicions about a therapist's ability to help an alcoholic:

> Personally, I think that the therapy of the clinic is damn superficial in many respects. They operate according to knowledge acquired from books, but they don't have the kind of field experience that we have. Here some other guy has got experience from the field, so to speak, that can broaden your mind much more than an educated person.

The same appreciation of practical knowledge is reflected in the way the members seem to boast about their total amount of "field experience." Paradoxically, even though the guild is an institution propagating sobriety, the one who used to drink the most is highly valued because of his experience:

> PA: Somehow I feel that in the guild, a guy who has drunk less or who has gone to the dogs for a shorter time is being mitigated, almost like, "that ain't nothing, I drank more."
> Where have you heard something like that?
> PA: I have heard it right here. During the time I have spent in these very meetings.
> Well, it is always for the good of a guy who sooner gets it to his head that he has to seek help.
> Dumber's the one who has drunk longer. Must be dumber.
> PA: But do some men boast with that, that they are dumber?
> One colors the situation for one's own advantage that I have drunk longer than you have. Let's take two guys in the guild, one guy who has drunk a year and another one who has drunk two

years. The first one who has drunk only a year has already at that point realized that he better seek help. . . . And me, I myself am so dumb that I did not get it after a year, I had to go on. And I put it to him this way: "What are you after all, I'm a little better, I know all this crap a little better."
But we always say that it's better to come on time; it is spelled out straight.

Though it is true that members do not accept the line of thought that contends that a heavy ex-drinker is considered to be a cherished expert in the area of both alcoholism and sobriety, it nonetheless sheds light on the mystery of why the life stories told in the guild concentrate on experiences of drinking rather than those of sobriety, and why they tend to have a boasting tone. However, there is another reason for this, as well: namely, that the guild members do not totally disengage themselves from their previous selves as drunkards. From this vantage point, the heroic stories of past drinking emphasize a characteristic feature of traditional Finnish boozing: the presentation of the man in question as a free-wheeling buddy who has the guts to shock other people and to break social norms if they are too restrictive. In that light, some of the blunders of one's previous life can be partially accepted or at least laughed at afterward. It is a way of linking one's past with one's present without having to totally deny and disapprove of a phase in one's life that could be quite long. The men reason is that some change has to take place, but a total change is neither desirable nor possible:

Lahtinen said once, that sobriety does not change a person one bit. I agree that the booze itself doesn't change a man in any direction. On the other hand one could I say that if one cannot change in any way, cannot change one's way of thinking or behaving, then continuous sobriety is impossible. The personality of an alcoholic has to change one way or another if one is going to stay sober.
One has to keep one's everyday life on the rails without booze.
Drinking is a way of life. I now have a way of life which booze doesn't belong to, but I'm still as crazy as I used to be. In that respect I haven't changed one bit. Your way of thinking does change, though. I might be even more crazy today, but there are things. . . . I crawled around on the main street on all fours, with my suspenders in the mud, or so my buddies told me afterwards.

A man wouldn't do that kind of thing sober, but I'm really still crazy in the same way. I'm still as proud as someone who owned Europe, even though, deep down you know that you are nothing. You came here empty and you're empty when you leave.

TECHNIQUES OF DESIRE

When considered in connection with the case studies of blue-collar taverns discussed in chapter 3, and the study of blue-collar alcoholism presented in chapter 4, the case of the guild helps us draw the outline for a theory of blue-collar alcoholism. I also suggest that the general pattern could be applied to other types of alcohol problems, which are always socially and culturally conditioned.

The workers' drinking habits and views of drinking must be considered in the context of their whole way of life. Their desire and craving for drinking stems from the place of alcoholic drinks in the whole way of life. For them, drinking is a symbol and realization of freedom and independence, a profane manifestation of their social philosophy and identity formation.

Tavern-going signifies a desire for personal freedom, a protest toward a restricted, middle-class way of life, and heavy drinking manifests opposition to the demand for use of self-control. Admittedly, not every worker goes to the tavern that often, and heavy drinking is a rare occasion among many blue-collar men. But these ideas, which blue-collar drinking expresses, are central features of working-class culture. They can be expressed in a variety of other ways; in chapter 4, for instance, we discussed smoking and infidelity as ways to put a desire for independence into words in a life story.

When central elements of a man's philosophy of life are attached to drinking, it is understandable that it is hard for him to give up drinking even when it causes social and health problems. This is especially so because we are not dealing with false beliefs of drinking or of alcoholic effects on the human metabolism. Rather, we are dealing with identity formation. When the men, say, conceive uncontrolled drinking as freedom, as a state in which they do not have to use self-control, that is what freedom is for them. There is no "true" freedom, quite like there is no "real" self. We are all engaged in a cultural construction of our identity, and that can be done only so that we incorporate our ideas into various practices and objects.

I do not mean to say that we can voluntarily construct our identity the way we want it. This is because we inherit most of our ideas of the good life from previous generations or from contemporaries. And the same goes for the practices and artifacts with which we attempt to realize our ideals. The elements of identity formation have their ideal and physical limitations; their social meanings can be somewhat bent or twisted, but this can be done only in terms of the artifacts' previous meaning structures. Even if drinking is made expressive of something that is different from its earlier uses, the others' responses and measures follow the old patterns. And finally, many habits, such as drinking, have physical effects, which may, among other things, force individuals to reconsider their view of life.

The guild philosophy has been developed as an outcome of such reconsiderations. Like any treatment modality, it is an attempt to redefine the clients' state and situation, to provide a framework in terms of which they can reconstruct their past, their whole identity. Because most guild members share a working-class view of life, the guild "program" is a reworked version of it. It is most of all based on an extended cultural critique of the bourgeois "rat race," on the insight that heavy drinking is just another form of it.

Like any mode of indigenous treatment, the guild philosophy has been construed in a spontaneous, partly unconscious fashion. Though it is a partial disengagement from the members' cultural background and from their previous life, even the new elements in it are in concert with the cultural context from which they stem. Many features of the guild philosophy are not outcomes of conscious and practical reasoning, but the results of an interplay between conscious planning and symbolizing. Because gaining sobriety has been the initial goal of the men, it has forced them to direct their collective energies and imagination toward working out an inner logic of life, in terms of which they could stay temperate. Once such a logic is found, it gets a life of its own. It creates a symbolic imagination that uses the available materials—a range of collective articulations, symbolic systems, attitudes, rituals, expressive artifacts, and concrete objects—and picks up the ones that fit in. They, in turn, reinforce the totality.

As an indigenous treatment modality, the A-guild has the advantage that there is little cultural distance between the "clients" and the guild philosophy. The members are not required to "buy" a totally new view of life in order to make the program work for them. On the other hand, it may be assumed that the ideology suits best for a relatively small group of people. Theoretically, all treatment modalities, including the professional ones, have the same problem. They are always reflections of, and reflect on, the social meanings attached to the drinking habits and drinking problems of a social group. But widespread programs have the advantage that they rely on prevalent, widely known, and generally approved theories of the nature of alcohol problems. They make sense for quite different individuals, because they have contributed to constructing these individuals' alcohol problems. A self-help ideology has seldom the required publicity for that.

And even apart from that, it is always difficult for modern individuals to believe in an offered reconstruction of their life story and identity. Since persons in the modern world are constantly faced by a need to reconsider their values and identity; any offered identity appears as just another grand narrative, a fashion or a style rather than their long awaited true personality.

A particular difficulty in believing in such an indigenous treatment ideology, as the guild philosophy is, stems from its distance from the dominant ideas and ideology. There are striking discrepancies between the guild view of life and dominant notions of "sensible" or "rational" thinking. Boasting by one's prior drinking in a group that propagates sobriety, or bragging about one's laziness in a society that places a high value on work, are cases in point. Though the tendency to do such things is perfectly in accordance with the inner logic of the guild philosophy, they appear as strange or irrational on a conscious and rational level.

It is no wonder that the guild ideology presents itself as a creed for a newcomer or for anyone who does not "get it." In fact the dividing line does not run between individuals but inside them. During moments of doubt and suspicion, the moments when one gets the temptation to drink, the guild lines of thought appear as irrational normative rules, supervised by other guild members. There are certainly many people who have tried the guild but have not been able to "buy" their creed. Then there are others who go there on and off, without totally believing in the ideology. Even though it is publicly said that it is left up to the individual to make up his mind whether one sets teetotalling or controlled drinking as his goal, deviations from the actual norm of sobriety are seldom discussed in the group:

MK: Do you discuss the others' drinking?
Yes, but that's a difficult situation over there, as you can see a big

bunch, so usually we don't. In a private discussion with someone you can talk, but in the group very private matters cannot be discussed. It's so general.

MK: What do the others say?

Some say, not a drop. It's against the principles of the guild: "A way of life free from alcohol problems." A couple of beers should be okay, if it doesn't cause a problem. Others are of another opinion.

Still others have a binge every now and then, and go to the guild in the meanwhile. Drinking is a way of life, as one of the guild members said above. It has its own inherent logic, with the concomitant structure of feelings and emotions, a logic that which includes a desire and craving for alcohol. The guild philosophy is another one, and these two discourses, with contradictions inherent in both of them, fight each other in the minds of the men.

However, there are many individuals out there who have gained sobriety through the guild. They have been able to make it work for them, each having found a view of life in which there's no room for an overwhelming desire to drink:

To become modest is a long process. Take me, for example, I'm such a damn self-satisfied guy, all the time pretending to be a Big Caesar. One thing I'm pleased with is that I came here once to these tables to ask only that my craving for booze would be taken away from me. And now I've got that. What's happened after that, that I have found a desire to develop as a human being, that's all just a very nice extra.

Chapter 7

ALCOHOLISM AS A CULTURE-BOUND SYNDROME

PROBLEM DRINKING AND THE ALCOHOLISM FRAME

In her study dealing with hallucinogenic healing in the Peruvian Amazon, Marlene Dobkin de Rios (1972, 108) describes the case of a patient, Rosa. When Rosa was eighteen and lived in a jungle hamlet near the Brazilian border she suddenly became, as Dobkin de Rios with her Western cultural bias puts it, a "secret alcoholic." Without telling anyone in her family, she would drink about two pints of cane alcohol a day. When her drinking finally came to the attention of her family, her aunt took her to the community *ayahuasquero* for help. Under the effects of the drug used in the healing method, she saw a vision that explained her problem. According to it, her drinking had been caused by a young man who had proposed marriage to her. She had refused the boy. The boy had, as revenge, secretly prepared a white powder and slipped it into her *chicha*, a fermented corn drink. This powder caused her heavy drinking. When Rosa told the healer of her visions, he interpreted the details concerning her bewitchment for her, and told her that he would return the evil to the young man. Rosa gave up drinking and had no occasion to consult a healer for many years.

Let us now compare the Peruvian case to a mode of Western alcoholism treatment. In an article reporting on his study of Alcoholics Anonymous (AA) (see Denzin 1987a; 1987b), Norman K. Denzin cites a fragment of a confessional self-story of a recovering AA alcoholic (Denzin 1986, 328):

> I'm an alcoholic and will be one until the day I die. I'll do any damned thing I have to not to drink. When I drink I go insane. I get violent. I go back to the past and get filled up with hate and resentments. It took me three tries at this program to finally get it straight. I had to go out the last time for three years and damned near drink myself to death. Finally I surrendered to my alcoholism. Today I have a new way of living and I wouldn't trade it for a bottle of booze.

As vignettes from very different cultures, these two cases can be compared from a number of viewpoints. Let us use the contraposition of the two cases as a prism to break down the self-evident Western view on drinking problems into its component parts.

In the Peruvian case, reflecting the worldview of the people living in the slums of Iquitos, illnesses and other troubles are believed to be caused by bewitchment, a bad spell cast by a malevolent person. Therefore, the cure is brought about by a counter-spell. In the American case, in concert with the view of life of Western people, alcoholism is believed to be caused by a personal allergy to the substance of ethyl alcohol. The recovery from the disease of alcoholism is believed to be only partial, based on a surrender to one's alcoholism, and on developing a new identity as a recovering alcoholic. In the Peruvian case, alcoholism is viewed as a short-term problem, whereas in the case of AA, it is perceived as a permanent trait of an individual, a unitary disease.

The source of recovery in the two cases is completely different. Among the poor people of Iquitos, another person causes the problem. Therefore the cure is sought in supernatural powers which can change the constellation of social relations. Among the members of AA, the recovery is assumed to be in one's mind and soul, in the spiritual awakening of an individual. Although it is true that AA believes in the importance of "the higher power" and group-support in bringing about substantial change, the ultimate decision is nevertheless up to the individual. The AA group and "God, as we understand him" only help an individual who is willing to help himself.

Reflecting the Western alcoholism frame, AA views heavy drinking as a disease in its own right. Heavy, or otherwise deviant drinking is not perceived within the everyday-life frame—as a code of conduct that, despite its extreme form, can be understood as communication, and made intelligible by relating it to the meaning structure of ordinary drinking. Rather, heavy drinking is explained in terms of a totally different framework—a frame that is applied only to abnormal drinking. The alcoholism frame shifts attention away from the role of drinking as just another medium of communication, or as a symbol and realization of the social organization of everyday life. Instead, AA focuses on an individual's particular drinking style as proof of a personal pathology.[1]

Although the Peruvian people do not apply the notion of sorcery to all incidents, it is nonetheless an integral part of their everyday life. It is part of their everyday-life frame. They do not think that heavy drinking is caused by a pathology of the drinker or, for that matter, even the pathology of the person that casts the bad spell. Among the Peruvian people, bewitchment is used as a weapon in resolving interpersonal conflicts; there is nothing pathological about it. Therefore they think that a drinking problem is just one example of misfortune caused by the curse of a malevolent person. The point could be clarified by comparing Rosa's case with other *ayahuasca* patients. The same solution is used in other cases, such as infidelity. Just like a desire for alcohol, a desire for another woman or man is thought to be caused by witchcraft, and cured by the healer's magic. That is exemplified in the case of Berta, a woman of thirty-seven who had been happily married for several years. She had found herself suddenly wanting to respond to the sexual advances of an older man. A drug-induced vision revealed that her desire for the older man had been caused by a potion he had given her. Since it turned out that the desire was caused by the other man's bewitchment, her husband threw the older man out of the house, and the marriage was rescued.

ALCOHOLISM AND INDIVIDUALISM

The alcoholism frame is rooted in the cultural forms of Western societies in several ways. It is a reflection of the opposition of "individual" to "society"; or inner "urges" and "desires" to "will-power" and "super-ego." Second, the alcoholism frame reflects the modern person's search for individuality through the means of what I call biographical reasoning. Since personalities are increasingly understood as fragile, cultural constructions, the identity of an alcoholic gives, in a paradoxical way, continuity to threatening uncertainty and change. The alcoholism frame pays attention to an individual's deviant drinking habits, to the tension or contradiction between the individual's drinking and the larger society, and to the individual's personality.

"Society" as a concept came into use in the sixteenth century in its present meaning, referring to an object that has a life of its own and its own laws (Trilling 1978, 19). The concept "civilization" was an invention of the French Physiocrats of the latter half of the eighteenth century (Elias 1978, 44). The Physiocrats argued that there is not much an individual or even a government can do to alter the course of social life dictated by the natural laws of society. The "civilized" way of life, therefore, sought to find out about these laws and to act in concert with them.

Society and individual are both abstractions of a particular kind, and as opposites in a polarity they are dependent on each other. They form a pair which was brought about in one and the same process. The individual is a person who takes part in the game of "societal life" as its pawn. A modern individual, a human being having an individuality, is an abstraction in the sense that the individual is neither a man nor a woman, neither a peasant nor a lord. The individual is an abstraction of the different persons who serve as examples of the concept of individual.[2] The concept "personality" is an abstraction of the possible traits that are connected with an individual. This is the object of one of the new scholarly disciplines of the modern era, psychology.

As modern persons, it is very difficult for us to imagine any way to conceive of human beings other than the way we do. In other words, it is very difficult to realize that our conceptions of human beings and of the self are culture-bound. We cannot see their limits because they lie behind a horizon of taken-for-grantedness. One way to understand the limits of our worldview is to look at extreme examples of other ways of thinking. It is often for this purpose that one makes cultural comparisons: not entirely to understand a foreign culture in its own terms, but in order to make our own cultural patterns visible.

In order to highlight the modern concept of the self, consider Marcel Mauss's (1979) study of notions of the self among primitive tribes in North and South America and Australia. Among the Pueblo people there are a limited number of first names which are given in accordance with clan divisions. The names express the name holder's exact position and role in the community. Among the Pueblo, as among other primitive tribes, people are identified and given names as collective stereotypes, as "roles" or *personages*, and not as persons in the modern sense of the word: "on the one hand the clan is conceived of as constituted by a *certain number of persons*, actually roles; and, on the other, the purpose of all these roles is really to symbolize, each in its own portion, the pre-figured totality of the clan" (ibid, 65).

I do not mean to suggest that two and only two types of persons exist, the modern individual on one side and the personage on the other. Rather, these two constitute the extreme positions in a continuum. In point of fact, it is obvious that "traditional persons," if there ever were any, conceive of themselves as unique individuals in some respects, and that "modern individuals" have experiences of some kind of belonging. "Modern individuals" define themselves, and are defined by others, according to their relative position in the ranking system in their community or society.[3] However, it is useful to view the modernizing process as a gradual shift from personages to individuals.

The emergence of the notion of "individual" and "society" has provided us with the framework within which we conceive of human social conduct, and of the "personality structure" of the individual. The modern individuals experience a tension or contradiction between the "needs" or "desires" of the individual and the constraints of the "society." Similarly, modern individuals experience a tension or contradiction *within* themselves. For example, there is an *internal* tension between individual "desires" and a sense of duties toward society and other people. Modern thought, building on older Christian ideas, also conceives of a tension or conflict between the "natural" or "animalistic" part of the individual, and the "conscious" or "human" or "civilized" part.

The active, conscious part in the individual is commonly termed the "will." Alcoholism and other addictions can be seen as reflections of this generally conceived tension between desire and will or between inner urges and super-ego. The conception of inner division and inner struggle is not unique to the alcoholism frame but it has been especially well-developed by people and organizations who think and talk about alcoholism and addiction.

INDIVIDUALITY AND BIOGRAPHICAL REASONING

The modern ideology of individuality stresses individual uniqueness and urges self-inspection and self-determination. It is easy to point out the distinctive character of every human being as an organism. Consider, for instance, an individual's fingerprints. But as individuality is discussed on the level of personality, a sort of biographical consciousness is needed. I suggest that individuality and a sense of personal continuity in time is constructed by means of what I call biographical reasoning.

Individuality as I am discussing it is linked with individualism—they are aspects of the same modernizing process Christopher Hill (1980, 217) points out when discussing England in the seventeenth century: "All roads in our period have led to individualism. More rooms in better-off peasant houses, use of glass in windows . . . use of coal in grates, replacement of benches by chairs, all this made possible greater comfort and privacy for at least the upper half of the population. Privacy contributed to the introspection and soul-searching of radical Puritanism, to the keeping of diaries and spiritual journals, to George Fox and Samuel Pepys. Possibly even the mirror may have aided self-consciousness." Hill could have quite well added life stories to his list right after the diaries.

A number of scholars have studied the rise and history of autobiographies as a reflection or indicator of the rise of individualism (Misch 1969; Weintraub 1975;1978; Neumann 1970; Delany 1969). Weintraub (1975, 834) points out that autobiography is inseparably linked to the problem of self-conception: "The manner in which men conceive of the nature of the self largely determines the form and process of autobiographic writing." Autobiographies reveal the gradual emergence of that form of self-conception called individuality. For instance, Delany (1969) notes that the emergence of autobiographies in Italy was preceded by family histories. And the same goes for Britain: "In early British autobiographies we often find similar transitions from genealogy to autobiography; by placing his own story in the context of family tradition the writer could avoid giving the appearance of an unseemly egotism" (ibid., 12). The histories of autobiography suggest that individuality is a specifically modern form of self-conception, which began in the Renaissance and developed into full blossom at the time of Goethe (Misch 1969; Weintraub 1975; 1978).[4] However, autobiographies are more than just a reflection of individuality. Rather, modern individuals construct their identity with the help of their life stories. I am not referring specifically to written or spoken autobiographical stories. Instead I am focusing on every individual's autobiographical consciousness, one's way of conceiving oneself by construing a "reading" of one's own life history. The rise of a larger modern autobiographical consciousness is the reason for written autobiographies, for the birth of the literary genre of autobiography. An individual's identity is a product of his autobiography, his life story. I mean this not in the conventional sense, according to which the individual's personality is formed during childhood and youth, but rather in the sense that the personal autobiography is a reconstruction of the past. The autobiography constructs "identity" and makes it real.

What is meant by the concept of identity? On a general level one can say that by the identity of an object (or a person) we refer to the relative stability of at least some of its features. In order to consider oneself as, say, a jealous person, one has to recall situations which prove that one indeed has that character trait. The concept of individuality means that one has personal experience with a measure of continuity. However, modern ideology also emphasizes an individual's will and ability to renew oneself, to free oneself from all kinds of inner and outer obstacles. Personal change is also central to modern notions of identity. In short, the dividing line between permanent character traits and the conception of identity or personality as a structure is vague and ambiguous.

The idea that an individual's identity is a product of his or her life story does not mean that people have ready-made autobiographies in their back pockets. In fact most people can imagine several life stories or autobiographies to tell.

Consider such very simple questions as: Are you afraid of darkness? Are you short-tempered? Do you smoke? Posing such questions does not mean that we want to know whether a person right now is afraid of darkness, has gotten angry, or is having a smoke. We want to know whether the person has regularly feared darkness, gotten angry pretty fast, or smoked cigarettes. It is not clear whether a single case makes it justified for a person to say that he is afraid of darkness. And what is the definition of a smoker? As difficult as these interpretations and characterizations of the self may be, individuals have to be able to make them in order to delineate their identity and individuality.

I do not mean to suggest that these self-definitions we make are necessarily imaginary, arbitrary, or even subjective. Individuals usually have no doubt whether they are a smoker or not. And in case of doubt, they can always try not to smoke. These self-definitions are always dependent on, or even constituted by, social conventions. Modern individuals make these conventions real in everyday life. When an individual who defines himself and is defined by others as having an "addiction" for smoking or drinking, that is a "hard fact."

The notion of "addiction" shifts attention from the everyday social and cultural meaning of the act, or the situation in which it is accomplished, to the function of such acts as a personality characteristic. The recurrent acts are not explained in terms of the everyday-life frame but in terms of a general addiction frame that draws on the notion of the tension between desire and will-power. If persons then want to "get rid" of an "addiction," a "complex," or a "neurosis," they have to narrate their life story anew one more time, so that the problem in question gets a new meaning in their life. Their life gets a new meaning or at least a new historical background. Take the AA-clubs: an essential part of their "program" is the requirement that a newcomer learn to tell his life story according to a set formula, a particular genre of life stories which always begins: "Hello, I'm Joe and I am an alcoholic." In this case, a particular variant of the alcoholism frame is used as the organizing principle of the individual's whole life. "Alcoholism" is preserved as a cornerstone of the individual's new identity, despite the fact that the purpose of the renewal is to remain abstinent.

The life story formula presents the new identity in a narrative form. The rewritten identity is not more unreal, or artificial, than the "original" identity. All identities can be regarded as cultural constructions and presented in a story format. Conversely, any life story may be "translated" into an identity structure.

There are no naive autobiographies. That is one of the most difficult problems for the modern individual. One reflects on oneself, has doubts about everything, including one's own sincerity and authenticity. Therefore it is not easy to find a worldview which rules and structures individuals' conception of their life history, and which they can also believe in. We live in an age where it is increasingly felt that an individual's life history is nothing but a narrative, a story which is made real by believing in it. This also means that personalities become understood as fragile, cultural constructions.

Chapter 8

NOTES TOWARD A CULTURAL THEORY OF ALCOHOLISM

The studies presented in this book have been more suggestive and questioning than hypothesis-testing of their nature. Yet I believe that the points being made by these studies give us cause to talk about a cultural theory of alcoholism, emerging in the social studies on alcohol. By making a uniting review of the main suggestions and hypotheses developed on the way, I will now draw an outline of this emerging theory, and raise some further themes and questions.

THE ALCOHOLISM FRAME AND ALCOHOLISM

We could start by going back to the guild case study presented in chapter 6. As a somewhat exceptional case, the guild treatment philosophy illustrates the relation of the alcoholism frame to alcoholism.

Because of the guild members' abundant "field experience" about all kinds of alcoholism treatment institutions, they do know how to use the psychologistic talk about "the alcoholic's character traits." For example, when they were asked to interpret why laziness is such a prevalent feature or topic in the guild, one of them said it is because "alcoholics are damn bitter and envious toward one another." In employing such interpretations about themselves, they can be likened to the regulars of the taverns studied in chapter 3. They also had their doubts about the "real" reason why they go to the tavern; maybe it was not the company or the view of life, but the alcohol. Some of the storytellers even openly declared that they are alcoholics. However, in the case of the A-guild, such ad hoc interpretations are of a second order, and of secondary importance, when compared to the way their "program" actually works. In their profane cultural forms, they are able to resist the alcoholism frame, and relate their alcohol problems to the everyday life frame. They have come up with another way of articulating the meaning of drinking with their cultural world; a view of life in terms of which drinking is not that tempting. For the tavern-goers, drinking was an expression of a desire for personal freedom, and a profane protest of Puritan work and consumer ethics, of a way of life where one is constantly striving for new commodities, bigger and better, so that one never really has time to live one's life, to enjoy. Against this background, the treatment ideology of a blue-collar self-help group, the A-guild, makes sense; it claims that drinking is just another form of the same rat race, that to really be able to step out of it one has to give up drinking.

Yet their alcohol problems have been initially structured by the alcoholism frame. On the basis of the case studies discussed in this work, it seems plausible to think that alcoholism is the product of a particular accounting strategy here called the alcoholism frame. By that I do not just refer to the notion that the existence of alcoholism is "diagnosed" by the criteria provided by the alcoholism frame. The alcoholism frame also organizes, structures, and guides behavior, and in that sense produces the empirical phenomenon.

Nonetheless, alcoholism is far from the only possible view of drinking and drinking problems. The desire to drink or get drunk is not an inborn human characteristic. It cannot be explained by a particular, universal function it always serves in a community or individual, or by a particular psychological or physical pathology. People drink and like to get drunk for various reasons. However, individual differences must be related to the culture; to the roles and symbols that alcoholic drinks have in various everyday life situations; to the structures of meaning in terms of which individuals learn the general meaning of drinking, create the taste for it, and maybe learn to make a distinction between normal and abnormal. If drinking is perceived within the notion of desire, people's desire to drink may stem from different meaning structures. Drinking must be conceived in its cultural context.

People do not necessarily, in every culture, like to drink heavily. And even if they do in a particular culture, they do not necessarily conceive of it as a moral problem, or think that drinking causes problems.[1] In other words, it is not inevitable that a community or society controls people's desire to drink, or that the individuals themselves feel that they have to impose self-control on themselves—that is, that they would like to drink more than what they think is acceptable.

However, in many Western societies people treat drinking as a moral question, and they experience, at least occasionally, a tension between their desire to drink and their conception about acceptable drinking. This state of affairs does not necessarily lead to the notion of alcoholism as an accounting strategy of unacceptable drinking. People may well treat heavy drinking as a sin, or as a crime, as has been the case in the history of Finland (Bruun 1971) and the United States (Conrad and Schneider 1980; Schneider 1978). However, in both of these countries there has been a trend, wherein a form of nonnormative behavior is labeled first a "sin," then a "crime," and finally a "sickness."

But even more important than such fluctuations in the conceptions of heavy drinking and habitual drunkenness is the individualization and pathologization of drinking. As was discussed in chapter 2, in the case of Finland this development had to do with the shift from state control to individual control, or from a "repressive" to a more "conditioning" control. On the level of legitimations, it coincided with a shift from asceticism to hedonism. Along with a shift from a negative to positive concept of human nature, it became common to think that abnormal drinking must be due to a personal pathology or bad social conditions. The beginning of the hedonist era gave rise to the distinction between normal and pathological, which is the main characteristic of the alcoholism frame—or a more general addiction frame. In the alcoholism frame, the crossing of the limits of normality is defined as pathological.

In other words, "alcoholism" is a reinterpretation, a product of an accounting strategy of socially unacceptable drinking habits. The general alcoholism frame does not view drinking within the frames that make it clear to society's members "what is going on" in a particular situation. It rather appraises drinking within a different framework, which shifts the attention from the situation to *drinking* as a particular topic; the concern is for *individuals* and their drinking *habits*; in the particular way individuals play their role in a social situation that includes alcoholic drinks.

Compared to the other frames within which drinking can be understood, the alcoholism frame is a special case in certain respects. It centers reflexive attention on individual behavior, assessed from the viewpoint of normality, and on the use of one particular chemical substance. Its particularity is of course only relative; it is an example of the frames by which the modern individual and individuality are socially produced and reproduced. The history and social genesis of the notion of the modern individual was outlined in the previous chapter. In our daily practices, we construct individuality by now and again shifting our attention from the attempt to understand what people "mean," or what idea or message they are trying to convey, to the individual style with which individuals accomplish the acts. The individual "traits" thus found are then used, both by the individual and by others, to identify a person.

Yet it can be argued that as a relatively recent invention the alcoholism frame does not organize our perceptions and behavior as much as the everyday life frame does. From this point of view, getting to be an alcoholic could be interpreted as a process where the alcoholism frame becomes more dominant and more automatically used in interpreting social situations.

As the Finnish examples discussed in chapters 3 and 4 showed, the everyday life frame—which is ordinarily used to make sense of drinking contexts—reflects social organization and people's way of life. In chapter 3 it was shown that the men's attitude toward drinking, and the meaning of their other activities in the tavern, were in a homologous relationship with their attitudes toward other aspects of their life. In other words, their drinking habits reflected their overall view of life. For the darts players, the activities in the tavern were a symbolic way of dealing with the tensions and contradictions between work, family life, and their own preferences stemming from the cultural tradition. As a group these men tried to achieve a view of life in terms of which they would resolve or at least relieve the contradictions, maintain control over their life, and preserve their self-esteem. For them, going to the tavern was at once a symbol and a realization of a measure of personal freedom. Moreover, darts and beer were an alternative to the bourgeois way of life, to the asceticism of "collecting the pennies." The storytellers, on the other hand, had developed a slightly different view of life. Being similar to the darts players in many respects, they did not think that it is necessary—or even sensible, for that matter—to control their drinking. On the contrary, for them to be free meant that a man frees

himself from self-control, and in organizing his life relies on the manipulation of external control. This way of thinking was called the logic
of freedom.

The logic of freedom can be seen as an example of a coping strategy. Since individuals in modern society often have to act in an instrumental fashion, there are different coping strategies, and a drinking
bout is an example and a symbol of one of them: it represents an effort
to get rid of personal responsibilities by instead preferring open and
naked control. This coping strategy is used especially by the manual,
blue-collar workers, who work under close supervision and control,
and cannot control or plan their work. Instead, since it is expected of
those doing "mental work" to be their own "bosses," it is typical of the
middle and upper class to make a virtue of necessity another way
around: by trying to convince oneself that the tasks one accomplishes
are what one has always wanted to do, that no outer control or forcing
oneself is needed. Following Weber, it could be called the "logic of calling." Coupled with these two strategies, there is the logic of self-control,
which tries to render the need to force oneself a positive thing by
emphasizing the strong character such self-control and self-denial
requires. Such an attitude toward drinking and life in general could be
seen among the darts players discussed in chapter 3.

In addition to the occupational differences, there are also historical
fluctuations as to the popularity of these coping strategies. As was discussed in chapter 2, the logic of control or "cult of self-control" was
particularly popular at the turn of the century, whereas the last decades
have seen the rise of an ideology of hedonism. However, these coping
strategies live side by side, and they are all used, to a greater or lesser
degree, by a single individual. As was discussed in chapter 4, the notion
of "loss of control," which is the cornerstone of the notion of alcoholism,
may be seen an effect of a clashing of two coping strategies: in their
behavior persons follow the "logic of freedom" but appraise or diagnose
it from the viewpoint of the logic of calling, or the logic of control.

Thus, the use of the alcoholism frame always serves a function. It
is a way of trying to come to terms with problems created or associated
with an individual's heavy, socially unacceptable, drinking habits. To
become an alcoholic is to begin to conceive of one's drinking within
the alcoholism frame. If individuals drink in an unacceptable way often
enough, their behavior is no more interpreted as an extreme case of
"normal" drinking. It is interpreted—by others and possibly by themselves—within the alcoholism frame.

There are always certain culture-specific interpretive rules that are applied to make a distinction between normal and pathological drinking. In the case of the Finnish blue-collar men studied in chapter 4, it was found that to continue with one's drinking in the morning was one of the signs that makes the wife and the drinker himself consider the use of the alcoholism frame. The usefulness of the alcoholism frame as an accounting strategy was due to its ability to overcome a cognitive dissonance. Drinking, when primarily interpreted as expressing the desire to cut loose and to be personally free, is contradictory to the man's will to preserve his marriage. In such a case drinking may be redefined as a symptom of a senseless craving for alcohol. In such a case the alcoholism frame works as a self-fulfilling prophecy. When it is generally applied to a person, it structures social relations and situations, and gives them a new meaning.

THE DOUBLE EPISTEMOLOGY OF THEORIES OF ALCOHOLISM

This leads us to the notion of a double epistemological status of the theories of alcohol problems. All theories about the nature of drinking problems are, or can be treated as, efforts to deal with them.

Any alcoholism theory that makes sense at least to some people provides some elements of a framework in which various signs, incidents, or feelings that belong to an individual's past or present life are selected and interpreted as "symptoms" of sickness. The picture, thus obtained, represents an individual variant of a universal illness, as defined by the alcoholism frame being used. As an explanatory model, such a framework provides, not only a theory of the etiology and nature of alcoholism but also outlines for an effective cure. In other words, the theories of alcoholism, employed by the parties who try to deal with the problem, construct and reconstruct the illness itself. The attempts to deal with alcohol problems therefore become an essential part of the problem.

The attention paid to certain signs, feelings, or forms of behavior, to be later defined as symptoms of alcoholism, is from the very beginning due to a common conviction that they are somehow problematic. People try to define the situation since it is a first step toward removing the problem. Or, as a matter of fact, a definition of the situation is an *aspect* of the cure. In that sense we could say that alcoholism, as a cultural construct, consists of the measures, taken both by the identified patient and by others, by which people try to handle drinking habits deemed problematic. Paradoxically, alcoholism—as a phenomenological experience of an inability to control oneself—is the product of the alcoholism frame.

In its different variants, the function of the alcoholism frame has been to help the victim. Earlier in history, it was thought that to deem drunkenness a sin would bring drunkards to their senses; make them realize that drinking is not only foolish but also immoral. Later it was reasoned that the people who more and more often voluntarily admit their alcohol problems and submit to treatment must not be any more punished by calling them criminals or sinners; it was thought that alcohol problems can be resolved or eased by removing the stigma of alcoholics. That was done by opposing a "moral model"—in terms of which drunkards are treated as criminals or sinners—and by instead treating alcohol problems as an individual sickness.[2]

There are some factors in the social development of Western societies that increase the use of the alcoholism frame, or a more general addiction frame. One of them, the shift from state control to individual control, was already discussed. Another one is a growing proportion of the people who are doing "mental" work, of those who are self-employed, or whose work requires self-control as opposed to external control. The more that individuals have to lose if they start to drink, the more irrational heavy drinking seems, and the more the alcoholism frame makes sense.[3]

As was discussed in chapter 7, the overall modernization process toward individualism and individuality also makes the general addiction frame suitable to the modern era. In the era of the modern person, we construct individuality by assessing the style with which an individual accomplishes certain acts. Not all acts are useful as individual characteristics. The acts that deviate from the norm, which can be made in different, "personal" ways, or in the case of which culture makes a distinction between "normal" and "abnormal," are the most useful. From this standpoint, when the notion of "addiction" is used, the attention has totally shifted to the function of an act as a personality characteristic.

In this sense, the distinction made between normal and abnormal can be seen as part of what may be called the modernizing or civilizing process of Western societies (Elias 1978; 1982; Foucault 1973a; 1973b; 1979). When perceived in this perspective, this development is linked with individuation, which is furthermore connected to the increased importance of market relations and panoptic power relations as the bases for social relations and interaction. These profound transformations have not only brought about a renaming of certain problems; they have also produced us as individual subjects trying to make sense of various phenomena.

The increased importance of market relations enhances the use of the addiction frame by making utilitarian rationality and self-interest a self-evident framework. The risks of alcohol abuse are discussed in terms of this individualist perspective. Should, then, an informed person fail to follow the advised rational course of action, it is taken as proof of a pathology such as alcoholism. From this individualist perspective it makes sense to think that "the problem is in the man, not in the bottle."[4]

All in all, there are many reasons why the division into normal and pathological gains currency in all walks of life. In the social science literature, this trend is called *medicalization* of social control. Changes in the definition of such illnesses or phenomena as hyperkinesis (Conrad 1975), wife battering (Kurz 1987), sexuality (Galliher and Tyree 1985; Tiefer 1986; S. Bell 1987) infanticide (O'Donovan 1984), infant mortality (van Daalen 1985), alcoholism (Room 1983), and compulsive gambling (Rosecrance 1985) have been discussed in the literature. The exponents of this line of thought have been specifically concerned about the way daily life has become increasingly medicalized; consumer dependence on professional medical remedies has been fostered (Calnan 1984), and the medical profession has gained jurisdiction over matters that earlier were the sole domains of religion, politics; or criminal law (Katz and Abel 1984).

Let me, however, suggest that the strengthened authority of the medical profession is only of secondary importance, or a secondary effect of the development outlined above. The normal/pathological dichotomy is not employed by medical doctors only, and even less is it restricted to the vulgar conception of, say, "addiction" as a physical disease. In Finland, for instance, alcoholism treatment has not become, and is probably not becoming, a domain of medical doctors. Yet one can for a good reason argue that Finnish conceptions about problem drinking are increasingly organized by the alcoholism frame, and that unacceptable drinking is perceived as a personal pathology. In this instance, instead of medicalization we could talk about pathologization. Medicalization is only a special case of it, since the line drawn between normal and pathological phenomena is part of medical practice.

As was already implied, the role of the alcoholism frame in structuring social reality is not restricted to producing the victims of the alcoholism frame—that is, alcoholics. It is not only applied to obviously extreme situations or deviant drinking habits. People use it generally in interpreting and assessing others' and their own drinking. Therefore it tends to structure all drinking situations to a degree.

In this sense, pathologization may have far-flung consequences to Western civilization. It may be that individual behavior is increasingly appraised in terms of the division into the normal and the abnormal. This increases the number of illnesses—whether they be conceived as physical or psychological—by enlarging the scope of aspects of human life that are appraised from the perspective of healthiness or normality. And not only is the healthiness of more and more habits and vices scrutinized by natural scientific measurements; an individual's willingness or inability to avoid apparently unhealthy or otherwise harmful habits is conceived of as a disease in its own right.

It could be argued that this development enlarges the scope of the notion of addiction as a particular, modern culture-bound syndrome. It may lead to a somewhat modified conception of the individual. Let me elaborate on this.

If an individual's habit, perceived to be expressive of an individual's ability to control his or her desires, is within the addiction frame deemed abnormal, it is then interpreted within a framework that radically differs from the ones applied to "ordinary" behavior. Depending on the case and individual preferences, the "addiction" may be related to the individual's "early experiences," to the "family system," and so forth. If the new frameworks become widely used in everyday life, it follows that they begin to structure it quite like the everyday-life frame. Imagine, for instance, that certain acts are automatically perceived as "slips of the tong" and interpreted within the Freudian "dictionary." Gradually these "slips of the tong" begin to be used to express certain ideas. A similar development has in fact happened in the case of those who have come to realize that they are "alcoholics," "sex addicts," and so on. However, this far the everyday-life frame, as we have called it, has provided the basis for mutual understanding. It may be that this is changing; that everyday life gets increasingly structured by the addiction frame, that "normal" behavior is defined on the basis of the addiction frame rather than the other way around.

THE DISEASE CONCEPT AND EVERYDAY LIFE

Medical science has certainly had an impact on our understanding of health and illness. We should not, however, overemphasize the opposition between the "medical model" and everyday life frame. As was pointed out, the addiction frame also has its roots in Western cultural tradition. As a folk model of the West, the "medical model" has to acquire its explanatory power from its ability to make sense of certain social problems in terms of the Western cultural tradition. The AA, for example, is in many ways a religious movement. Even though it defines alcoholism as a disease, an essential element in its program is nonetheless the requirement—quite comparable to many revivalist movements—that individuals confess their alcoholism (read: sins) and repent. This is in fact contradictory to the claim made by the AA that alcoholics are sick persons not responsible for their behavior or condition. Indeed, the apparent contradiction between these statements is eased by the creed that alcoholics cannot help themselves without group support and "a Power greater than ourselves" (Blumberg 1977; Maxwell 1962).

It could be suggested that the way in which AA is presented as a treatment model that is based on—or in accordance with—scientific, medical knowledge about "the disease of alcoholism" is a legitimation strategy. As the AA's ingenious invention to call itself a "spiritual" rather than a "religious" movement, its insistence to call alcoholism a disease—which is in fact treated as a sin—gives the movement an air of modernity and scientificness in a secularized, rational era.

Mutatis mutandis, the same could be said of the A-guild. Even though they totally reject religion, it is interesting how the mid-nineteenth century Finnish Pietists had similar ideas about the good and ethical way of life. These ideas could be seen in the way the revivalist movement's leading figures responded to criticism leveled against them by the Fennoman nationalist movement. The revivalists did not accept dance, drinking, or card plying. One of the leading figures of the Fennoman movement, Elias Lönrot, criticized them for their denial of all devotions and joys of life, and accused them of concentrating so much on their devotional exercises that they did not have time to work. In his reply Jonas Lagus, a famous Protestant minister and religious leader, said that these true Christians do take care of their work, but they do not want to gather vast riches (Ylikangas 1979, 219-33).

By these two cases I do not mean to suggest that, knowingly or unknowingly, admitting it or not, the philosophies of self-help groups always stem from religion. That would be precisely as foolish as to argue that, say, the AA view stems from Western medicine. The point is that, for instance, "medicine" and "religion" are much closer to each other than we tend to think.[5]

It seems that secularization and rationalization are only superficial phenomena. Take, for instance, the blue-collar men's life stories analyzed in chapter 4. They show how superficially the alcoholism frame had been connected to the thinking of the men with alcohol problems. It did not organize the narrative structure, and could only be seen on the level of evaluative clauses. The narrative structure—and the meaning of drinking in it—reflected the everyday-life frame shared by all blue-collar men.

This can, of course, be a particular Finnish feature, an indicator of Finland's "backwardness" in this respect. The situation might be different in, for instance, the United States. In the U.S.A., the native country of AA, the strongest proponent of the disease model, the AA ideology has acquired a semiofficial position, and AA programing has become a cornerstone of virtually all rehabilitation efforts.[6] However, the degree to which this has had an impact on character formation cannot just be assumed. Proper research would be needed.

Whatever the degree to which theories of alcohol problems have structured the problematic itself, it is obvious that they have to be seen as part of it, not as observations or theories about a disease per se. Yet provided that the phenomenon is perceived in this perspective, the case studies discussed in this work suggest that alcohol problems can be approached—and maybe resolved—from the point of view of a cultural theory of alcoholism. As a treatment program, this would mean that the frames and discourses that define and organize the problem itself should be reconstructed and deconstructed so the problem is rooted in the everyday life frame.

THE FUTURE OF ALCOHOLISM

The analysis presented here is, of course, itself a view on alcoholism. Like any other alcoholism theory, it obviously contributes to modifying the prevalent concept of alcoholism. The practical, especially therapeutic, uses of a cultural or metatheory do not exist so far, but it seems plausible to assume that the rise of such theory reflects the (post)modern era we live in. It may reflect the increasing difficulties of modern individuals and identified alcoholics in believing in any offered explanatory model of alcoholism; a model that would both make sense and provide an explicit program of recovery.

The options for the future of alcoholism seem to be many. On one side, the development appears to be favorable for an expansion of the pathologizing view. It may be assumed that social and cultural distinctions used in identity formation tend to be deprived of their contents due to the demands for equality. Therefore drinking problems tend to be perceived as unique and individual, rather than socially and culturally conditioned. It may be that alcoholism is increasingly perceived as a pathology in the universalistic relation of an abstract individual to a chemical substance.

Yet in the (post)modern era, we can discern aspects that may work against "alcoholism" as a particular disease. Along with a growing disbelief of all metanarratives, we may begin to question if our personality and identity is only a product of our biographical reasoning, of a story we tell ourselves. This would also mean that we become distrustful of a personal continuity, of a true story about individual development. Therefore, it may also be that "alcoholism" melts in the air of disbelief. Or that it is increasingly considered as a shallow sign of our personal lifestyle; that all persons have their personal addiction, be it gambling, sex addiction, or alcoholism, or that an individual can be identified as a personality by a unique combination of different addictions. The anonymous participation in AA-type self-help groups may be becoming a way of searching for a personal lifestyle and personality. In a way, the implications of the brief therapy approach point in the same direction. In it, etiologies and future prospects of a problem are consciously considered as stories we tell ourselves and believe in, and the aim of the therapy is to invent a story in which the problem has been solved or disappeared. Along with these developments, all these addictions are losing much of their authenticity and innocence.

Chapter 9

THEORETICAL APPENDIX:
SOCIAL MEANING, SOCIAL NORMS,
AND THE DESIRING SUBJECT

Though we have only looked at the social construction of one specific phenomenon, this study has produced some theoretical starting points and insights that are, I suggest, generally relevant in sociological theory and cultural studies. One of the things I have learned by doing this study has been that we must not take for granted the culturally prevalent conception of individuals as desiring subjects, according to which personalities can be characterized by a tension between instinctual urges, on the one hand, and social control or self-control, on the other. Instead, we must treat "desire" and "self-control" as *notions* Western culture uses, notions that produce us in their own image as desiring subjects. Another, related insight is that we must not confuse social norms with social meaning. Or, to use Peter Winch's (1971) concepts, one must make a distinction between regulative and constitutive rule.[1]

In this theoretical appendix, I will first discuss and critique the Freudian and post-Freudian views of civilization. Then, I will elaborate on a different account of modernization and character modification, and the role of the notions of "desire" and "self-control" in it. Finally, by taking examples of the studies of this book, I will discuss the function and meaning of expressly stated regulative rules—that is, social norms in a strict sense of the word—may have.

THE FREUDIAN AND POST-FREUDIAN VIEWS OF CIVILIZATION

In the social science literature, Sigmund Freud was probably the first to pay serious attention to the modern individual as a subject of desire. According to Freud, civilization consists of the constraints individuals impose on their natural instincts, and the human psyche consists of a tension between the "libido" and the "super-ego." In this respect, "primitive man" is less disciplined:

> If civilization imposes such great sacrifices not only on man's sexuality but on his aggressivity, we can understand better why it is hard for him to be happy in that civilization. In fact, primitive man was better off in knowing no restrictions of instinct. [Freud, 1978: 115]

The Freudian view of social life is also expressed and further developed in Norbert Elias's theory of the civilizing process (Elias, 1978; 1982). According to Elias, the civilizing process is best understood as a gradual internalization of outer constraints into self-restraint. By studying books giving instructions about civilized manners, he shows that there is a general pattern in the history of changing manners and conceptions of civilized behavior. The "overall shape of the curve" corresponds, according to Elias, to the growing importance and strength of the central power of a nation—that is, the state as a power monopoly. Along with state formation, and the growing importance of an exchange economy, networks of mutual dependence become denser, and that is the reason for the individual's need for greater discretion.

According to Elias, the civilizing process means that the regulation of drives becomes stricter. That is why the people of the Middle Ages appear to us like savages, or children. In the Middle Ages, too, society exerted formative pressure on individuals, Elias admits, even if in different ways. "But above all, the control and restraint to which the instinctual life of adults was subjected was considerably less than in the following phase of civilization, as consequently was the difference in behavior between adults and children" (Elias 1978, 140-41).

The problem with Elias's line of reasoning is that he fails to explain why table manners, natural functions, spitting, blowing one's nose, relations between the sexes, and aggression, were the things that became increasingly controlled. He gives a symbolic explanation only when discussing the innumerable prohibitions and taboos surrounding the use of the knife.

First of all he remarks that the knife is a weapon of attack. According to him, the social attitude toward the knife and the rules governing its use are primarily emotional in nature, because the knife is a symbol of violence. And as was said, according to Elias the civilizing process is caused by state formation—that is, the formation of a monopoly of violence. But here Elias goes even further, when explaining the prohibition on eating fish with a knife—circumvented by the introduction of a special fish knife. According to Elias, it "seems at first sight rather obscure in its emotional meaning, though psychoanalytical theory points at least in the direction of an explanation (p. 124)." A measure of discretion, wonderfully in line with the object of the study, has kept Elias from disclosing the symbolic meaning of fish in psychoanalytical theory.

However, such a symbolic interpretation of an object of prohibitions is an exception for Elias. Otherwise he just presents us with two parallel histories: one about the history of manners (volume one), and another one about state formation (volume two). The way he connects the two together has the typical weakness of a functionalist explanation, "a cannibalism of form by function," as Sahlins (1976, 83) has put it. Only, in the case of Elias, the contents of manners and the areas in which self-control is increasingly used, are of interest only as *indicators* of a tightening control of individuals' drives and of the heightened threshold of embarrassment.

Yet there is, in Elias's work, an underlying theory of the reason why behavioral education and changes in factual manners have been concentrated on these particular issues. For Elias, the civilizing process is a gradual sublimation of ahistorical, basic human needs and drives. When adopting more refined manners, and developing feelings of shame, man advances further and further away from the state of nature. That is why a Middle Ages man—or a savage—is childlike.

As unable as Elias is in cutting totally loose from the self-concept of the Western man, he is perfectly aware of the problems of his theory, which is not quite as simple as was described above. Not all individual urges are "natural:" they might be sublimations or deformations of drives:

The modification of the manner of spitting, and finally the more or less complete elimination of the need for it, is a good example of the malleability of psychic life. It may be that this need has been compensated by others (e.g., the need to smoke) or weakened by certain changes of diet. [1978, 159]

In other words, human needs *are* historical for Elias, even though they are modifications of "original," natural needs. Moreover, Elias even doubts whether the contraposition of "civilization" and "nature" is nothing more than an expression of the tensions of the civilized psyche itself. "At any rate, the psychic life of 'primitive' peoples is no less historically (i.e., socially) stamped than that of 'civilized' peoples, even if the former are scarcely aware of their own history. There is no zero point in the historicity of human development, just as there is none in the sociality, the social interdependence among men" (1978, 160). And in volume two Elias notes that a condition of totally uncontrolled drives, of an absolute "beginning" simply does not exist (1982, 86). He even remarks that historical changes should be grasped qualitatively.

Despite these qualifications, it is fair to say that Elias pictures the civilizing process quantitatively, as a process whereby "the regulation of the whole instinctual and affective life by steady self-control becomes more and more stable, more even and more all-embracing" (ibid, 230). In his view, man can be understood best as an animal, with his drives, instincts, and needs, which are kept in check and more or less modified by the civilization in which he lives. The specificity of the Western civilization is, in Elias's theory, that outer constraints are internalized into self-restraint, and original drives are—by feelings of shame—pushed from the consciousness into the unconscious. His study is meant to be a natural history of the personality structure Freud has described in his writings.

The French structuralist and poststructuralist theory of desire, based on Jacques Lacan's reading of Freud, and developed especially by Gilles Deleuze and Felix Guattari in their book *Anti-Oedipus* (1977), is critical of the naturalism of the position outlined above. It rejects the simplistic notion of certain identifiable "human instincts" or "basic needs" which direct our urges. In this position, desire is understood as a *flux* with no determinate goal, and it differs from lacking, which is organized. The paradox is that every time we speak about our desires within discourse, we name and define them, and in that way channel desire, transform it into "need" or "lack." In this instance, Deleuze and

Guattari speak about *socius* rather than discourse. For them socius denotes the forms of Power (Österberg 1988, 228). As Deleuze and Guattari (1977, 33) put it: "The prime function incumbent upon the socius has always been to codify the flows of desire, to inscribe them, to record them, to see to it that no flow exists that is not properly dammed up, channeled, regulated." Socius tries to *territorialize* human beings, to make them belong to a determinate position. Desire responds by attempts to fly and escape, by *de-territorialization*. Generally, socius's activities of coding are met with desire's de-coding, until this liberating moment is met by *re-territorializing*. This is how the struggle between desire and socius goes on.

Deleuze and Guattari's theory of desire differs from the old Freudian view discussed in the previous pages. Unlike Freud, Deleuze and Guattari do not presuppose any natural instincts. They even oppose prevalent Freud-Marxist doctrines, which combine psychology and economics in order to show how the *libido* is suppressed, channeled, or sublimated through confronting the socio-economic order (Österberg 1988, 228). Deleuze and Guattari instead stress that the *social* is itself a mode of desire. They argue that desire does not confront external institutions which inhibit it; desire inhibits itself through its self-made institutions. But despite the differences, in many respects the two views are similar. They both conceive of desire as human energy flowing from somewhere "below," and modified by something "above" or "on the surface." They conceptualize "life" for all humans by the concept of desire; and "social life" or "discourse" by the idea of constraints that channel and modify desire.

THE FOUCAULDIAN VIEW OF MODERNIZATION

Michel Foucault approaches the question of the desiring subject from a slightly different point of view. In many of his studies he traces the historical genesis of the conceptual division into the Same and the Other—the realms of knowledge and normality, on the one hand, and madness and pathology on the other—and how modern subjects are constituted by this division. It is in fact the same duality that finds its expression in the Eliasian notion of a tension between desire and self-control discussed above.

In *Madness and Civilization* Michel Foucault (1973, 247) notes that in the late eighteenth century a new concept of madness, and a new method of healing the mad, was invented. The madmen were freed from all chains, but only at the expense of being punished for any manifestations of madness. In this way the asylum organized for the madman a consciousness of himself; a consciousness of the man of reason, of the Other—that is, his own madness.

In *Discipline and Punish* Foucault (1979) discusses the same phenomenon on a more general level by noting that throughout the seventeenth and eighteenth centuries, there was a gradual extension of the mechanisms of discipline; their spread throughout the social body, and the formation of what might be called the disciplinary society. This meant that people were ever more effectively produced as disciplined individuals, as individuals who are conscious of constant but unverifiable surveillance, and of the possibility of punishment. Such an arrangement assures the automatic functioning of power; it becomes unnecessary to use force to constrain the convict to good behavior, the madman to calm, or the schoolboy to application. "He who is subjected to a field of visibility, and who knows it, assumes responsibility for the constraints of power; he makes them play spontaneously upon himself; he inscribes in himself the power relation in which he simultaneously plays both roles; he becomes the principle of his own subjection" (Foucault 1979, 202-3).

In other words, it was freedom, coupled with the awareness of the possibility of surveillance and punishment, that made the human subjects adopt the viewpoint of their overseers; that made desires strange to the desiring subjects themselves. Allured by external freedom, individuals began to "take responsibility" for their actions—that is, to become their own controls, and to reunite their *self* with the motives and objectives of their overseers, generalized as pure *reason*.

Along with the emergence of the disciplinary or panoptic society and power structure, there also emerges the notion of individuals as personalities who more or less effectively keep their desires in check.[2] For Foucault, this notion of personality emerged as an effect of the disciplinary techniques, and it was conceptually formulated by the sciences of man organized by the panoptic "gaze." Individualizing surveillance, first practiced by the police, and later on continued by various disciplines, was generalized into a form of knowledge. By the end of the eighteenth century, the disciplinary techniques attained a level at which the formation of knowledge and the increase of power regularly reinforce one another in a circular process:

First the hospital, then the school, then, later, the workshop were not simply "reordered" by the disciplines; they became, thanks to them, apparatuses such that any mechanism of objectification could be used in them as an instrument of subjection, and any growth of power could give rise in them to possible branches of knowledge; it was this link, proper to the technological systems, that made possible within the disciplinary element the formation of clinical medicine, psychiatry, child psychology, educational psychology, the rationalization of labour. [Foucault 1979, 224][3]

THE USES OF "SELF-CONTROL"

The Foucauldian view of modernization and character formation has important methodological implications. It shows the theoretical relevance of a social constructionist approach to such notions as "desire," "self-control," or "alcoholism." When studying concrete cases this means, for instance, that when there are public demands for self-control, one must analyze the social meaning and function of such demands.

According to Foucault, one of the consequences of the history by which modern individuals are constituted as desiring subjects is an inability to conceive of desires as historically changing. As the power of society on the individual is conceptualized as outer restraints—or internalized self-restraint—imposed by society, the desire to be held in check is conceived as a constant. Sexuality, for instance, has been seen as such a constant; it has been thought that the historically singular forms, in which it was manifested, were due to various forms of repression to which it was bound to be subjected in every society. As an effect of such a conception of power and of sexuality, *"desire and the subject of desire were withdrawn from the historical field,* and interdiction as a general form was made to account for anything historical in sexuality" (Foucault 1985, 4; italics added).

To break with that conception of the individual as a subject of desire, we have to bracket the self-evident notions of "desire" or "self-control," to stand detached from them, and to analyze the role of these notions in constituting us as modern individuals. In Foucault's case, this led into an analysis of the history of the notion of sexuality; how the use of the term was established in connection with other phenomena: the establishment of a set of rules and norms; and changes in the way individuals were led to assign meaning and value to their conduct. "In

short, it was a matter of seeing how an 'experience' came to be constituted in modern Western societies, an experience that caused individuals to recognize themselves as subjects of a 'sexuality,' which was acces-
sible to very diverse fields of knowledge and linked to a system of rules
and constraints" (Foucault 1985, 4). Later, in order to understand how
the modern individual could experience himself as a subject of a "sexuality," Foucault first decided to determine "how, for centuries, Western
man had been brought to recognize himself as a subject of desire" (Foucault 1985, 6). In a similar vein, in this study, I have analyzed the way in
which modern individuals are brought to understand themselves as
subjects of a desire or a craving to drink, and as possible subjects of
"alcoholism."

The social constructionist approach employed in this book has
also helped me to see self-control as a notion people at times use for various reasons. In chapter two, it was shown how, at the turn of the nineteenth century, the Finnish temperance movement's public urge for the
use of self-control had a legitimating function. It contributed to rendering the individualist behavioral code morally acceptable by emphasizing the difficulty of living up to the new ideals. It stressed the strong
willpower it takes to be able to resist the temptations of individual
drives and needs. The stress laid on the difficulty in achieving the new
moral standard tended to dampen the individual gains of it.

THE MEANING OF SOCIAL NORMS

The discussion above has shown that we cannot take it for granted
that modern character formation is the consequence of social constraints, existing in the form of social norms, and internalized as self-
restraint. Social constraints or social norms—that is, regulative rules,
are not the glue or cement that keeps a society in one piece and makes
individuals into social subjects. But although social norms are not
"effective" in that sense, there exist explicitly expressed social norms in
practically all social interaction. People at least try to make each other
act in certain ways, and express their disapproval of some other ways of
speaking or behaving. What is, then, the function of the normative
aspect of social life? A new look at the case study of the A-guild, presented in chapter six, will shed light on these questions. It shows that
regulative rules may have several social functions and meanings.

The case study showed that the effect of the guild on its members' ability to abstain from drinking was not based on a normative pressure the group imposed on its members. It was shown that the guild members did not force themselves to abstain or support others in doing so; rather, by developing a reinterpretation of the sense and meaning of drinking, they attempted to get rid of their desire to drink. However, that does not mean that there are no examples of regulative rules or normative pressure within the group.

For instance, there was a normative aspect in the members' habit of telling stories and anecdotes of their previous lives as drunkards or alcoholics. The tone of these often humorous stories was somewhat boasting, even though they did describe in a plain way the hardships and degradation which heavy drinking repeatedly brought about to the guild members. The men seemed to boast even with the amount of hardships they faced when drinking. Stories about a more "civilized" drinking were mitigated, along with the individuals who told such stories. In such cases, then, it was disapproved to openly undermine the experiences of others, in a spirit of tolerance toward individual differences. In other words, there was an openly expressed norm which forbids undermining the seriousness of others' previous drinking problems. Every time someone did that, he was disapproved and reminded that it is inappropriate to do so.

Another example was the members' attitude toward laziness. Although they were quite active, and arranged many kinds of activities in addition to the ordinary meetings, they repeatedly made complaints about the laziness of the guild members. The laziness of the members was in fact one of the favorite topics in the conversations. "How lazy this bunch can be," was an expression that was often heard. There were always things to be done together, but the problem was that the members seemed to have developed the avoidance of all work into an art form. One could say that the leading figures of the guild tried to impose normative pressure on the members in order to get things done, and the fact that laziness was a general topic showed that they had succeeded. There was a social norm that obliged the members to do their share of the common tasks.

The guild philosophy also refused to spell out any fixed theory of alcoholism, or a treatment ideology they subscribed to. This could be seen in the prevailing social norm not to say a good word about professional psychotherapy.

One of the most central pieces of advice the guild members gave to newcomers was that—before getting a job—they should first "clear

their head," to step out of the "squirrel wheel" or the rat race by deliberately staying unemployed at least for a half year. That piece of advice
also had a status of a social norm. That could be noted in the fact that
the only man in the guild who had held on to his job throughout his
drinking career and recovery was suspected of never really changing his
views, of never stepping out of the squirrel wheel.

What is the meaning of these social norms in the guild "program"? To answer that we first have to understand the inner logic of the
guild philosophy.

For instance, these men who strove for sobriety tended to boast
with their previous drinking because of their rejection of theoretical
knowledge detached from concrete practice. By boasting with their previous drinking the members cherished their "field experience." For the
same reason they disapproved of any member saying that professional
alcoholism treatment or psychotherapy has helped them; in such cases
others often reminded such a member of his later setbacks and
relapses—that is, of the failures of professional treatment. The common
topic of the guild members' laziness and the need to force the members to take care of the common tasks could be seen as an effect of the
guild philosophy, of the idea that, to get rid of the craving for drinking,
one has to step out of the squirrel wheel which entails hard work associated with heavy drinking. That the members were lazy and even
boasted with their laziness showed that they have created a new relation to work, that they have "gotten the idea."

As the social norms prevailing in the guild are perceived within
the guild philosophy as a whole, we can distinguish at least two different cases. First, in some cases a need to prohibit certain attitudes or
modes of speech derives from a striking discrepancy between the inner
logic of the view of life of a cultural group and dominant notions of
"sensible" or "rational" thinking. The ban on apparent boasting about
one's prior drinking and the consequent norm not to undermine the
experiences and the severity of drinking problems of a person who has
not totally "gone to the dogs" are cases in point. Though the tendency to
do such things is perfectly in accordance with the inner logic of the
guild philosophy, and though these norms are repeatedly broken, the
norms prevail in the spirit of tolerance toward different cases because—
and this is the main point—boasting about drinking in a group that
propagates sobriety does not make any sense whatsoever on a conscious and rational level. The guild members' relation to laziness is
another example of this: in a culture where hard working is a self-evi-

dent, underlying value, it is hard to openly challenge the "Protestant work ethic" and build one's social identity on a different relation to work. That is why the guild members cover the credit they give to each other for being able to "step out of the squirrel wheel" in constant complaints about the members' laziness.

Second, in some cases the expression of a social norm shows that the culture's members consciously defend their way of thinking and account of the world. That is the case, for instance, when the guild members disapprove of a member defending the usefulness of professional psychotherapy.

There are also certainly cases where a group member has doubts about the sense of the world view offered by the guild, or there are newcomers who have not understood or seen the relevance and inner logic of the guild philosophy. In such cases or during the members' moments of doubt, the moments when one gets the temptation to drink, the guild lines of thought appear as irrational normative rules, supervised by other guild members.

On a more abstract level, I suggest that the existence of a social norm is an expression of a legitimation crisis of some sort. When people are aware of at least two alternative options in their thinking and conduct, and when they grant some legitimacy to both of them, they account for their actual conduct by referring to a social norm. Either they comply with a normative rule, and resist the temptation to do otherwise, or they repeatedly break a social norm but reproduce it in social interaction by saying that they themselves or others "should" do otherwise. In the latter case the appearance of a social norm is the outcome of negotiated thinking: by normatively restricting forms of behavior that are in too stark a contrast with the dominant, "rational" lines of thought a social group pays tribute to the cornerstones of prevailing social order. The existence of a norm might be sheer lip service paid to the prevailing social order, but it nevertheless shows that the cultural forms of the group are not strong enough to openly challenge the rationality of the prevailing social order.

DISCUSSION

This chapter has dealt with two questions. First, I discussed different accounts of the civilizing process. Then I moved over to discuss the meaning and function social norms—or regulative rules—may have in social intercourse. In both discussions we are concerned with the same theme: modern character formation. The Foucauldian view suggests that we must not conceive of "civilization" or "society" simply as constraints imposed upon "individuals." We must bracket these self-evident notions, consider them as cultural constructions within which we have learned to perceive us as modern individuals, to assign meaning and value to our conduct.

Instead of thinking of socialization and modernization in terms of social norms, some of which are internalized and repressed from the consciousness into the "subconscious," let me rather suggest that the emergence of regulative rules is an indicator of a legitimation crisis. When a shared worldview and view of life disintegrates, some of its aspects come to be seen as regulative rules. Where there are interdictions or "moral obligations," there is negotiated thinking involved. When we force ourselves into following a regulative rule, we are aware of an alternative. Or when we acknowledge that we "should" do otherwise, we deviate from the prevailing morals but simultaneously give some credit to its legitimacy. Therefore, it cannot be taken for granted that finally new social norms are internalized and come to be seen as "natural" behavior. It may of course be that a norm is forgotten because everybody automatically complies with it. But it may quite well be that "breaking the norms" slowly becomes the standard behavioral code and, as part of a changed view of life, it is no more morally suspect. In this case, the norms are forgotten because everybody breaks them.

From this perspective, norms are an interesting object of sociological analysis. However, by simply listing the norms existing in a cultural group we cannot get a good picture of its view of life, because norms do not point out the central aspects of a culture. Instead, norms emerge in "places" where a group's forms of behavior or lines of thought are in a stark contrast with the dominant, "rational" way of thinking. As such indicators of breaches in the hegemonic cultural order, they manifest social and cultural trends. Norms and interdictions are not the principal way in which behavior modification takes place, or how subjects are constituted, but they do structure and direct our urges and wants by representing outer restraints to be resisted or duties to be complied with. The cultural analysis of alcoholism made in this book is an example of how this view of norms can be applied, but it may quite well be employed in other areas of social research.

NOTES

CHAPTER 1

1. Harry Levine (1990) argues that there is a distinct group of countries—the "temperance cultures"—in which alcoholic drink and drunkenness symbolically represent the dangers people fear and experience from loss of individual self-control and self-regulation. The temperance cultures developed large-scale, ongoing temperance movements in the nineteenth and early twentieth centuries. These countries are the United States, Britain, Canada, Australia, New Zealand, and the Nordic countries—Finland, Sweden, Norway, and Iceland. These temperance cultures have been shaped by the culture of Protestantism, and have been or still are places where people drink a considerable portion of their alcohol in liquor. Levine suggests that the original temperance cultures retain today a distinctive and strong cultural focus on the problematic consequences of alcoholic drink. The earlier temperance movement concerns with alcohol have been changed, so that chief among the developments of the public concern with drinking during the past ten or fifteen years "neotemperance" era has been the spread of the philosophy of Alcoholics Anonymous.

2. In his later works, Foucault was interested in the history of these notions. In his uncompleted study dealing with the history of sexuality, his main question was, how it came to be taken for granted that subjects, desires, and interdictions were given as concepts for explaining history and society. For a more detailed discussion of this, see the Theoretical Appendix of the book at hand.

CHAPTER 2

1. Ways of thinking and behaving do not change overnight. Sulkunen (1986, 23-24) notes that the people who had migrated to the towns carried on

their habit of daily "aperitifs" also in their new role as free and independent wage laborers. The conditions were, however, totally different. They could not have their daily drink at home with a meal. Instead, the workers had to go to a tavern after the working day. In the new context the old drinking norms could not be applied, and new ones were not available.

2. During 1878-1917, the total consumption of the rural population was 0.8 liters (of 50% spirits), whereas that of the industrial population was 5 liters. The industrial workers decreased their consumption dramatically in the beginning of the 20th century: from 7.9 liters in 1887-1900 to 2.6 in 1901-1917 (Turpeinen 1977, 59-60).

3. That is due to the doctrine the movement adopted in the 1860s, according to which the community of believers has "the keys to the kingdom of God." By that they meant that the members of the movement had the power to forgive a member's sins, or to make him or her do more repentance work (Raittila 1976; Suolinna 1969; Miettinen 1942).

4. The relation of *herännäisyys* to drinking reflected a change in public attitudes during the 19th century, and this ambiguity culminated in the person of Paavo Ruotsalainen, its charismatic leader (see Ruokanen 1989). Throughout his life, he preserved a habit of occasional, rather heavy drinking. In the beginning of the 19th century the movement was not that concerned about drinking, but the attitude changed in the middle of the century. The old leader's drinking was criticized increasingly, and it was tolerated only because of his unchallenged spiritual authority. The younger leaders of the movement, particularly Henrik Renqvist (1789-1866) were active also in the rising temperance movement. Reinforced by the influence of another movement, *lestadiolaisuus*, which fought strongly against drunkenness from the middle of the 19th century onward, all revivalist movements adopted the idea that wherever there are two or three gathered around glasses of beer or spirits, there is also the devil with them.

5. This means that the boys went on their night visits in one or more groups and visited several girls during the same trip. In going to the girls' sleeping quarters a formal endeavor ceremony was performed with its knocks, endeavor rhymes, and lines (Sarmela 1969, 155).

6. Kurikka had to resign from Työmies in 1899, but that was only partly due to his Tolstoyist thoughts, and it did not end the influence of Tolstoyism in the workers' movement, not even in Työmies (Nokkala 1958, 221, 224-25).

7. This often seems to be the only reason why temperance societies exist. Many of them operate under political parties, as their branches, and it is generally known that they are often "paper organizations," founded by the parties to

collect the subsidy they get from the state. That was one of the two main themes in criticism directed against the temperance movement in the press in 1984, studied by Kirsi (1989). The other theme was the bureaucratization of temperance work. By that the critics remarked that the activities, like publicity campaigns, are only due to the laws that govern temperance work. An increasing number of posts for particular "temperance secretaries" and for other temperance officials have been established in local communes, and municipal "temperance boards" were obligatory until 1989. Consequently, the organization of the special "temperance week" of 1984, studied by Kirsi and Piispa (1985) depended almost totally on the work of the municipal temperance officials: temperance societies organized their own events or were active in cooperation with the municipal sector only in less than a third of the local communes studied.

8. The public rather seems to be annoyed by the existence of temperance organizations, as far as public discussion in the press is concerned (see Piispa and Kirsi 1986). The temperance movement is argued to be meaningless or even harmful, and the tax revenue allotted to the organizations is claimed to be a national economic waste. The temperance activists defend themselves by remarking that the temperance movement is renewed, and that the public interest for temperate and healthy ways of life is growing.

9. Indeed, the object of temperance work has come to be defined more broadly in this respect. Until the 1950s the only intoxicant mentioned in the programs was alcohol. Drugs were added in the 1972 program, and tobacco in the 1983 program. And in addition to the "intoxicants policy program," the movement has, since the 1970s, had a separate social policy program and a cultural policy program (ibid., 15-16).

10. It was as early as 1951 that the World Health Organization recognized alcoholism as a disease, and the American Medical Association followed suit in 1956 (Room 1983). Since then, several other comparable individual problems have been given the status of a disease; in 1980, for instance, the American Psychiatric Association formally defined compulsive gambling as a disorder in impulse control (Rosecrance 1985).

11. In the Finnish (Lutheran) state church, the "secular" concept of person seems not to have emerged until after World War II, when one of its ministers, Erkki Niinivaara, strongly promoted a new conception of the relation of the church to *culture* (see Niskanen 1988). In his writings, Niinivaara came to oppose the Pietist alienation from life: "Unlike Pietist thought, Niinivaara did not take into account the badness, fall, and the reality of sin that works in the world" (ibid., 58). For him, *culture* was also God's creation, and from that viewpoint he promoted a kind of cultural optimism. Niinivaara's writings caused many heated debates, but in the end he was left quite alone in church circles,

still very much influenced by the revivalist movements.

12. Daniel Bell (1976) notes that the American hedonistic age, which is often associated with the 1960s generation, has in fact its roots in the Young Intellectuals' attack on petty bourgeois values, and can be seen as an extension of the hedonism of the 1950s. As in the Finnish case, he associates American hedonism with an opposition of prohibition, since it was the last major effort by small town and traditionalist forces to impose a specific value, the prohibition of liquor, on the rest of society.

13. In *Discipline and Punish* (1979) and in *Madness and Civilization* (1973) Michel Foucault talks about the same mechanism, about the way in which the loosening of external control and the strengthening of "disciplinary" techniques also leads to the disciplinary question of the normal and the abnormal.

CHAPTER 3

1. For more detailed reports of the case studies, consult Alasuutari and Siltari (1983) and Sulkunen, Alasuutari, Nätkin, and Kinnunen (1985, chapter 6) for the darts club ethnography. The study dealing with the storytellers of Katajanmarja is reported in Alasuutari (1985) and in Sulkunen, Alasuutari, Nätkin, and Kinnunen (1985, chapter 8).

2. This view is supported in a study of Finnish boozing, which was based on film material (see Falk and Sulkunen 1983).

3. For a more detailed discussion of these themes, see Alasuutari and Siltari 1983; Kortteinen 1982.

4. For instance Rosenzweig 1983; Stedman Jones 1983; Ames 1985; LeMasters 1975.

CHAPTER 4

1. The interviewees were asked to draw a continuous line depicting the ups and downs of their life, and then to explain them in an unstructured interview. The metal workers and the members of the A-guild were interviewed by myself and two research assistants, whereas the workers who had come to search for help with alcohol problems were interviewed by therapists at the beginning of therapy.

2. A-clinics, the first of which were established in 1954, are outpatient treatment units operating in most Finnish cities. There are altogether 39 A- clinics in the country (Immonen et al. 1980). Characteristic of A-clinics is that, while

treatment is based upon close cooperation between psychiatrists, social workers, physicians, and nurses, the work is guided by an explicitly nonmedical working philosophy concerning alcoholism (Bruun 1963; 1971).

3. In addition to the life story interviews, a group of alcoholics' wives was also interviewed by a female research assistant. These in-depth, unstructured interviews will be used as additional data in the last section of the chapter. For a more detailed, Finnish-language report of this study, see Alasuutari 1986b. An earlier version of this chapter was published in 1986 (see Alasuutari 1986a).

4. According to Pierre Bourdieu (1977), habitus is a generative principle, modus operandi, that is at the same time a system that generates perceptions and a system that generates practices.

5. There are, of course, exceptions, such as van Dijk 1980 and Chafe 1980.

6. The applying of Propp's method did not and could not, of course, mean a mechanical copying of it. As tape-recorded interviews, the data of this study was so different from that of Propp that it had to be treated in a special way suggested by studies in the ethnography of speech (Labov and Waletsky 1973; Labov 1972) before the analysis of narrative structures could be undertaken. The so-called free and restricted clauses that do not describe the development of the plot were separated from the text that was to be analyzed as a narrative. Their content and meaning will be discussed later, under the title "identity." But, whatever the adjustments in solving particular problems have been, the basic Proppian principles have been the methodological base of sociological studies dealing with narratives (see Wright 1973; Radway 1984; Alasuutari and Kytömäki 1986).

7. Propp (1975, 5) criticized sharply such classifications of folk tales: "The most common division is a division into tales with fantastic content, tales of everyday life, and animal tales. At first glance everything appears to be correct. But involuntarily the question arises, "Don't tales about animals sometimes contain elements of the fantastic to a very high degree?" And conversely, "Don't animals actually play a large role in fantastic tales?" Is it possible to consider such an indicator as sufficiently precise?"

8. The stories do include "flashbacks" in the sense that men sometimes return to a phase they already mentioned, but in such a case they make the phase clear in the chronological order of events they are referring to. The narrative analysis, then, deals with the expressed chronological order of events, not the literary form of the presentation.

9. Propp (1975), with a slightly different definition, called the component parts functions, while Dundes (1964) entitled them as motifs.

10. Chafe (1977) finds a similar structuring principle in the folk tales of Caddo Indians from his schema-theoretical point of view. They are composed of "scenes," much like scenes in a play. Interestingly, each scene appears to be organized according to the same schema. At the beginning of each scene there is someone on stage doing something. Then there is the arrival of a visitor, followed by a conversation between the visitor and the person already there. Then the host does something to or for the visitor, and finally the visitor leaves. The same schema "may even constitute the organizing principle for the chunking at a higher level—that is, for the story as a whole rather than for individual scenes within it" (Chafe 1977, 223). According to the explanation Chafe gives to this phenomenon, the Caddo, like other American Indian groups, have traditionally spent a great deal of their time visiting. As a familiar pattern of behavior it has found its way into tales.

11. For a similar interpretation of the Finnish culture, see Falk and Sulkunen (1983). A monograph consisting of ethnographic case studies dealing with these issues has also been published in the Finnish language (Sulkunen et al. 1985). For an article based on one of them, written in English, see Alasuutari 1985.

12. Gareth Stedman Jones, for example, talks about the remaking (referring to the first "making" studied by Thompson 1980, originally 1963) of the English working class in 1870-1900 in London. According to him, the shift from work-centered culture to a culture oriented toward the family and the home had to do with the growing separation between home and work place due to the vast migration of the skilled working class from the city to the suburbs. This happened simultaneously with an increase in both leisure time and earnings. As a consequence, at least the wives of skilled workers stayed at home. The home increasingly became the wife's sole domain, and the association of mother with home became increasingly axiomatic. The wife also became the decision-maker in all household expenditure (Stedman Jones 1983, 217-19.) In a similar vein, Roy Rosenzweig (1983) describes in his social history of the city of Worcester, Massachusetts, the emergence of the primarily male leisure space, the saloon. The fact that leisure, at the beginning of the 20th century more and more turned into a family occasion—picnics in the park, the movies, etc.—has not seemed to change the proper location of traditional drinking that belongs outside the family sphere. The results of the study by Haavio-Mannila and Holmila (1986) could be interpreted to show, in the Finnish case, that the emergent habit of companion drinking among spouses explains why new, "light" drinking habits seem to be additional to, rather than substitutional for, traditional heavy drinking (Mäkelä 1975, 350-53; 1978, 341).

13. Room (1985c; 1985b) has argued that cultural and structural changes, which tend to accompany industrialization and the mobilization of labor, increase the demand for sobriety and self-control, and in this way bring about

both the idea of addiction and the existential experience of loss of control.

14. In a similar vein Stedman Jones (1983, 217-19) explains the consequences of the wife becoming the decision-maker in household expenditure. In many households the husband was only entrusted with pocket money to be spent on fares, beer, tobacco, and a trade union or club subscription.

15. The data include also other clues. In any oral narrative, there are—in addition to the "narrative clauses" that make up the plot—the so-called evaluative clauses in which storytellers present their personal point of view on the events described in the plot. Even if one tells a story, a legend for example, one usually gives a motive for telling the particular story, and more or less comments on or evaluates the events of the story while telling it. Even the same story may have a different point, function, or morale, when told in different situations (Allen 1979; Murase 1975; Siikala 1984). The evaluative clauses reflect one's identity, the way one makes sense of and organizes one's everyday life in the perceived living conditions as expressed in the narrative structure of the story. The evaluative clauses can easily be identified by testing how the place of the clause is fixed in the story. The order of narrative clauses is totally fixed in the sense that changes in their order result in an unintelligible or different kind of plot. The evaluative clauses, instead, are "free" or "restricted" in nature. The place of free clauses can be freely changed, whereas the restricted clauses can be placed between certain narrative clauses without changing the original plot (Labov and Waletsky 1973; Labov 1972). As outlined above, the personal evaluations of the events told in a story are often embedded in the way the narrative events are told, in the choice of words, emphases, and phrases (Robinson 1981).

16. Particular items or habits, like drinking habits, do not of course only express one's view of life; the elements in a cultural relationship also influence and modify each other (Willis 1978, 201-3). Heavy-drinking habits, say, expressing one's view of life, lead a man into conflicts that sooner or later result in changes in his living conditions. They, in turn, make him adjust his way of making sense of the reality.

17. See, for example, Scott and Lyman (1968), who distinguish four modes of excuse and six modes of justification. The study of people's rationalizations for their behavior is indeed interesting in showing what mode of an account is regarded legitimate in a particular case, culture, or era (Room 1984b). But to explain why some acts require accounting and others do not, and why certain modes of accounts do while others do not, one has to study the collective subjectivity on which accounts are based and from which they derive their sense. From this perspective, the power of culture does not lie in the accounts; they are only clues to the underlying cultural structures and forms of identity.

18. The relations between the meaning of drinking, gender, and manual

labor are, in the case of Finnish blue-collar men, discussed in detail by Alasuutari (1986b). A similar structure of meanings, concerning English working-class cultural forms, is presented by Willis (1977) and Corrigan and Willis (1980). According to them, the specific articulation of the distinctions between male/female on the one hand, and mental/manual labor on the other, is of focal importance in explaining why Western class societies can exist in the free form of democracy. Should all people really try to get mental work, which is generally valued as superior to manual labor, the blue-collar population would be a real, disappointed, and dissatisfied lower caste. The social order would have to be secured at gunpoint. Those socialized into the working-class culture thereby reject mental work; according to Corrigan and Willis, this rejection is the main feature of working-class culture. Among blue-collar men this reversal of the dominant value system is achieved by associating manual labor with the social superiority of masculinity, and mental labor with the social inferiority of femininity.

19. Gusfield (1979) describes a similar kind of pride in an ethnographic study dealing with drunken driving. A norm of "competent" drinking prevails in the bars that were studied. It was not regarded as incompetent to limit one's drinking, to avoid driving, or to be drunk as long as the drinker can indicate that the determination of the state of incompetence is his self-recognition, that it is not forced upon him. From this perspective, paradoxically, the one who does not fall behind in drinking may regard himself as more competent to drive. Falling behind is taken as a sign that one is getting drunk.

20. This meaning of heavy drinking could be clearly seen in a case study I conducted, dealing with a group of regular customers in a suburban pub (Sulkunen et al. 1985, chapter 8). These men despised customers who just hastily dropped into the pub and left. Accordingly, a member of the group, leaving before the closing time, feels a need to explain why. Paradoxically, such an organization of everyday life presupposes the existence of outer controllers or limits. Often, a man might wonder what is wrong because his wife had not yet come to take him home.

21. In a similar vein to those life stories, such a medical model of alcoholism was reflected in AA-influenced movies analyzed by Room (1985a): the motivation for the characters' alcoholism and drinking remains obscure. The present study suggests why the motivation for alcoholism should remain mysterious, either in AA or in the everyday life of the men studied. In addition to excluding the guilt and blaming often connected with alcohol problems, it seems to offer a logical solution to the cognitive dissonance outlined above. The AA program, based on such a medical model, has proved to be a successful means of recovery. Paradoxically—at least in the case of the alcoholics studied here—the very solution creates much of the problem.

22. The question of reliability has to be posed—in my view—another way around: a "bias" could be shown by presenting a better, more consistent way of organizing the "clues" into a coherent interpretation. That is, by somehow falsifying the theoretical model presented here.

CHAPTER 5

1. Analytically, three levels of abstraction can be distinguished in this respect. First, "alcoholism" itself is a historical cultural construct (see Levine 1978b), a popular EM, based on the distinction between "normal" and "pathological" drinking, and to a large extent shared both by patients and healers in the West. Second, the explanatory models of alcoholism among different social groupings such as professionals and laymen are shared by individuals, or let us say that they are constructed in terms of the same dimensions of meaning. Third, there are the EMs of *individual* patients and practitioners involved in *particular* illness situations at a particular time. This chapter deals with a particular illness called alcoholism by analyzing individual accounts, but the emphasis is laid on the shared dimensions or maps of meaning as well as cultural logics in terms of which "alcoholism" is explained and dealt with. Therefore, the concept of explanatory model is here used to refer to this more abstract level as well (see Kleinman 1980:106).

2. The figures, dealing with the demographic structure of the clientele, are given only in percentages, not in absolute numbers. However, otherwise in the report it is announced that in 1984 the total number of clients was 9,488, and in 1985 it was 9,390. The tables presenting the demographic structure of the clientele by age and marital status did not allow cross-tabulation of these two variables.

3. During the years 1971-1985, the proportion of single clients was at its highest in 1973 at 32%, and at its lowest in 1978 at 28.3%. In 1985 the figure was 31.6 %. Though the proportion of single clients has risen during the early 1980s, it is possible that the figures do not reflect the actual situation, because cohabiting and common-law marriages have gained more popularity during the 1970s and 80s. The proportion of widows has not changed remarkably; it was 2% in 1971 and 1.9 % in 1985.

4. The baby boomers adopted a new pattern also regarding marital behavior. The greatest changes took place during 1966-74, the years when this generation reached the age of marriage. The amount of new marriages reached its peak at that time, and the amount of divorces rose rapidly. That is mainly because of the advanced economic independence of these women. At the same time, the number of women with families who worked outside the home

increased markedly. Whereas 42% of married women with children held jobs in 1960, by 1975 the figure had risen to 66% (Jallinoja 1980).

5. The annual reports of the A-clinic of Tampere 1975-1984. Note that the mean percentage is calculated as the mean of the yearly percentages, not as the percentage of manual workers and married clients of the total number of clients throughout the ten year period. In this way, the variation in the yearly number of clients does not have an effect on the figures that try to present the average yearly situation. In the outpatient clinic the number of clients reached its peak in 1977, when there were 1,967 clients. In the detoxification station, the peak of the ten year period was reached in 1976, when there were 775 clients. In the residential facility, the highest number of clients was reached both in 1975 and 1983, when there were 55 men. In 1984 the outpatient clinic had 1,239, the detoxification station 660, and the residential facility 54 clients. The female clients are a minority in the A-clinic. The residential facility does not have female clients at all, whereas the proportion of women has been around 10% in the outpatient clinic and the detoxification station.

6. Max Weber (1971) for example made the petit bourgeoisie the classic example of "workaholics."

7. The occupations of the men were a construction worker, a farmer, a porter, and a retired entrepreneur. Two of the women were presently working outside the home, one as a nurse and another as a secretary, whereas one had retired from their family firm just like her husband, and one worked on the family farm beside her husband.

8. According to Toivonen (1988, 82), the proportion of white-collar workers has risen from 8% in 1930 to 46% in 1985. According to Kortteinen (1985), who classifies jobs into those in primary production, industrial sector, information sector, services, and other work, calculated that by 1980 "information work" had become the largest sector. Its proportion of all occupations was 15% in 1960, 21.8% in 1970, and 30.5% in 1980 (ibid., 88). He characterizes information as mental rather than manual.

CHAPTER 6

1. Kaihovaara 1986. In the light of these figures, it seems that the A-guilds are a slightly but not a remarkably smaller institution than AA. According to Kalervo (1986), in 1985 there were almost 500 AA groups in 180 towns, and the total number of active members was approximately 8,000.

2. In Finland coffee did not replace spirits as a substance generally used in daily life until the latter half of the 19th century (Roberts 1982; Kuusanmäki 1954).

CHAPTER 7

1. Psychological theories maintain that alcoholism is only a secondary disease or a symptom of a "personality disorder" or of an "alcoholic personality" (see Cox 1985). For learning theorists, the abnormality does not reside in the drinkers' defected capacities for learning or unlearning, but in what they have learned; that they have repeatedly engaged in conduct that has harmful or antisocial consequences (see Marlatt and Donovan 1982). The family systems theorists do not even locate the pathology or "dysfunctioning" in the "identified patient," but in the family system (Hoffman 1981). But nonetheless, the distinction between normal and abnormal is a prevalent characteristic of Western views of unacceptable drinking. And as an individual's behavior is deemed abnormal, it is interpreted in terms of a framework that differs from the everyday-life frame. However, this does not mean that the alcoholism frame would be totally apart from the cultural structures of everyday life in the modern world. After all, it is generally used as a means of making sense of drinking problems. It is so prevalent precisely because in the case of recurrent unacceptable drinking it makes more sense than the frame that renders ordinary drinking occasions intelligible. Both the everyday-life frame and the alcoholism frame are rooted in the social and cultural forms of Western societies.

2. In this instance, Bryan Turner (1986) talks about *individuation*, the bureaucratic practices and disciplines which individuate citizens for purposes of exact taxation, social regimentation, and political surveillance. He argues that bureaucratic individuation, brought about by the growth of universal citizenship, undermines the relevance of particularistic features of individuals: "One effect of the spread of universalistic standards of citizenship has been the erosion of ascriptive categorizations of persons. Gender, age and ethnicity become increasingly irrelevant for the continuity of capitalist production" (ibid., 13).

3. The modern system of name-giving is admittedly different. There are no strict rules for name-giving, even if one has to admit that, for instance, there is a statistical relationship between first names and different generations of children. A modern person's first name is one of the "values" he or she gets in the scale of "first names." However, a modem person's last name or surname still reflects the old system—described by Mauss—where a person is known for his or her relative rank in a predefined and stable social structure. Yet the modern notion of abstract person would be hostile to all evidence which shows that a person's opportunities are affected by his or her name.

4. It has even been argued that the era of an inner-directed bourgeois personality is over. Neumann (1970) argues that in this century, evidenced by a new type of autobiography, the independent individual is lost for the time being. The new biographies do not include a consistent story line or reflect on

the development of a personality; they consist of a repertoire of social roles. According to his interpretation, this is due to late-capitalist development (ibid., 186). This line of thought treats life stories as one-to-one reflections of real personality types, as pictures of individuals' inner world. The fact that late modern autobiographies are not necessarily organized by a logical and chronological story line is interpreted as proof of a disintegration of the subject. However, if one analyzes the changing genre of autobiographies as stories told by individual authors, the interpretation does not sound very well-founded. Instead, it could be argued that the authors are increasingly aware of the literary tradition of autobiographies. In a modernist spirit, they refuse to write their own story, and thus express their identity and personality, by using the same narrative structure already used by so many authors that it has become a recognizable, conventional literary genre. By breaking the confines of the already conventionalized genre they want to underline their uniqueness. In that sense such new types of autobiographies could be argued to reflect the ever-more self-reflective nature of (post)modern individuals. This development is at once a sign of a "postmodernist" loss of confidence in the grand narratives Lyotard (1984) talks about, and a continuation of the Christian tradition of soul-searching. By rejecting the conventional formula of life stories, the authors want to deny their mediocrity as individuals, to assert that their "true self" cannot be conveyed by describing it in a way that has proved to be a recognizable narrative form. There is an underlying belief that one's "authentic self" must be found outside or beyond language, but on the other hand modern individuals are haunted by a gnawing feeling that personalities are just narrative constructs.

CHAPTER 8

1. In a review of drinking and drunkenness in transcultural perspective, Heath (1986) notes: "A major finding, in cross-cultural perspective, is that alcohol-related problems are really rare, even in many societies where drinking is customary and drunkenness is commonplace."

2. However, one has to bear in mind that both in the "moral model" and in the "medical model" the cause of problems is thought to be found in the "identified patient." In other words, both models treat heavy drinking as an individual problem. When placing the moral model in a sorry past, the proponents of the medical model miss the point that the moral element in premodern thinking dealt mainly with public morals and communal values rather than immorality of individual subjects. The moral doom of the Finnish workers' temperance movement was, for instance, laid on other classes or the social and political system as a whole, not on the victims. In other words, the main dimension of historical changes regarding views of health and illness is, I suggest,

communal vs. individual rather than moral vs. medical. The kind of moral model often opposed to the medical one is, in fact, a modern construct, a reconstruction of the past that serves as a label in disapproving of the dark side of modern medical and therapeutic practice, as the findings of Tournier's (1985) survey in fact show. The uneasy union of moral and medical elements in modern therapeutic practice is embedded in the individualist worldview that underlies it.

3. It is for this reason, I suggest, that the middle class is more apt to conceive of alcohol problems as a disease. According to Rodin's (1981) study, the modal group subscribing to AA as the best treatment model tended to be higher in social class and to endorse the disease model in its entirety more strongly than other groups.

4. This was one of the main slogans of Alcoholics Anonymous, the self-help organization that greatly contributed to establishing the disease concept of alcoholism in American society. According to Room (1985a) this overall premise of the AA was neatly attuned to general concerns and experiences of its creators, the American middle-class "wet generation" that came of age by the early 1920s. Since alcohol and drinking had in their youth become symbols of their revolt "against the shibboleths of Victorian morality," they could not blame the bottle for the hardships many of them were to face. However, the success of the medical model as the one employed in explaining an increasing number of various "dis-eases" needs to be accounted for on a more general level.

5. Farber (1987) in fact notes that the normal/pathological dichotomy is essentially a religious concept; the notion of pathology is based on the inference that there has been a breach of the natural (God-given) order. He also claims that mental illness is, as a concept, a secularized variant of the myth of the Fall.

6. According to a nationwide survey of U.S. state hospitals carried out in 1966, AA was used as a primary therapy instrument in 88% of the institutions surveyed, and as a follow-up modality in 82% (Tournier 1979, 231).

CHAPTER 9

1. Though it is true that society or a social group imposes certain norms, or regulative rules, on individuals, who may then behave in accordance with the norms, it is important to note that people follow certain culture-bound rules also when there are no norms involved, or when the norms are broken. When I, for instance, follow the linguistic rules of English to say what I want to say, I am not following regulative but rather constitutive rules, which give meaning to my sentences.

2. Simultaneously, there is an interesting shift in the location of the "ego." While the people in the Middle Ages seemed to be familiar with their wants, and unaccustomed to forcing themselves to do anything, from the sixteenth century onwards the position begins to get reversed. Take, for example, Emanuel Le Roy Ladurie's (1979) study of Montaillou, a French village at the turn of the thirteenth and fourteenth centuries. Among the peasants, the notion of self-discipline was hardly known. Even though they appreciated living on their own work, they worked only as much as was needed to survive. If something more interesting happened, the work could be interrupted for weeks. The peasants' conception of sin was in concert with their relation to work. If, say, prostitution or an extramarital relation attracted both parties, it was conceived as innocent. As soon as it became unpleasant, it was understood to become a sin. The later Protestant notion of sin was quite the opposite. Especially in Calvinism, everything sensual and emotional was prohibited as sinful; not only sexuality—which was accepted only if its function was to multiply—but all diversions and even an interest in high culture were suspect. Work was conceived as a profane form of sacred devotions (Weber 1971).

3. Initially, notions of personality and tensions between individuals' self-discipline and desires were conceived of as religious questions, and questions of moral conduct. Heavy drinking, for instance, was not perceived as a sign of a disease or a "loss of control;" it was condemned as immoral behavior, as a sin. But from early on, Christian asceticism also included the idea that certain behaviors, especially pleasures, represent *nature* in the individual, and that is why they have to be overcome, controlled by *reason*. According to Weber (1971: 118-19), Western monasticism had, in the rules of St. Benedict, with the monks of Cluny, again with the Cistercians, and most strongly the Jesuits, become emancipated from otherworldliness and self-torture:

> It had developed a systematic method of rational conduct with the purpose of overcoming the *status naturae*, to free man from the power of irrational impulses and his dependence on the world and on nature. It attempted to subject man to the supremacy of a purposeful will, to bring his actions under constant self-control with a careful consideration of their ethical consequences.

Originally the term *personality* only referred to those who were able to control their urges and impulses (Weber 1971, 119). However, nowadays the term is usually used in another meaning; it is thought that everybody has a personality, the only question is, what is it like. In other words, *personality* is one of the scales by which an individual is identified. One of the factors we refer to in that concept is the particular way in which individuals keep their urges in

Notes   195

check, or the way in which they have modified them. This is especially true of personality theories with a Freudian influence. Cattell (1950), for example, conceives of personality as a system composed of an individual's "ergic level," comprising basic instincts or needs, and his or her "sentiment level" and "attitude level."

BIBLIOGRAPHY

Aalto, Eeva
   Päihdeongelmaisen hoidosta [About the treatment of a person with drug problems]. 1976. *Tiimi* (no volume number) no. 1:14-19.

A-klinikkasäätiön toimintakertomus 1985
   [The annual rept of the activities of the A-clinic foundation]. 1985. Helsinki: A-klinikkasäätiö.

Alapuro, Risto
   Uskonto ja poliittinen mobilisoituminen maaseudulla [Religion and political mobilization in the countryside]. 1977. Matti Kussi, Risto Alapuro, and Matti Klinge (eds.): *Maailmankuvan muutos tutkimuskohteena* [The changing worldview as the object of research]. Helsinki: Otava. Pp. 121-47.

Alapuro, Risto, and Henrik Stenius
   Kansanliikkeet loivat kansakunnan [The social movements created the nation]. (*Kansa liikkeessä* [The folk in movement]. 1987. Risto Alapuro, Ilkka Liikanen, Kerstin Smeds, and Henrik Stenius (eds.). Helsinki: Kirjayhtymä. Pp. 7-49.

Alasuutari, Pertti
   The Male Suburban Pub-Goer and the Meaning Structure of Drinking. 1985. *Acta Sociologica* 28, 87-97.

———.
   Alcoholism in Its Cultural Context: The Case of Blue-collar Men. 1986a. *Contemporary Drug Problems* 13, 641-86.

———.
   Työmiehen elämäntarina ja alkoholismi. Tutkimus alcoholismin suhteesta emokulttuuriin [The male worker's life-story and alcoholism. A study on

197

the relation of alcoholism to the parent culture]. 1986b. Department of Sociology and Social Psychology, University of Tampere, Finland, Ser. A no. 9.

———.

Erinomaista, rakas Watson. Johdatus yhteiskuntatutkimukseen [Elementary, dear Watson. An introduction to social research]. 1989a. Helsinki: Hanki ja Jää.

———.

Kvalitatiivinen analyysi kulttuurisen kieliopin etsimisenä [Qualitative analysis as a search for a cultural grammar]. 1989b. *Sosiologia* 26, 267-76.

Alasuutari, Pertti, and Jorma Siltari
Miehisen vapauden valtakunta [The realm of male freedom]. 1983. University of Tampere, Research Institute for Social Sciences, Publications, ser. B 37.

Alasuutari, Pertti, and Juha Kytomäki
Pahuus on tappava bumerangi. Vanha Kettu—televisiosarjan maailmankuva ja juonirakenne [Badness is a deadly boomerang. The worldview and narrative structure of the television seris "Der Alte"]. 1986. *Kymmenen esseetä elämäntavasta* [Ten essays on the way of life]. Kalle Heikkinen (ed.). Lahti: Oy Yleisradio Ab, 139-50.

Allen, Barbara
The Personal Point of View in Orally Communicated History. 1979. *Western Folklore* 38, 110-18.

Ames, Genevieve
American Believes about Alcoholism: Historical Perspectives on the Medical-moral Controversy. 1985. *The American Experience with Alcohol. Contrasting Cultural Perspectives.* Linda A. Bennett and Genevieve M. Ames (eds.). New York: Plenum Press. Pp. 23-40.

Ames, Genevieve M., and Craig R. Janes
Heavy and Problem Drinking in an American Blue-Collar Population: Implications for Prevention. 1987. *Social Science and Medicine* 25 (8), 949-60.

Anonymous
Kahviko korviketta—ei kai? [Coffee, a substitute?—never . . .] *Vesiposti.* 1985. no. 3, 30-31.

Beaugrande, Robert
Text, Discourse and Process. 1980. Toward a Multidisciplinary Science of Texts. London.

Bell, Daniel
    The Cultural Contradictions of Capitalism. 1976. London: Heinemann.

Bell, Susan E.
    "Changing Ideas: The Medicalization of Menopause." 1987. *Social Science and Medicine* 24, 535-42.

Blumberg, Leonard
    The Ideology of a Therapeutic Movement: Alcoholics Anonymous. 1977. *Journal of Studies on Alcohol* 38, 2122-43.

Bourdieu, Pierre
    Outline of a Theory of Practice. 1977. Cambridge: University Press.

Bowen, Murray
    Alcoholism as Viewed through Family Systems Theory and Family Psychotherapy. 1974. *Annals New York Academy of Sciences.*

Brémond, Claude
    Morphology of the French Folktale. 1970. *Semiotica* vol. 2, no. 2, 247-76.

Bruun, Kettil
    Outcome of Different Types of Treatment of Alcoholics. 1963. *Quarterly Journal of Studies on Alcohol* vol. 24, no. 2, 280-88.

————.

    Finland: The Non-Medical Approach. 1971. In Kiloh, L. G., and D. S. Bell (eds.) *Alcoholism and Drug Dependence:* 29th International Congress. Sydney: Butterworths. Pp. 545-59.

Calnan, Michael
    Women and Medicalisation: An Empirical Examination of the Extent of Women's Dependence on Medical Technology in the Early Detection of Breast Cancer. 1984. *Social Science and Medicine* 18, 561-69.

Campbell, Colin
    The Romantic Ethic and the Spirit of Modern Consumerism. 1987. Oxford: Basil Blackwell.

Casswell, Sally, and Alistair Gordon
    Drinking and Occupational Status in New Zealand Men. 1984. *Journal of Studies on Alcohol* vol. 45, no. 2, 144-48.

Cattell, Raymond B.
    An Introduction to Personality Study. 1950. London: Hutchinson's University Library.

Chafe, Wallace L.
    The Recall and Verbalization of Past Experience. 1977. *Current Issues in*

Linguistic Theory. Roger W. Cole (ed.). Bloomington and London. Pp. 215-46.

Chafe, Wallace L. (ed.)
The Pear Stories. Cognitive, Cultural, and Linguistic Aspects of Narrative Production. 1980. Norwood: ABLEX Publishing Corporation.

Clarke, John, and Tony Jefferson
The Politics of Popular Culture: Culture and Sub-Culture. 1973. University of Birmingham, Centre for Contemporary Cultural Studies, Stencilled Occasional Paper no. 14.

Conrad, Peter
The Discovery of Hyperkinesis: Notes on the Medicalization of Deviant Behavior. 1975. *Social Problems* 23:12-21.

Conrad, Peter, and Joseph W. Schneider
Deviance and Medicalization. From Badness to Sickness. 1980. St. Louis: C. V. Mosby Company.

Corrigan, Philip, and Paul Willis
Cultural Forms and Class Mediations. 1980. *Media, Culture and Society* 2, 297-312.

Cox, W. Miles
Personality Correlates of Substance Abuse. 1985. In Mark Galizio and Stephen A. Maisto, *Determinants of Substance Abuse: Biological, Psychological, and Environmental Factors*. New York: Plenum Press. Pp. 209-46.

van Daalen, R.
The Start of Infant Health Care in Amsterdam: Medicalization and the Role of the State. 1985. *The Netherlands' Journal of Sociology* 21, 126-39.

Davis, Donald, et al.
The Adaptive Consequences of Drinking. 1974. *Psychiatry* 37:209-15.

Delany, Paul
British Autobiography in the Seventeenth Century. 1969. London: Routledge & Kegan Paul.

Deleuze, Gilles and Felix Guattari
Anti-Oedipus. Capitalism and Schizophrenia. 1977. New York: Viking Press.

Denzin, Norman K.
Interpretive Interactionism and the Use of Life Stories. 1986. *Revista Internacional de Sociologia*, volumen 33, fasciculo 3, 321-37.

————.

The Alcoholic Self. 1987a. California: Sage, Sociological Observations vol. 18.

————.

The Recovering Alcoholic. 1987b. California: Sage, Sociological Observations vol. 19.

van Dijk, Teun A.
Macrostructures. An Interdisciplinary Study of Global Discourse, Interaction, and Cognition. 1980. Hillsdale, N.J.: Lawrence Erlbaum Associates.

Dobkin de Rios, Marlene
Visionary Vine. Hallucinogenic Healing in the Peruvian Amazon. 1972. Prospect Heights, Ill.: Waveland Press.

Dundes, Alan
The Morphology of North American Indian Folktales. 1964. Helsinki: FF Communications no. 195.

Elias, Norbert
The History of Manners. The Civilizing Process: Volume I. 1978. New York: Pantheon Books.

————.

Power and Civility. The Civilizing Process: Volume II. 1982. New York: Pantheon Books.

Eskola, Antti
Persoonallisuustyypeistä elämäntapaan. Persoonallisuuden tutkimuksen metodologisia opetuksia [From personality types to way of life. Methodological lessons of personality research]. 1985. Juva: WSOY.

Falk, Pasi, and Pekka Sulkunen
Drinking on the Screen. An Analysis of a Mythical Male Fantasy in Finnish Films. 1983. *Social Science Information* vol. 22, no. 3, 387-410.

Farber, Seth
"Transcending Medicalism; An Evolutionary Alternative." 1987. *The Journal of Mind and Behavior* 8, 105-32.

Foucault, Michel
Madness and Civilization. A History of Insanity in the Age of Reason. 1973. New York: Vintage Books.

————.

Discipline and Punish. The Birth of the Prison. 1979. New York: Vintage Books.

———.
The History of Sexuality. Volume I: An Introduction. 1980. New York: Vintage Books.

———.
The Use of Pleasure. Volume 2 of The History of Sexuality. 1986. New York: Viking.

Freud, Sigmund
Civilization and Its Discontents. *The Standard Edition of the Complete Psychological Works of Sigmund Freud,* vol. 21. London: 1978. Hogarth Press. Pp. 57-146.

Galliher, John F., and Cheryl Tyree
"Edwin Sutherland's Research on the Origins of Sexual Psychopath Laws: An Early Study of the Medicalization of Deviance." 1985. *Social Problems* 33, 100-113.

Geertz, Clifford
The Interpretation of Cultures. 1973. New York: Basic Books.

Gergen, Mary, and Kenneth Gergen
The Social Construction of Narrative Accounts. 1984. *Historical Social Psychology.* Kenneth J. Gergen and Mary M. Gergen (eds.). Hillsdale, N.J.: Lawrence Erlbaum Associates. Pp. 173-89.

Giddens, Anthony
The Constitution of Society. 1984. Outline of the Theory of Structuration. Cambridge: Polity Press.

Goffman, Erving
Frame Analysis. An Essay on the Organization of Experience. 1974. Cambridge: Harvard University Press.

Gordon, Andrew J.
The Cultural Context of Drinking and Indigenous Treatment for Alcohol Problems in Three Migrant Hispanic Cultures. 1981. *Journal of Studies on Alcohol* Suppl. no. 9:217-40.

Gusfield, Joseph R. (assisted by Joseph Kotarba and Paul Rasmussen)
The World of Drinking-Driving. A Report to the National Science Foundation Law and Society Program. Part One: Managing Competence: The Ethnography of Bars in the Drinking-Driving Context. 1979. Manuscript.

Haavio-Mannila, Elina, and Marja Holmila
Juomiskumppanuus ja juomisen rajoittaminen perhesuhteiden ilmaisijana [Drinking companionship and the controlling of drinking as indi-

cators of conjugal relations]. 1986. *Sosiologia* 23: 117-26.

Hall, Roberta L.
Alcohol Treatment in American Indian Populations: An Indigenous Treatment Modality Compared with Traditional Approaches. 1986. In Thomas F. Babor (ed.), *Alcohol and Culture: Comparative Perspectives from Europe and America*. New York: Annals of New York Academy of Sciences, vol. 472:168-78.

Hästesko, F. A.
Suomen nuorisoseuraliikkeen historia. 1931. Helsinki.

Hauge, Ragnar, and Olav Irgens-Jensen
Alkohol i Norden. 1987. Helsingfors: Alko & NAD.

Heath, Dwight B.
Drinking and Drunkenness in Transcultural Perspective. 1986. *Transcultural Psychiatric Research Review* 23: 7-42 (Part I); 103-26 (Part II).

Helman, Cecil
Culture, Health and Illness: An Introduction for Health Professionals. 1984. Bristol: John Wright & Sons Ltd.

Hill, Christopher
The Century of Revolution: 1603-1741. 1980. Surrey: Nelson.

Hoffman, Lynn
Foundations of Family Therapy: A Conceptual Framework for Systems Change. 1981. New York: Basic Books.

Immonen, Erkki J., Lasse Murto, Sisko Pajunen, and Ingalill Österberg
A-klinikkasäätiö 1955-1980 [The foundation of A-clinics 1955-1980]. 1980. Kouvola.

Jackson, Don
The Question of Family Homeostasis. 1957. *Psychiatric Quarterly* Supplement 31:79.

Jallinoja, Riitta
Miehet ja naiset [Men and women]. In Valkonen et al. *Suomalaiset, Yhteiskunnan rakenne teollistumisen aikana* [The Finns, the structure of society during industrialization]. 1980. Juva: WSOY.

Jellinek, E. M.
The Disease Concept of Alcoholism. 1960. New Haven: College and University Press.

Jilek-Aal, Louise
Acculturation, Alcoholism and Indian-Style Alcoholics Anonymous. 1981.

Journal of Studies on Alcohol Suppl. no. 9:143-58.

Joe, V. C.
Review of the Internal-External Control Construct as a Personality Variable. 1971. *Psychological Reports* 28, 619-40.

Kaihovaara, Kyösti
A-kiltatoiminnasta apua alkoholiongelmiin [The A-guild activities help you in alcohol problems]. 1986. *Sinua tarvitaan. Vapaaehtoistoiminnan vuosikirja 1984-1985* [You are needed. A yearbook of voluntary activities 1984-1985]. Helsinki: Sosiaaliturvan keskusliitto. Pp. 74-79.

Kalervo
Yhteistyökumppanina AA [AA as a parner in cooperation]. 1986. *Sinua tarvitaan. Vapaaehtoistoiminnan vuosikirja 1984-1985* [You are needed. A yearbook of voluntary activities 1984-1985]. Helsinki: Sosiaaliturvan keskusliitto. Pp. 85-89.

Kallio, Tarja
Alkoholin käytön hallittavuuden käsitys. Alkoholiongelmaisten laitoshoitojakson aikana tapahtuvan muutoksen tarkastelua [Drinking-related locus of control-mittarilla. The concept of drinking control. An investigation of the change during an impatient treatment period as measured by the drinking-related locus of control test]. 1989. Terveydenhuollon pro gradu—tutkielma [unpublished master's thesis in health care]. Helsingin yliopisto, Yleislääketieteen laitos.

Katz, Janet, and Charles F. Abel
The Medicalization of Repression: Eugenics and Crime. 1984. *Contemporary Crises* 8, 227-41.

Kirsi, Tapio
Mitä on tämän päivän raittiuslaate? [What is the temperance ideology of today?]. 1988. *Alkoholipolitiikka* 53, 52-54.

————.
Raittiustyön arkea, päihdehuollon juhlaa ja raittiusliikkeen krapula. Tutkimus viikko—ja aikakauslehdistön raittius—ja päihdekirjoittelusta vuonna 1984 [Everyday temperance work, feast of intoxicant services, and hangover of the temperance movement. A study of the writings of weeklies and periodicals dealing with temperance and intoxicants in 1984]. 1989. Tampere: Ukk-instituutti.

Kirsi, Tapio, and Matti Piispa
Selvä peli. Tutkimus raittiusviikon toteuttamisesta [Fair play. A study of the arrangement of the temperance week]. 1985. Vammala: Suomen Raittiusjärjestöjen Liitto.

Klee, Linnea, and Genevieve Ames
Reevaluating Risk Factors for Women's Drinking: A Study of Blue Collar Wives. 1986. Manuscript.

Kleinman, Arthur
Patients and Healers in the Context of Culture. 1980. Berkeley: University of California Press.

Kortteinen, Matti
Lähiö. Tutkimus elämäntapojen muutoksesta [The suburb. A study of the ways of life in transition]. 1982. Helsinki: Otava.

————.
Turhapuro-syndrooma [The Turhapuro syndrome]. 1983. *Alkoholipolitiikka* 48, 60-67.

————.
Uusi yhteiskuntamuoto? [A new form of society?]. 1985. *Sosiologia* 22 (2), 87-105.

Koski-Jännes, Anja, and Jan Johansson
Drinking after Treatment and the Externalization of Control among Finnish Alcoholics. 1989. Paper presented at the 15th Annual Alcohol Epidemiology Symposium in Maastricht, Netherlands, 11-17 June.

Kunitz, Stephen J., and Jerrol E. Levy
Changing Ideas of Alcohol Use among Navaho Indians. *Quarterly Journal of Studies on Alcohol.* 1974. 35:243-59.

Kurtz, Ernest
Not-God. A History of Alcoholics Anonymous. 1979. Center City, Minn.: Hazelden Educational Services.

Kurz, Demie
"Emergency Department Responses to Battered Women: Resistance to Medicalization." 1987. *Social Problems* 34, 69-81.

Kuusanmäki, L.
Elämänmenoa entisaikaan [The way of life in the past]. 1954. Porvoo: WSOY.

Labov, William
Language in the Inner City. Studies in the Black English Vernacular. 1972. Philadelphia: University of Pennsylvania Press.

Labov, William, and Joshua Waletzky
Narrative Analysis: Oral Versions of Personal Experience. 1973. *Essays on the Verbal and Visual Arts.* J. Helm (ed.). San Francisco: American Ethnological Society.

LeMasters, E. E.
    Blue-Collar Aristocrats. Life-Styles at a Working-Class Tavern. 1975. Madison: Wisconsin University Press.

Le Roy Ladurie, Emanuel
    Montaillou, The Promised Land of Error. 1979. New York: Vintage Books.

Lender, Mark Edward, and Karen R. Karnchanapee
    'Temperance Tales'; Antiliquour Fiction and American Attitudes toward Alcoholics in the Late 19th and Early 20th Centuries. 1977. *Journal of Studies on Alcohol* 38, 1347-70.

Lévi-Strauss, Claude
    The Savage Mind. 1966. London: Weidenfeld and Nicholson.

——.
    Structural Anthropology. 1969. London: Allen Lane the Penguin Press.

Levine, Harry Gene
    Demon of the Middle Class: Self-Control, Liquor and the Ideology of Temperance in 19th-Century America. 1978a. Ph.D. dissertation. Berkeley: University of California, Department of Sociology.

——.
    The Discovery of Addiction: Changing Conceptions of Habitual Drunkenness in America. 1978b. *Journal of Studies in Alcohol*, vol. 39, no. 1, 143-74.

——.
    Temperance and Women in 19th-Century United States. 1980. Kalant, Oriana Josseau (ed.): Alcohol and Drug Problems in Women. *Research Advances in Alcohol and Drug Problems*, vol. 5. New York: Plenum Press.

——.
    The Alcohol Problem in America: From Temperance to Alcoholism. 1984. *British Journal of Addiction* 79, 109-19.

——.
    Temperance Cultures: Alcohol as a Symbol in Anglo and Nordic Societies. 1990c. Paper presented at the Society for the Study of Addiction seminar on "Substance Misuse—What Makes Problems." Windsor, Great Park, England, April 25-27.

Lyotard, Jean-François
    The Postmodern Condition. 1984. Manchester: Manchester University Press.

Mäkelä, Klaus
    Consumption Level and Cultural Drinking Patterns as Determinants of

Alcohol Problems. 1975. *Journal of Drug Issues* vol. 5, no. 4, 344-57.

———.

Alkoholipoliittisen mielipideilmaston vaihtelut Suomessa 1960—ja 1970—luvulla [Fluctuations in the climate of opinion concerning alcohol control measures in Finland in the 60s and 70s]. 1976. Helsinki: Reports from the Social Research Institute of Alcohol Studies 98.

———.

Level of Consumption and Social Consequences of Drinking. 1978. Yedi Israel et al. (eds.), *Research Advances in Alcohol and Drug Problems* vol. 4, New York: Plenum. Pp. 303-48.

Malinowski, Bronislaw
Argonauts of the Western Pacific. 1961. New York: E. P. Dutton.

Mandler, Jean Matter
Stories, Scripts, and Scenes: Aspects of Schema Theory. 1984. Hillsdale, N.J.: Lawrence Erlbaum Associates.

Mäntylä, Ilkka
Suomalaisen juoppouden juuret. Viinanpoltto vapaudenaikana [The roots of Finnish drunkenness. The distillation of spirits in the era of liberalism]. 1985. Helsinki: Suomalaisen kirjallisuuden seura.

Marlatt, G. Alan, and D. M. Donovan
Behavioral Psychology Approaches to Alcoholism. 1982. E. M. Pattison and E. Kaufman (eds.): *Encyclopedic Handbook of Alcoholism.* New York: Gardner Press.

Mauss, Marcel
A Category of the Human Mind: The Notion of Person, the Notion of "Self." 1979. *Sociology and Psychology. Essays.* London: Routledge & Kegan Paul. Pp. 57-94.

Maxwell, Milton A.
The Washingtonian Movement. 1950. *Quarterly Journal of Studies on Alcohol* vol. 11, no. 3, 410-51.

———.

"Alcoholics Anonymous: An Interpretation." 1962. Pittman, David J., and Charles R. Snyder (eds.), *Society, Culture, and Drinking Patterns.* New York: John Wiley & Sons.

Merton, Robert K.
The Sociology of Science, Theoretical and Empirical Investigations. 1973. Chicago: University of Chicago Press.

Miettinen, Martti E.
    Lestadiolainen heräysliike. I, Perustajan aika [The leastadian revivalist move-
    ment. I, The time of the founder]. 1942. Helsinki: Otava.

Misch, Georg
    Geschichte der Autobiografie, I-IV. 1969. Frankfurt am Main: Verlag G.
    Schulte-Bulmke.

Murase, Anne
    Personality and Lore. 1975. *Western Folklore* 34:3, 171-85.

Neumann, Berndt
    Identität und Rollenzwang. Zur Theorie der Autobiographie. 1970. Frankfurt:
    Atheneum Verlag.

Niemelä, Jorma
    Uskonnolliset tekijät alkoholismin syissä ja hoidossa II [Religious factors
    in the causes and treatment of alcoholism, II]. 1983. *Alkoholipolitiikka* 48,
    337-42.

Niskanen, Hannu
    Erkki Niinivaaran avautuminen kulttuurikysymyksiin 1944-1952 [Erkki
    Niinivaara's interest in cultural questions 1944-1952]. 1988. Kurten, Tage:
    Kirkko Suomalaisessa kulttuurissa [The church in Finnish culture]. Kirkon
    tutkimuskeskus, sarja A no. 49, pp. 54-63.

Nokkala, Armo
    Tolstoilaisuus Suomessa. Aatehistoriallinen tutkimus [Tolstoyism in Finland.
    A study in the history of ideas]. 1958. Helsinki: Tammi.

Notkola, Irma
    *Luonnollisesta hedelmällisyydestä lapsirajoitukseen. Mikrodemografinen
    tutkimus hedelmällisyyden transitiosta* [From natural fertility to family
    limitation. A family reconstitution study of fertility transition in Fin-
    land]. 1989. Publications of the Finnish Demographic Society no. 12,
    Kuopio.

Numminen, Jaakko
    Suomen Nuorisoseuraliikkeen historia I. Vuodet 1881-1905 [The history of
    Finnish youth societies movement. The years 1881-1905]. 1961. Helsinki:
    Otava.

O'Donovan, Katherine
    The Medicalisation of Infanticide. 1984. *Criminal Law Review*, 259-64.

Öjesjö, Leif
    An Epidemiological Investigation in a Total Population; The Lundby Study.

1983. Lundi Institutionen for Social- och Rättpsykiatri, Lunds Universitet [Institute for Social and Juridical Psychiatry, Lund University].

Österberg, Dag
    Metasociology. An Inquiry into the Origins and Validity of Social Thought. 1988. Oslo: Norwegian University Press.

Pascarosa, Paul, and Sanford Futterman
    Ethnopsychedelic Treatment for Alcoholics: Observations in the Peyote Ritual of the Native American Church. 1976. *Journal of Psychedelic Drugs* 8:215-21.

Piispa, Matti
    Alkoholiliberalismin suuri linja [The trend in alcohol liberalism]. 1990. *Alkoholipolitiikka* 55:6, 277-83.

Piispa, Matti, and Tapio Kirsi
    Raittiustyön muodot ja merkitykset. Tutkimus lehdistön raittiuskirjoittelusta [The forms and meanings of temperance work. A study on the press writings dealing with temperance]. 1986. Vammala: Tampereen yliopisto, Yhteiskuntatieteiden tutkimuslaitos.

Prince, Gerald
    A Grammar of Stories. 1973. Belgium: Mouton.

Propp, Vladimir
    Morphology of the Folktale. 1975. Austin and London: University of Texas Press.

Radway, Janice A.
    Reading the Romance. Women, Patriarchy, and Popular Literature. 1984. Chapel Hill: University of North Carolina Press.

Raittila, Pekka
    Lestadiolaisuus 1860—luvulla. [The leastadian movement in the 1960s]. 1976. Helsinki: Akateeminen Kustannusliike.

Raivio, Ahti
    Säkeniä itsekasvatustyön ahjosta [Sparkles from the center of self-education]. 1975. Kokkola: Keski-Pohjanmaan kirjapaino.

Riesman, David
    The Lonely Crowd. 1977. New Haven: Yale University Press.

Roberts, Fredric Marc
    Under the North Star: Notions of Self and Community in a Finnish Village. 1982. Ph.D. dissertation, City University of New York.

Robinson, John A.
Personal Narratives Reconsidered. 1981. *Journal of American Folklore* vol. 94, no. 371, 58-85.

Rodin, Miriam
Alcoholism as a Folk Disease; The Paradox of Beliefs and Choice of Therapy in an Urban American Community. 1981. *Journal of Studies on Alcohol* 42:822-35.

Room, Robin
Sociological Aspects of the Disease Concept of Alcoholism. 1983. *Research Advances in Alcohol and Drug Problems* vol. 7. New York and London: Plenum Press. Pp. 47-91.

———.

Alcohol and Ethnography: A Case of Problem Deflation? 1984a. *Current Anthropology* vol. 25, no. 2, April, 169-91.

———.

How Good an Excuse is Drunkenness? 1984b. Seminar presentation at the Institute of Law, University of Helsinki, May 10. Manuscript.

———.

Alcoholism and Alcoholics Anonymous in U.S. Films, 1945-1962: The Party Ends for the "Wet Generations." 1985a. Paper presented at an International Group for Comparative Alcohol Studies Conference on Cultural Studies on Drinking and Drinking Problems, Helsinki, September 24-28.

———.

Dependence and Society. 1985b. *British Journal of Addiction* vol. 80, 133-39.

———.

Drugs, Consciousness and Society: Can We Learn from Others' Experience? 1985c. *Alcohol, Drugs, and Tobacco: An International Perspective—Past, Present, and Future.* Proceedings of the 34th International Congress on Alcohol and Drug Dependence, vol. 2. Edmonton: Alberta Alcohol and Drug Abuse Commission, 174-76.

Rosecrance, John
Compulsive Gambling and the Medicalization of Deviance. 1985. *Social Problems* 32, 275-83.

Rosendal, Maunu
Suomen herännäisyyden historia. I osa (1796-1835) [The history of the Finnish revivalist movement. Part I]. 1902. Oulu: B. B. Bergdahl.

Rosenzweig, Roy
Eight Hours for What We Will. Workers and Leisure in an Industrial City 1870-1920. 1983. Cambridge: Cambridge University Press.

Rotter, J. B.
Generalized Expectancies for Internal Versus External Locus of Reinforcement. 1966. Psychological Monographs: General and Applied, Whole no. 609, 1-28.

Rumelhart, David E.
Notes on a Schema of Stories. Representation and Understanding. 1975. Studies in Cognitive Science. Daniel G. Bobrov and Allan Collins (eds.). Academic Press. Pp. 211-36.

Ruokanen, Tapani
Paavo Ruotsalainen, talonpoikain herättäjä [Paavo Ruotsalainen, the revivalist of peasants]. 1989. Porvoo: WSOY.

Sahlins, Marshall
Culture and Practical Reason. 1976. Chicago: University of Chicago Press.

Sarmela, Matti
Reciprocity Systems of the Rural Society in the Finnish-Karelian Culture Area. 1969. Communications 207. Helsinki: FF.

Schmidt, Wolfgang, Reginald G. Smart, and Marcia K. Moss
Social Class and the Treatment of Alcoholism: An Investigation of the Social Class as a Determinant of Diagnoses, Prognosis, and Therapy. 1968. Toronto: University of Toronto Press.

Schneider, Joseph W.
Deviant Drinking as Disease: Alcoholism as a Social Accomplishment. 1978. Social Problems 25, 361-72.

Scott, Marvin B., and Stanford M. Lyman
Accounts. American Sociological Review 1968. vol. 33, no. 1, 46-62.

Siikala, Anna-Leena
Tarina ja tulkinta. Tutkimus kansankertojista [Story and interpretation. A study on folk storytellers]. 1984. Mänttä.

Silvennoinen, Taisto
Miksi Jeppe jatkaa? [Why does Jeppe continue his drinking?] 1979. Tiimi (no volume number) no. 1:12-13.

Silverman, Joan L.
"I'll Never Touch Another Drop": Images of Alcoholism and Temper-

ance in American Popular Culture, 1874-1919. 1980. Ph.D. dissertation, New York University; London: University Microfilms International.

Singer, Merrill
Christian Science Healing and Alcoholism: An Anthropological Perspective. 1982. *Journal of Operational Psychiatry* 13:1, 3-12.

Singer, Merrill, and Maria Borerro
Indigenous Treatment of Alcoholism: The Case of Puerto Rican Spiritism. 1984. *Medical Anthropology* 8:246-73.

Sosiaalihallitus (National Board of Social Welfare)
Tilastotiedotus [Statistical report] 1986:2. Helsinki: Valtion Painatuskeskus.

Stedman Jones, Gareth
Languages of Class. Studies in English Working Class History 1832-1982. 1983. Cambridge: Cambridge University Press.

Steinbring, Jack
Alcoholics Anonymous: Cultural Reform among the Saulteaux. 1980. John Hamer and Jack Steinbring (eds.): *Alcohol and Native Peoples of the North.* Washington: University Press of America. Pp. 89-106.

Steinglass, Peter
A Life History Model of the Alcoholic Family. 1980. *Family Process* 19:211-26.

Steinglass, Peter, Sheldon Weiner, and Jack Mendelson
A Systems Approach to Alcoholism: A Model and its Clinical Implications. 1971. *Archives of General Psychiatry* 24:401-8.

Stevens, Susan M.
Alcohol and World View, A Study of Passamaquoddy Alcohol Use. 1981. *Journal of Studies on Alcohol* 9, 122-42.

Sulkunen, Irma
Väckelserorelserna som ett förskede i organiseringens historia [Revivalist movements as a preface in the history of social organization]. 1983. *Historisk Tidskrift* 1, 1-15.

———.
Raittius kansalaisuskontona. Raittiusliike ja järjestäytyminen 1870—luvulta suurlakon jälkeisiin vuosiin [Temperance as a civic religion. The temperance movement and popular organization in Finland from the 1870s to the years after the great strike of 1905]. 1986. Helsinki: Societas Historica Finlandiae.

Sulkunen, Irma, and Risto Alapuro
Raittiusliike ja työväestön järjestäytyminen [The temperance movement and the organizing of the workers]. 1987. *Kansa liikkeessä* [The folk in movement]. Risto Alapuro, Ilkka Liikanen, Kerstin Smeds, and Henrik Stenius (eds.). Helsinki: Kirjayhtymä. Pp. 142-56.

Sulkunen, Pekka
Alkoholin kulutukseen vaikuttavista tekijöistä eri maissa [Factors influencing the consumption of alcohol in different countries]. 1975. *Alkoholikysymys* no. 2, 47-57.

———.
Abstainers in Finland 1946-1976. A Study in Social and Cultural Transition. 1979. Reports from the Social Research Institute of Alcohol Studies no. 133.

Sulkunen, Pekka, Pertti Alasuutari, Ritva Nätkin, and Merja Kinnunen
Lähioravintola [The suburban pub]. 1985. Keuruu: Otava.

Suolinna, Kirsti
Yhteiskunnan ja uskonnollisten liikkeitten suhteista [On the relation of society to religious movements]. 1969. Institute of Sociology, University of Helsinki, Research Reports no. 119.

———.
Uskonnollisten liikkeitten asema sosiaalisessa murroksessa. [The position of religious movements in social change]. 1975. Institute of Sociology, University of Helsinki, Research Reports No. 203.

Suuniitty, Mirja
Keski-Suomen nuorisoseurojen historia [The history of the youth societies of central Finland]. 1976. Jyväskylä: Gummerus.

Talvi, Veikko
Pohjois-Kymenlaakson teollistuminen. Kymin Osakeyhtiön historia 1872-1917 [The industrialization of northern Kymmene valley. The history of Kymmene corporation 1872-1917]. 1979. Kouvola: Kymi Kymmene Oy.

———.
Tampereen A-klinikan vuosikertomukset 1975-1984 [The annual reports of Tampere A-clinic].

Thompson, E. P.
The Making of the English Working Class. Harmonthsworth, Middlesex: Pelican Books.

Thompson, Paul
The Voice of the Past. Oral History. 1978. Bristol: Oxford University Press.

Thune, Carl E.
   Alcoholism and the Archetypal Past. A Phenomenological Perspective
   on Alcoholics Anonymous. 1977. *Journal of Studies on Alcohol* vol. 38, no. 1,
   75-88.

Tiefer, Leonore
   "In Search of the Perfect Penis. The Medicalization of Male Sexuality."
   1986. *American Behavioral Scientist* 29, 579-99.

Toivonen, Timo
   *Rakennemuutos 1930-1985. Aineistoa toimiala-, luokka- ja kerrostumaraken-
   teen tutkimukseen* [Structural change 1930-1985. Data and material on
   transformation of industries, social classes, and strata]. 1988. Publications
   of the Turku School of Economics, series A-1.

Tournier, Robert E.
   Alcoholics Anonymous as Treatment and as Ideology. 1979. *Journal of
   Studies on Alcohol* 40:230-39.

────── .

   The Medicalization of Alcoholism: Discontinuities in Ideologies of
   Deviance. 1985. *Journal of Drug Issues*, Winter, 39-49.

Trilling, Lionel
   Sincerity and Authenticity. 1978. Cambridge: Harvard University Press.

Turner, Bryan S.
   The Body and Society. Explorations in Social Theory. 1984. Oxford: Basil
   Blackwell.

────── .

   Personhood and Citizenship. 1986. *Theory, Culture and Society* 3, 1-16.

Turner, Terence S.
   Narrative Structure and Mythopoesis: A Critique and Re-formulation of
   Structuralist Concepts of Myth, Narrative and Poetics. 1977. *Arethusa*,
   vol. 10, 103-63.

Turpeinen, Oiva
   Viinaan kuolleet Suomessa vuosina 1802-1877 [Alcohol Deaths in Finland
   in 1802-1877]. 1975. Helsinki: Alkoholipoliittisen tutkimuslaitoksen
   tutkimusseloste no. 90.

────── .

   Viinaan kuolleet Suomessa vuosina 1878-1917 [Alcohol deaths in Finland in
   1878-1917]. 1977. Helsinki: Alkoholipoliittisen tutkimuslaitoksen
   tutkimusseloste no. 110.

Turunen, Sakari
"Hyvä ihminen—kunnon kansalainen"—Nuorisoseuraliikkeen ohjelmallinen kehittyminen 1890-luvulla ja ensimmäisellä sortokaudella ["A good person—a decent citizen"—The programatic development of the youth societies movement in the 1890s and during the first era of Russian oppression in 1899-1905]. 1979. Suomen historian pro gradu—tutkielma, Tampereen yliopisto.

Watzlawick, Paul, John H. Weakland, and Richard Fish
Change: Principles of Problem Formation and Problem Resolution. 1974. New York: Norton.

———.
Sociology. Volume One. 1978. Berkeley: University of California Press.

Weber, Max
The Protestant Ethic and the Spirit of Capitalism. 1971. London: Unwin University Books.

Weibel-Orlando, Joan
Indians, Ethnicity, and Alcohol. Contrasting Perceptions of the Ethnic Self and Alcohol Use. 1985. The American Experience with Alcohol. Contrasting Cultural Perspectives. Linda A. Bennett and Genevieve M. Ames (eds.). New York: Plenum Press. Pp. 201-26.

Weintraub, Karl Joachim
Autobiography and Historical Consciousness. 1975. Critical Inquiry. Pp. 821-48.

———.
The Value of the Individual. Self and Circumstance in Autobiography. 1978. Chicago: University of Chicago Press.

Willis, Paul
Learning to Labour. How Working Class Kids Get Working Class Jobs. 1977. Hampshire: Gover.

———.
Profane Culture. 1978. London: Routledge & Kegan Paul.

Winch, Peter
The Idea of a Social Science and Its Relation to Philosophy. 1958. Routledge & Kegan Paul.

Wittman, Friedner
Alcoholism and Architecture: The Myth of Specialized Treatment Facilities. 1971. Paper presented at the American Institute of Architects meeting, Los Angeles, January.

Wright, Will
Sixguns and Society. A Structural Study of the Western. 1977. Berkeley and Los Angeles: University of California Press.

Ylikangas, Heikki
Körttiläiset tuomiolla. Massaoikeudenkäynnit heränneitä vastaan Etelä-Pohjan-maalla 1830—ja 1840—lukujen taitteessa [Körttiläiset on trial. The mass trials against the revivalists in Etelä-Pohjanmaa at the turn of the 1830s and 1840s]. 1979. Helsinki: Otava.

INDEX

medical model, 163, 192n2
Murase, A., 187n15
myth: definition of, 54
Mäkelä, K., 60, 186n12

N

narrative: structure, 61-63, 185n5,
185n6, 187n15; analysis, 184n6;
clauses, 187n15. *See also* life
story
nature culture division, 15-16
needs, 16. *See also* desire and self-
control
Neumann, B., 154, 191n4
Niemelä, J., 88
Niinivaara, E., 183n11
Niskanen, H., 183n11
Nokkala, A., 15, 182n6
normal pathological division, 4, 5,
18-20, 60, 158, 159, 163, 164,
173, 184n13, 191n1; and
civilized primitive division, 18-
19; drinking, 4, 162; drinking,
and the alcoholism frame, 2;
family life, and dry/wet
dichotomy, 103-104; and
religion, 193n5
Notkola, I., 16
Numminen, J., 12
Nätkin, R., 21, 184n1

O

O'Donovan, K., 164
Öjesjö, L., 83
Österberg, 173
Other, the, 173-175
outer constraints, 170, 172, 176, 180

P

panoptic power relations, 164, 174-
175
Pascarosa, P., 85
pathological. *See* normal
pathological division
pathologization, 168; definition of,
164-165
pathology, notion of, 4. *See also*
normal pathological division
person: ascriptive categorizations
of, 191n2; and individual, 152,
191n2; and name-giving, 153,
191n3. *See also* individual
personage, 153
personality, 154; definition of, 152;
history of, 172, 174, 194n3; and
identity, 155; notion of, 194n3
personality frame, 2. *See also*
alcoholism frame; addiction frame
phase, of a story. *See* function
Piispa, M., 182n7, 183n8
pleasurable submission, 43-49, 52;
and women, 46-48. *See also* logic
of freedom
post-Freudian view of civilization,
169, 172-173
postmodernity, 167-168
Prince, G., 61-63
prohibition, 20, 87, 184n12; working
class support for, 11
Propp, V., 61-63, 185n7, 185n9,
185n6
psyche, 3, 4; and Freud, 3
psychoanalytical theory, 171
public sphere. *See* gender
purposive rationality and desires,
tension between, 71. *See also*
desire and self-control